Hands-On High Performance with Go

Boost and optimize the performance of your Golang
applications at scale with resilience

Bob Strecansky

Packt>

BIRMINGHAM - MUMBAI

Hands-On High Performance with Go

Commissioning Editor: Richa Tripathi
Acquisition Editor: Alok Dhuri
Content Development Editor: Pathikrit Roy
Senior Editor: Storm Mann
Technical Editor: Pradeep Sahu
Copy Editor: Safis Editing
Project Coordinator: Francy Puthiry
Proofreader: Safis Editing
Indexer: Tejal Daruwale Soni
Production Designer: Joshua Misquitta

First published: March 2020

Production reference: 1230320

Published by Packt Publishing Ltd.
Livery Place
35 Livery Street
Birmingham
B3 2PB, UK.

ISBN 978-1-78980-578-9

www.packt.com

To my wife Bree, who made all of this (plus many other things!) possible.

Packt.com

Subscribe to our online digital library for full access to over 7,000 books and videos, as well as industry leading tools to help you plan your personal development and advance your career. For more information, please visit our website.

Why subscribe?

- Spend less time learning and more time coding with practical eBooks and Videos from over 4,000 industry professionals

- Improve your learning with Skill Plans built especially for you

- Get a free eBook or video every month

- Fully searchable for easy access to vital information

- Copy and paste, print, and bookmark content

Did you know that Packt offers eBook versions of every book published, with PDF and ePub files available? You can upgrade to the eBook version at www.packt.com and as a print book customer, you are entitled to a discount on the eBook copy. Get in touch with us at customercare@packtpub.com for more details.

At www.packt.com, you can also read a collection of free technical articles, sign up for a range of free newsletters, and receive exclusive discounts and offers on Packt books and eBooks.

Contributors

About the author

Bob Strecansky is a senior site reliability engineer. He graduated with a computer engineering degree from Clemson University with a focus on networking. He has worked in both consulting and industry jobs since graduation. He has worked with large telecom companies and much of the Alexa top 500. He currently works at Mailchimp, working to improve web performance, security, and reliability for one of the world's largest email service providers. He has also written articles for web publications and currently maintains the OpenTelemetry PHP project. In his free time, Bob enjoys tennis, cooking, and restoring old cars. You can follow Bob on the internet to hear musings about performance analysis:

Twitter: @bobstrecansky
GitHub: @bobstrecansky

About the reviewer

Eduard Bondarenko is a long-time software developer. He prefers concise and expressive code with comments and has tried many programming languages, such as Ruby, Go, Java, and JavaScript.

Eduard has reviewed a couple of programming books and has enjoyed their broad topics and how interesting they are. Besides programming, he likes to spend time with the family, play soccer, and travel.

> *I want to thank my family for supporting me during my work on the book and also the author of this book for an interesting read.*

Packt is searching for authors like you

If you're interested in becoming an author for Packt, please visit `authors.packtpub.com` and apply today. We have worked with thousands of developers and tech professionals, just like you, to help them share their insight with the global tech community. You can make a general application, apply for a specific hot topic that we are recruiting an author for, or submit your own idea.

Table of Contents

Preface   1

Section 1: Learning about Performance in Go

Chapter 1: Introduction to Performance in Go   11
  Technical requirements   12
  Understanding performance in computer science   12
    A brief note on Big O notation   13
    Methods to gauge long term performance   14
      Optimization strategies overview   14
    Optimization levels   16
  A brief history of Go   17
    The Go standard library   18
    Go toolset   19
      Benchmarking overview   21
  The ideology behind Go performance   21
    Goroutines – performance from the start   22
    Channels – a typed conduit   22
    C-comparable performance   22
    Large-scale distributed systems   23
  Summary   23

Chapter 2: Data Structures and Algorithms   25
  Understanding benchmarking   25
    Benchmark execution   26
    Real-world benchmarking   29
  Introducing Big O notation   30
    Practical Big O notation example   32
    Data structure operations and time complexity   33
    O(1) – constant time   34
    O(log n) - logarithmic time   35
    O(n) – linear time   37
    O(n log n) – quasilinear time   38
    O(n2) – quadratic time   40
    O(2n) – exponential time   41
  Understanding sort algorithms   43
    Insertion sort   44
    Heap sort   44
    Merge sort   45
    Quick sort   46

Understanding search algorithms   46
   Linear search   46
   Binary search   47
Exploring trees   48
   Binary trees   48
   Doubly linked list   49
Exploring queues   50
   Common queuing functions   50
   Common queuing patterns   51
Summary   51

Chapter 3: Understanding Concurrency   53
Understanding closures   53
   Anonymous functions   54
   Anonymous functions with respect to closures   55
   Closures for nesting and deferring work   57
   HTTP handlers with closures   57
Exploring goroutines   61
   The Go scheduler   61
   Go scheduler goroutine internals   62
     The M struct   63
     The P struct   63
     The G struct   63
   Goroutines in action   64
Introducing channels   65
   Channel internals   65
   Buffered channels   66
     Ranges over channels   68
   Unbuffered channels   69
     Selects   71
Introducing semaphores   73
Understanding WaitGroups   75
Iterators and the process of iteration   77
Briefing on generators   82
Summary   82

Chapter 4: STL Algorithm Equivalents in Go   83
Understanding algorithms in the STL   84
   Sort   84
   Reverse   85
   Min element and max element   86
   Binary search   88
Understanding containers   89
   Sequence containers   89
     Array   90
     Vector   90

Deque 91
List 92
Forward list 94
Container adapters 95
Queue 95
Priority queue 96
Stack 98
Associative containers 99
Set 99
Multiset 100
Map 102
Multimap 103

Understanding function objects 104
Functors 104
Iterators 106
Internal iterators 106
External iterators 107
Generators 108
Implicit Iterators 108

Summary 109

Chapter 5: Matrix and Vector Computation in Go 111
Introducing Gonum and the Sparse library 112
Introducing BLAS 112
Introducing vectors 113
Vector computations 113
Introducing matrices 115
Matrix operations 116
Matrix addition 116
A practical example (matrix subtraction) 117
Scalar multiplication 119
Scalar multiplication practical example 120
Matrix multiplication 121
Matrix multiplication practical example 122
Matrix transposition 124
Matrix transposition practical example 126
Understanding matrix structures 127
Dense matrices 127
Sparse matrices 127
DOK matrix 129
LIL matrix 129
COO matrix 130
CSR matrix 130
CSC matrix 132
Summary 133

Section 2: Applying Performance Concepts in Go

Chapter 6: Composing Readable Go Code   137
  Maintaining simplicity in Go   138
  Maintaining readability in Go   138
  Exploring packaging in Go   139
    Package naming   139
    Packaging layout   140
    Internal packaging   142
    Vendor directory   143
    Go modules   143
  Understanding naming in Go   146
  Understanding formatting in Go   148
  Briefing on interfaces in Go   150
  Comprehending methods in Go   151
  Comprehending inheritance in Go   154
  Exploring reflection in Go   156
    Types   156
    Kinds   157
    Values   158
  Summary   159

Chapter 7: Template Programming in Go   161
  Understanding Go generate   161
    Generated code for protobufs   162
      Protobuf code results   165
  The link toolchain   166
  Introducing Cobra and Viper for configuration programming 168
    Cobra/Viper resulting sets   171
  Text templating   172
  HTML templating   174
  Exploring Sprig   176
    String functions   176
    String slice functions   178
    Default functions   179
  Summary   181

Chapter 8: Memory Management in Go   183
  Understanding Modern Computer Memory - A Primer   183
  Allocating memory   184
    Introducing VSZ and RSS   185
  Understanding memory utilization   190
    Go runtime memory allocation   193
      Memory allocation primer   193
    Memory object allocation   194
  Briefing on limited memory situations   204
  Summary   205

Chapter 9: GPU Parallelization in Go   207
  Cgo – writing C in Go   207
    A simple Cgo example   209
  GPU-accelerated computing – utilizing the hardware   211
    CUDA – utilizing host processes   215
    Docker for GPU-enabled programming   215
  CUDA on GCP   217
    Creating a VM with a GPU   218
    Install the CUDA driver   223
    Install Docker CE on GCP   224
    Installing NVIDIA Docker on GCP   225
    Scripting it all together   226
  CUDA – powering the program   227
  Summary   233

Chapter 10: Compile Time Evaluations in Go   235
  Exploring the Go runtime   236
    GODEBUG   236
    GCTRACE   238
    GOGC   241
    GOMAXPROCS   243
    GOTRACEBACK   245
    Go build cache   247
    Vendoring dependencies   247
    Caching and vendoring improvements   247
    Debug   249
    PProf/race/trace   249
  Understanding functions   249
    KeepAlive   250
    NumCPU   250
    ReadMemStats   251
  Summary   254

Section 3: Section 3: Deploying, Monitoring, and Iterating on Go Programs with Performance in Mind

Chapter 11: Building and Deploying Go Code   257
  Building Go binaries   258
  Go build – building your Go code   259
    Build flags   259
    Build information   261
    Compiler and linker flags   263
    Build constraints   265
    Filename conventions   266
  Go clean – cleaning your build directory   267

Retrieving package dependencies with go get and go mod 269
Go list 270
Go run – executing your packages 274
Go install – installing your binaries 276
Building Go binaries with Docker 277
Summary 281

Chapter 12: Profiling Go Code 283
Understanding profiling 283
Exploring instrumentation methodologies 284
Implementing profiling with go test 284
Manually instrumenting profiling in code 285
Profiling running service code 285
Briefing on CPU profiling 287
Briefing on memory profiling 293
Extended capabilities with upstream pprof 295
Comparing multiple profiles 297
Interpreting flame graphs within pprof 299
Detecting memory leaks in Go 301
Summary 303

Chapter 13: Tracing Go Code 305
Implementing tracing instrumentation 305
Understanding the tracing format 306
Understanding trace collection 307
Movement in the tracing window 312
Exploring pprof-like traces 317
Go distributed tracing 321
Implementing OpenCensus for your application 322
Summary 328

Chapter 14: Clusters and Job Queues 329
Clustering in Go 330
K-nearest neighbors 331
K-means clustering 333
Exploring job queues in Go 337
Goroutines as job queues 337
Buffered channels as job queues 340
Integrating job queues 342
Kafka 342
RabbitMQ 346
Summary 351

Chapter 15: Comparing Code Quality Across Versions 353
Go Prometheus exporter – exporting data from your Go application 354

APM – watching your distributed system performance   360
    Google Cloud environment setup   360
    Google Cloud Trace code   363
SLIs and SLOs – setting goals   368
    Measuring traffic   372
    Measuring latency   372
    Measuring errors   372
    Measuring saturation   372
    Grafana   372
Logging – keeping track of your data   375
Summary   379

Appendix A: Other Books You May Enjoy   381
    Leave a review - let other readers know what you think   383

Index   385

Preface

Hands-On High Performance with Go is a complete resource with proven methodologies and techniques to help you diagnose and fix performance problems in your Go applications. The book starts with an introduction to the concepts of performance, where you will learn about the ideology behind the performance of Go. Next, you will learn how to implement Go data structures and algorithms effectively and explore data manipulation and organization in order to write programs for scalable software. Channels and goroutines for parallelism and concurrency in order to write high-performance codes for distributed systems are also a core part of this book. Moving on, you'll learn how to manage memory effectively. You'll explore the **Compute Unified Device Architecture (CUDA)** driver **application programming interface (API)**, use containers to build Go code, and work with the Go build cache for faster compilation. You'll also get a clear picture of profiling and tracing Go code to detect bottlenecks in your system. At the end of the book, you'll evaluate clusters and job queues for performance optimization and monitor the application for performance regression.

Who this book is for

This Go book is a must for developers and professionals who have an intermediate-to-advanced understanding of Go programming and are interested in improving their speed of code execution.

What this book covers

Chapter 1, *Introduction to Performance in Go*, will discuss why performance in computer science is important. You will also learn why performance is important in the Go language.

Chapter 2, *Data Structures and Algorithms*, deals with data structures and algorithms, which are the basic units of building software, notably complex performance software. Understanding them will help you to think about how to most impact fully organize and manipulate data in order to write effective, performant software. Also, iterators and generators are essential to Go. This chapter will include explanations of different data structures and algorithms, as well as how their big O notation is impacted.

Chapter 3, *Understanding Concurrency*, will talk about utilizing channels and goroutines for parallelism and concurrency, which are idiomatic in Go and are the best ways to write high-performance code in your system. Being able to understand when and where to use each of these design patterns is essential to writing performant Go.

Chapter 4, *STL Algorithm Equivalents in Go*, discusses how many programmers coming from other high-performance languages, namely C++, understand the concept of the standard template library, which provides common programming data structures and functions in a generalized library in order to rapidly iterate and write performant code at scale.

Chapter 5, *Matrix and Vector Computation in Go*, deals with matrix and vector computations in general. Matrices are important in graphics manipulation and AI, namely image recognition. Vectors can hold a myriad of objects in dynamic arrays. They use contiguous storage and can be manipulated to accommodate growth.

Chapter 6, *Composing Readable Go Code*, focuses on the importance of writing readable Go code. Understanding the patterns and idioms discussed in this chapter will help you to write Go code that is more easily readable and operable between teams. Also, being able to write idiomatic Go will help raise the level of your code quality and help your project maintain velocity.

Chapter 7, *Template Programming in Go*, focuses on template programming in Go. Metaprogramming allows the end user to write Go programs that produce, manipulate, and run Go programs. Go has clear, static dependencies, which helps with metaprogramming. It has shortcomings that other languages don't have in metaprogramming, such as __getattr__ in Python, but we can still generate Go code and compile the resulting code if it's deemed prudent.

Chapter 8, *Memory Management in Go*, discusses how memory management is paramount to system performance. Being able to utilize a computer's memory footprint to the fullest allows you to keep highly functioning programs in memory so that you don't often have to take the large performance hit of swapping to disk. Being able to manage memory effectively is a core tenet of writing performant Go code.

Chapter 9, *GPU Parallelization in Go*, focuses on GPU accelerated programming, which is becoming more and more important in today's high-performance computing stacks. We can use the CUDA driver API for GPU acceleration. This is commonly used in topics such as deep learning algorithms.

Chapter 10, *Compile Time Evaluations in Go*, discusses minimizing dependencies and each file declaring its own dependencies while writing a Go program. Regular syntax and module support also help to improve compile times, as well as interface satisfaction. These things help to make Go compilation quicker, alongside using containers for building Go code and utilizing the Go build cache.

Chapter 11, *Building and Deploying Go Code*, focuses on how to deploy new Go code. To elaborate further, this chapter explains how we can push this out to one or multiple places in order to test against different environments. Doing this will allow us to push the envelope of the amount of throughput that we have for our system.

Chapter 12, *Profiling Go Code*, focuses on profiling Go code, which is one of the best ways to determine where bottlenecks live within your Go functions. Performing this profiling will help you to deduce where you can make improvements within your function and how much time individual pieces take within your function call with respect to the overall system.

Chapter 13, *Tracing Go Code*, deals with a fantastic way to check interoperability between functions and services within your Go program, also known as tracing. Tracing allows you to pass context through your system and evaluate where you are being held up. Whether it's a third-party API call, a slow messaging queue, or an $O(n^2)$ function, tracing will help you to find where this bottleneck resides.

Chapter 14, *Clusters and Job Queues*, focuses on the importance of clustering and job queues in Go as good ways to get distributed systems to work synchronously and deliver a consistent message. Distributed computing is difficult, and it becomes very important to watch for potential performance optimizations within both clustering and job queues.

Chapter 15, *Comparing Code Quality Across Versions*, deals with what you should do after you have written, debugged, profiled, and monitored Go code that is monitoring your application in the long term for performance regressions. Adding new features to your code is fruitless if you can't continue to deliver a level of performance that other systems in your infrastructure depend on.

To get the most out of this book

This book is for Go professionals and developers seeking to execute their code faster, so an intermediate to advanced understanding of Go programming is necessary to make the most out of this book. The Go language has relatively minimal system requirements. A modern computer with a modern operating system should support the Go runtime and its dependencies. Go is used in many low power devices that have limited CPU, Memory, and I/O requirements.

You can see the requirements for the language listed at the following URL: `https://github.com/golang/go/wiki/MinimumRequirements`.

In this book I used Fedora Core Linux (version 29 during the time of writing this book) as the operating system. Instructions on how to install the Fedora Workstation Linux distribution can be found on the Fedora page at the following URL: `https://getfedora.org/en/workstation/download/`.

Docker is used for many of the examples in this book. You can see the requirements listed for Docker at the following URL: `https://docs.docker.com/install/`.

In `Chapter 9`, *GPU Parallelization in Go,* we discuss GPU programming. To perform the tasks of this chapter, you'll need one of two things:

- A NVIDIA enabled GPU. I used a NVIDIA GeForce GTX 670 in my testing, with a Compute Capability of 3.0.
- A GPU enabled cloud instance. Chapter 9 discusses a couple of different providers and methodologies for this. GPUs on Compute Engine work for this. More up to date information on GPUs on Compute Engine can be found at the following URL: `https://cloud.google.com/compute/docs/gpus`.

After you read this book; I hope you'll be able to write more efficient Go code. You'll hopefully be able to quantify and validate your efforts as well.

Download the example code files

You can download the example code files for this book from your account at `www.packt.com`. If you purchased this book elsewhere, you can visit `www.packtpub.com/support` and register to have the files emailed directly to you.

You can download the code files by following these steps:

1. Log in or register at `www.packt.com`.

2. Select the **Support** tab.
3. Click on **Code Downloads**.
4. Enter the name of the book in the **Search** box and follow the onscreen instructions.

Once the file is downloaded, please make sure that you unzip or extract the folder using the latest version of:

- WinRAR/7-Zip for Windows
- Zipeg/iZip/UnRarX for Mac
- 7-Zip/PeaZip for Linux

The code bundle for the book is also hosted on GitHub at `https://github.com/bobstrecansky/HighPerformanceWithGo/`. In case there's an update to the code, it will be updated on the existing GitHub repository.

We also have other code bundles from our rich catalog of books and videos available at `https://github.com/PacktPublishing/`. Check them out!

Code in Action

Code in Action videos for this book can be viewed at `http://bit.ly/2QcfEJI`.

Download the color images

We also provide a PDF file that has color images of the screenshots/diagrams used in this book. You can download it here: `https://static.packt-cdn.com/downloads/9781789805789_ColorImages.pdf`.

Conventions used

There are a number of text conventions used throughout this book.

`CodeInText`: Indicates code words in text, database table names, folder names, filenames, file extensions, pathnames, dummy URLs, user input, and Twitter handles. Here is an example: " The following code blocks will show the `Next()` incantation"

A block of code is set as follows:

```
// Note the trailing () for this anonymous function invocation
func() {
  fmt.Println("Hello Go")
}()
```

When we wish to draw your attention to a particular part of a code block, the relevant lines or items are set in bold:

```
// Note the trailing () for this anonymous function invocation
func() {
  fmt.Println("Hello Go")
}()
```

Any command-line input or output is written as follows:

```
$ go test -bench=. -benchtime 2s -count 2 -benchmem -cpu 4
```

Bold: Indicates a new term, an important word, or words that you see onscreen. For example, words in menus or dialog boxes appear in the text like this. Here is an example: "The **reverse algorithm** takes a dataset and reverses the values of the set"

Warnings or important notes appear like this.

Tips and tricks appear like this.

Get in touch

Feedback from our readers is always welcome.

General feedback: If you have questions about any aspect of this book, mention the book title in the subject of your message and email us at customercare@packtpub.com.

Errata: Although we have taken every care to ensure the accuracy of our content, mistakes do happen. If you have found a mistake in this book, we would be grateful if you would report this to us. Please visit www.packtpub.com/support/errata, selecting your book, clicking on the Errata Submission Form link, and entering the details.

Piracy: If you come across any illegal copies of our works in any form on the Internet, we would be grateful if you would provide us with the location address or website name. Please contact us at copyright@packt.com with a link to the material.

If you are interested in becoming an author: If there is a topic that you have expertise in and you are interested in either writing or contributing to a book, please visit authors.packtpub.com.

Reviews

Please leave a review. Once you have read and used this book, why not leave a review on the site that you purchased it from? Potential readers can then see and use your unbiased opinion to make purchase decisions, we at Packt can understand what you think about our products, and our authors can see your feedback on their book. Thank you!

For more information about Packt, please visit packt.com

Section 1: Learning about Performance in Go

In this section, you will learn why performance in computer science is important. You will also learn why performance is important in the Go language. Moving on, you will learn about data structures and algorithms, concurrency, STL algorithm equivalents, and the matrix and vector computations in Go.

The chapters in this section include the following:

- Chapter 1, *Introduction to Performance in Go*
- Chapter 2, *Data Structures and Algorithms*
- Chapter 3, *Understanding Concurrency*
- Chapter 4, *STL Algorithm Equivalents in Go*
- Chapter 5, *Matrix and Vector Computation in Go*

Introduction to Performance in Go 1

This book is written with intermediate to advanced Go developers in mind. These developers will be looking to squeeze more performance out of their Go application. To do this, this book will help to drive the four golden signals as defined in the *Site Reliability Engineering Workbook* (`https://landing.google.com/sre/sre-book/chapters/monitoring-distributed-systems/`). If we can reduce latency and errors, as well as increase traffic whilst reducing saturation, our programs will continue to be more performant. Following the ideology of the four golden signals is beneficial for anyone developing a Go application with performance in mind.

In this chapter, you'll be introduced to some of the core concepts of performance in computer science. You'll learn some of the history of the Go computer programming language, how its creators decided that it was important to put performance at the forefront of the language, and why writing performant Go is important. Go is a programming language designed with performance in mind, and this book will take you through some of the highlights on how to use some of Go's design and tooling to your advantage. This will help you to write more efficient code.

In this chapter, we will cover the following topics:

- Understanding performance in computer science
- A brief history of Go
- The ideology behind Go performance

These topics are provided to guide you in beginning to understand the direction you need to take to write highly performant code in the Go language.

Technical requirements

For this book, you should have a moderate understanding of the Go language. Some key concepts to understand before exploring these topics include the following:

- The Go reference specification: `https://golang.org/ref/spec`
- How to write Go code: `https://golang.org/doc/code.html`
- Effective Go: `https://golang.org/doc/effective_go.html`

Throughout this book, there will be many code samples and benchmark results. These are all accessible via the GitHub repository at `https://github.com/bobstrecansky/HighPerformanceWithGo/`.

If you have a question or would like to request a change to the repository, feel free to create an issue within the repository at `https://github.com/bobstrecansky/HighPerformanceWithGo/issues/new`.

Understanding performance in computer science

Performance in computer science is a measure of work that can be accomplished by a computer system. Performant code is vital to many different groups of developers. Whether you're part of a large-scale software company that needs to quickly deliver masses of data to customers, an embedded computing device programmer who has limited computing resources available, or a hobbyist looking to squeeze more requests out of the Raspberry Pi that you are using for your pet project, performance should be at the forefront of your development mindset. Performance matters, especially when your scale continues to grow.

It is important to remember that we are sometimes limited by physical bounds. CPU, memory, disk I/O, and network connectivity all have performance ceilings based on the hardware that you either purchase or rent from a cloud provider. There are other systems that may run concurrently alongside our Go programs that can also consume resources, such as OS packages, logging utilities, monitoring tools, and other binaries—it is prudent to remember that our programs are very frequently not the only tenants on the physical machines they run on.

Optimized code generally helps in many ways, including the following:

- Decreased response time: The total amount of time it takes to respond to a request.
- Decreased latency: The time delay between a cause and effect within a system.
- Increased throughput: The rate at which data can be processed.
- Higher scalability: More work can be processed within a contained system.

There are many ways to service more requests within a computer system. Adding more individual computers (often referred to as horizontal scaling) or upgrading to more powerful computers (often referred to as vertical scaling) are common practices used to handle demand within a computer system. One of the fastest ways to service more requests without needing additional hardware is to increase code performance. Performance engineering acts as a way to help with both horizontal and vertical scaling. The more performant your code is, the more requests you can handle on a single machine. This pattern can potentially result in fewer or less expensive physical hosts to run your workload. This is a large value proposition for many businesses and hobbyists alike, as it helps to drive down the cost of operation and improves the end user experience.

A brief note on Big O notation

Big O notation (https://en.wikipedia.org/wiki/Big_O_notation) is commonly used to describe the limiting behavior of a function based on the size of the inputs. In computer science, Big O notation is used to explain how efficient algorithms are in comparison to one another—we'll discuss this more in detail in Chapter 2, *Data Structures and Algorithms*. Big O notation is important in optimizing performance because it is used as a comparison operator in explaining how well algorithms will scale. Understanding Big O notation will help you to write more performant code, as it will help to drive performance decisions in your code as the code is being composed. Knowing at what point different algorithms have relative strengths and weaknesses helps you to determine the correct choice for the implementation at hand. We can't improve what we can't measure—Big O notation helps us to give a concrete measurement to the problem statement at hand.

Methods to gauge long term performance

As we make our performance improvements, we will need to continually monitor our changes to view impact. Many methods can be used to monitor the long-term performance of computer systems. A couple of examples of these methods would be the following:

- Brendan Gregg's USE Method: Utilization, saturation, and errors (`www.brendangregg.com/usemethod.html`)
- Tom Wilkie's RED Metrics: Requests, errors, and duration (`https://www.weave.works/blog/the-red-method-key-metrics-for-microservices-architecture/`)
- Google SRE's four Golden Signals: Latency, traffic, errors, and saturation (`https://landing.google.com/sre/sre-book/chapters/monitoring-distributed-systems/`)

We will discuss these concepts further in `Chapter 15`, *Comparing Code Quality Across Versions*. These paradigms help us to make smart decisions about the performance optimizations in our code as well as avoid premature optimization. Premature optimization plays as a very crucial aspect for many a computer programmers. Very frequently, we have to determine what *fast enough* is. We can waste our time trying to optimize a small segment of code when many other code paths have an opportunity to improve from a performance perspective. Go's simplicity allows for additional optimization without cognitive load overhead or an increase in code complexity. The algorithms that we will discuss in `Chapter 2`, *Data Structures and Algorithms*, will help us to avoid premature optimization.

Optimization strategies overview

In this book, we will also attempt to understand what exactly we are optimizing for. The techniques for optimizing for CPU or memory utilization may look very different than optimizing for I/O or network latency. Being cognizant of your problem space as well as your limitations within your hardware and upstream APIs will help you to determine how to optimize for the problem statement at hand. Optimization also often shows diminishing returns. Frequently the return on development investment for a particular code hotspot isn't worthwhile based on extraneous factors, or adding optimizations will decrease readability and increase risk for the whole system. If you can determine whether an optimization is worth doing early on, you'll be able to have a more narrowly scoped focus and will likely continue to develop a more performant system.

It can be helpful to understand baseline operations within a computer system. *Peter Norvig*, the Director of Research at Google, designed a table (the image that follows) to help developers understand the various common timing operations on a typical computer (`https://norvig.com/21-days.html#answers`):

Execute typical instruction	1/1,000,000,000 sec = 1 nanosec
Fetch from L1 cache memory	0.5 nanosec
Branch misprediction	5 nanosec
Fetch from L2 cache memory	7 nanosec
Mutex lock/unlock	25 nanosec
Fetch from main memory	100 nanosec
Send 2K bytes over 1Gbps network	20,000 nanosec
Read 1MB sequentially from memory	250,000 nanosec
Fetch from new disk location (seek)	8,000,000 nanosec
Read 1MB sequentially from disk	20,000,000 nanosec
Send packet US to Europe and back	150 milliseconds = 150,000,000 nanosec

Having a clear understanding of how different parts of a computer can interoperate with one another helps us to deduce where our performance optimizations should lie. As derived from the table, it takes quite a bit longer to read 1 MB of data sequentially from disk versus sending 2 KBs over a 1 Gbps network link. Being able to have *back-of-the-napkin math* comparison operators for common computer interactions can very much help to deduce which piece of your code you should optimize next. Determining bottlenecks within your program becomes easier when you take a step back and look at a snapshot of the system as a whole.

Breaking down performance problems into small, manageable sub problems that can be improved upon concurrently is a helpful shift into optimization. Trying to tackle all performance problems at once can often leave the developer stymied and frustrated, and often lead to many performance efforts failing. Focusing on bottlenecks in the current system can often yield results. Fixing one bottleneck will often quickly identify another. For example, after you fix a CPU utilization problem, you may find that your system's disk can't write the values that are computed fast enough. Working through bottlenecks in a structured fashion is one of the best ways to create a piece of performant and reliable software.

Optimization levels

Starting at the bottom of the pyramid in the following image, we can work our way up to the top. This diagram shows a suggested priority for making performance optimizations. The first two levels of this pyramid—the design level and algorithm and data structures level—will often provide more than ample real-world performance optimization targets. The following diagram shows an optimization strategy that is often efficient. Changing the design of a program alongside the algorithms and data structures are often the most efficient places to improve the speed and quality of code bases:

Design-level decisions often have the most measurable impact on performance. Determining goals during the design level can help to determine the best methodology for optimization. For example, if we are optimizing for a system that has slow disk I/O, we should prioritize lowering the number of calls to our disk. Inversely, if we are optimizing for a system that has limited compute resources, we need to calculate only the most essential values needed for our program's response. Creating a detailed design document at the inception of a new project will help with understanding where performance gains are important and how to prioritize time within the project. Thinking from a perspective of transferring payloads within a compute system can often lead to noticing places where optimization can occur. We will talk more about design patterns in Chapter 3, *Understanding Concurrency*.

Algorithm and data structure decisions often have a measurable performance impact on a computer program. We should focus on trying to utilize constant $O(1)$, logarithmic $O(\log n)$, linear $O(n)$, and log-linear $O(n \log n)$ functions while writing performant code. Avoiding quadratic complexity $O(n^2)$ at scale is also important for writing scalable programs. We will talk more about O notation and its relation to Go in Chapter 2, *Data Structures and Algorithms*.

A brief history of Go

Robert Griesemer, Rob Pike, and Ken Thompson created the Go programming language in 2007. It was originally designed as a general-purpose language with a keen focus on systems programming. The creators designed the Go language with a couple of core tenets in mind:

- Static typing
- Runtime efficiency
- Readable
- Usable
- Easy to learn
- High-performance networking and multiprocessing

Go was publicly announced in 2009 and v1.0.3 was released on March 3, 2012. At the time of the writing of this book, Go version 1.14 has been released, and Go version 2 is on the horizon. As mentioned, one of Go's initial core architecture considerations was to have high-performance networking and multiprocessing. This book will cover a lot of the design considerations that Griesemer, Pike, and Thompson have implemented and evangelized on behalf of their language. The designers created Go because they were unhappy with some of the choices and directions that were made in the C++ language. Long-running complications on large distributed compile clusters were a main source of pain for the creators. During this time, the authors started learning about the next C++ programming language release, dubbed C++x11. This C++ release had very many new features being planned, and the Go team decided they wanted to adopt an idiom of *less is more* in the computing language that they were using to do their work.

The authors of the language had their first meeting where they discussed starting with the C programming language, building features and removing extraneous functionality they didn't feel was important to the language. The team ended up starting from scratch, only borrowing some of the most atomic pieces of C and other languages they were comfortable with writing. After their work started to take form, they realized that they were taking away some of the core traits of other languages, notably the absence of headers, circular dependencies, and classes. The authors believe that even with the removal of many of these fragments, Go still can be more expressive than its predecessors.

The Go standard library

The standard library in Go follows this same pattern. It has been designed with both simplicity and functionality in mind. Adding slices, maps, and composite literals to the standard library helped the language to become opinionated early. Go's standard library lives within $GOROOT and is directly importable. Having these default data structures built into the language enables developers to use these data structures effectively. The standard library packages are bundled in with the language distribution and are available immediately after you install Go. It is often mentioned that the standard library is a solid reference on how to write idiomatic Go. The reasoning on standard library idiomatic Go is these core library pieces are written clearly, concisely, and with quite a bit of context. They also add small but important implementation details well, such as being able to set timeouts for connections and being explicitly able to gather data from underlying functions. These language details have helped the language to flourish.

Some of the notable Go runtime features include the following:

- Garbage collection for safe memory management (a concurrent, tri-color, mark-sweep collector)
- Concurrency to support more than one task simultaneously (more about this in Chapter 3, *Understanding Concurrency*)
- Stack management for memory optimization (segmented stacks were used in the original implementation; stack copying is the current incantation of Go stack management)

Go toolset

Go's binary release also includes a vast toolset for creating optimized code. Within the Go binary, the go command has a lot of functions that help to build, deploy, and validate code. Let's discuss a couple of the core pieces of functionality as they relate to performance.

Godoc is Go's documentation tool that keeps the cruxes of documentation at the forefront of program development. A clean implementation, in-depth documentation, and modularity are all core pieces of building a scalable, performant system. Godoc helps with accomplishing these goals by auto-generating documentation. Godoc extracts and generates documentation from packages it finds within $GOROOT and $GOPATH. After generating this documentation, Godoc runs a web server and displays the generated documentation as a web page. Documentation for the standard library can be seen on the Go website. As an example, the documentation for the standard library pprof package can be found at https://golang.org/pkg/net/http/pprof/.

The addition of gofmt (Go's code formatting tool) to the language brought a different kind of performance to Go. The inception of gofmt allowed Go to be very opinionated when it comes to code formatting. Having precise enforced formatting rules makes it possible to write Go in a way that is sensible for the developer whilst letting the tool format the code to follow a consistent pattern across Go projects. Many developers have their IDE or text editor perform a gofmt command when they save the file that they are composing. Consistent code formatting reduces the cognitive load and allows the developer to focus on other aspects of their code, rather than determining whether to use tabs or spaces to indent their code. Reducing the cognitive load helps with developer momentum and project velocity.

Go's build system also helps with performance. The `go build` command is a powerful tool that compiles packages and their dependencies. Go's build system is also helpful in dependency management. The resulting output from the build system is a compiled, statically linked binary that contains all of the necessary elements to run on the platform that you've compiled for. `go module` (a new feature with preliminary support introduced in Go 1.11 and finalized in Go 1.13) is a dependency management system for Go. Having explicit dependency management for a language helps to deliver a consistent experience with groupings of versioned packages as a cohesive unit, allowing for more reproducible builds. Having reproducible builds helps developers to create binaries via a verifiable path from the source code. The optional step to create a vendored directory within your project also helps with locally storing and satisfying dependencies for your project.

Compiled binaries are also an important piece of the Go ecosystem. Go also lets you build your binaries for other target environments, which can be useful if you need to cross-compile a binary for another computer architecture. Having the ability to build a binary that can run on any platform helps you to rapidly iterate and test your code to find bottlenecks on alternate architectures before they become more difficult to fix. Another key feature of the language is that you can compile a binary on one machine with the OS and architecture flags, and that binary is executable on another system. This is crucial when the build system has high amounts of system resources and the build target has limited computing resources. Building a binary for two architectures is as simple as setting build flags:

To build a binary for macOS X on an x86_64 architecture, the following execution pattern is used:

```
GOOS=darwin GOARCH=amd64 go build -o myapp.osx
```

To build a binary for Linux on an ARM architecture, the following execution pattern is used:

```
GOOS=linux GOARCH=arm go build -o myapp.linuxarm
```

You can find a list of all the valid combinations of GOOS and GOARCH using the following command:

```
go tool dist list -json
```

This can be helpful in allowing you to see all of the CPU architectures and OSes that the Go language can compile binaries for.

Benchmarking overview

The concept of benchmarking will also be a core tenant in this book. Go's testing functionality has performance built in as a first-class citizen. Being able to trigger a test benchmark during your development and release processes makes it possible to continue to deliver performant code. As new side effects are introduced, features are added, and code complexity increases, it's important to have a method for validating performance regression across a code base. Many developers add benchmarking results to their continuous integration practices to ensure that their code continues to be performant with all of the new pull requests added to a repository. You can also use the `benchstat` utility provided in the `golang.org/x/perf/cmd/benchstat` package to compare statistics about benchmarks. The following sample repository has an example of benchmarking the standard library's sort functions, at `https://github.com/bobstrecansky/HighPerformanceWithGo/tree/master/1-introduction`.

Having testing and benchmarking married closely in the standard library encourages performance testing as part of your code release process. It's always important to remember that benchmarks are not always indicative of real-world performance scenarios, so take the results you receive from them with a grain of salt. Logging, monitoring, profiling, and tracing a running system (as will be discussed in Chapter 12, *Profiling Go Code*; Chapter 13, *Tracing Go Code*; and Chapter 15, *Comparing Code Quality Across Versions*) can help to validate the assumptions that you have made with your benchmarking after you've committed the code you are working on.

The ideology behind Go performance

Much of Go's performance stance is gained from concurrency and parallelism. Goroutines and channels are often used to perform many requests in parallel. The tools available for Go help to achieve near C-like performance, with very readable semantics. This is one of the many reasons that Go is commonly used by developers in large-scale solutions.

Goroutines – performance from the start

When Go was conceived, multi-core processors were beginning to become more and more commonplace in commercially available commodity hardware. The authors of the Go language recognized a need for concurrency within their new language. Go makes concurrent programming easy with goroutines and channels (which we will discuss in Chapter 3, *Understanding Concurrency*). Goroutines, lightweight computation threads that are distinct from OS threads, are often described as one of the best features of the language. Goroutines execute their code in parallel and complete when their work is done. The startup time for a goroutine is faster than the startup time for a thread, which allows a lot more concurrent work to occur within your program. Compared to a language such as Java that relies on OS threads, Go can be much more efficient with its multiprocessing model. Go is also intelligent about blocking operations with respect to goroutines. This helps Go to be more performant in memory utilization, garbage collection, and latency. Go's runtime uses the GOMAXPROCS variable to multiplex goroutines onto real OS threads. We will learn more about goroutines in Chapter 2, *Data Structures and Algorithms*.

Channels – a typed conduit

Channels provide a model to send and receive data between goroutines, whilst skipping past synchronization primitives provided by the underlying platform. With properly thought-out goroutines and channels, we can achieve high performance. Channels can be both buffered and unbuffered, so the developer can pass a dynamic amount of data through an open channel until the value has been received by the receiver, at which time the channel is unblocked by the sender. If the channel is buffered, the sender blocks for the given size of the buffer. Once the buffer has been filled, the sender will unblock the channel. Lastly, the close() function can be invoked to indicate that the channel will not receive any more values. We will learn more about channels in Chapter 3, *Understanding Concurrency*.

C-comparable performance

Another initial goal was to approach the performance of C for comparable programs. Go also has extensive profiling and tracing tools baked into the language that we'll learn about in Chapter 12, *Profiling Go Code*, and Chapter 13, *Tracing Go Code*. Go gives developers the ability to see a breakdown of goroutine usage, channels, memory and CPU utilization, and function calls as they pertain to individual calls. This is valuable because Go makes it easy to troubleshoot performance problems with data and visualizations.

Large-scale distributed systems

Go is often used in large-scale distributed systems due to its operational simplicity and its built-in network primitives in the standard library. Being able to rapidly iterate whilst developing is an essential part of building a robust, scalable system. High network latency is often an issue in distributed systems, and the Go team has worked to try and alleviate this concern on their platform. From standard library network implementations to making gRPC a first-class citizen for passing buffered messaging between clients and servers on a distributed platform, the Go language developers have put distributed systems problems at the forefront of the problem space for their language and have come up with some elegant solutions for these complex problems.

Summary

In this chapter, we learned the core concepts of performance in computer science. We also learned some of the history of the Go computer programming language and how its inception ties in directly with performance work. Lastly, we learned that Go is used in a myriad of different cases because of the utility, flexibility, and extensibility of the language. This chapter has introduced concepts that will continually be built upon in this book, allowing you to rethink the way you are writing your Go code.

In Chapter 2, *Data Structures and Algorithms*, we'll dive into data structures and algorithms. We'll learn about different algorithms, their Big O notation, and how these algorithms are constructed in Go. We'll also learn about how these theoretical algorithms relate to real-world problems and write performant Go to serve large amounts of requests quickly and efficiently. Learning more about these algorithms will help you to become more efficient in the second layer of the optimizations triangle that was laid out earlier in this chapter.

Data Structures and Algorithms 2

Data structures and algorithms are the basic units of building software, notably complex, performance software. Understanding them helps us think about how to impactfully organize and manipulate data in order to write effective, performant software. This chapter will include explanations of different data structures and algorithms, as well as how their Big O notation is impacted.

As we mentioned in `Chapter 1`, *Introduction to Performance in Go*, design-level decisions very often have the most measurable impact on performance. The least expensive calculation is the one you don't have to make – if you work toward optimizing your design early on while architecting your software, you can save yourself from a lot of performance penalties down the line.

In this chapter, we will be discussing the following topics:

- Benchmarking by utilizing Big O notation
- Search and sort algorithms
- Trees
- Queues

Creating simple data structures that don't contain superfluous information will help you write practical, performant code. Algorithms will also help improve the performance of the data structures that you have.

Understanding benchmarking

Metrics and measurement are at the root of optimization. The adage *You can't improve what you can't measure* rings true with performance. To be able to make intelligent decisions about performance optimizations, we must continuously measure the performance of the functions we are trying to optimize.

As we mentioned in `Chapter 1`, *Introduction to Performance in Go*, the Go creators made performance a forethought in their language design. The Go testing package (`https://golang.org/pkg/testing/`) is used to test Go code in a systematic way. The testing package is a fundamental part of the Go language. This package also includes a helpful built-in benchmarking functionality. This functionality, which is invoked by `go test -bench`, runs the benchmarks that you've defined for your functions. The results from your tests can also be saved and viewed at a later date. Having previous results of benchmarks from your functions available allows you to track the long-term changes that you are making in your functions and their outcomes. Benchmarking dovetails nicely with profiling and tracing to retrieve an accurate report of the state of our system. We will learn more about profiling and tracing in `Chapter 12`, *Profiling Go Code*, and `Chapter 13`, *Tracing Go Code*. As we are benchmarking, it's important to note that CPU frequency scaling should be disabled (see `https://blog.golang.org/profiling-go-programs`). This will allow for more consistent benchmarking across benchmarking runs. An included bash script for disabling frequency scaling can be found at `https://github.com/bobstrecansky/HighPerformanceWithGo/blob/master/frequency_scaling_governor_diable.bash`.

Benchmark execution

Benchmarks in Go use the axiom of starting with the word `Benchmark` (with a capital B) in the function call to denote that they are a benchmark and that they should use the benchmark functionality. To execute the benchmarks that you've defined for your code in your test package, you can use the `-bench=.` flag in your `go test` execution. This testing flag ensures all your benchmarking tests are run. An example of a benchmark is shown in the following code block:

```
package hello_test
import (
    "fmt"
    "testing"
)
func BenchmarkHello(b *testing.B) { // Benchmark definition
    for i := 0; i < b.N; i++ {
        fmt.Sprintf("Hello High Performance Go")
    }
}
```

In this (admittedly simple) benchmark, we are iterating over our `fmt.Sprintf` statement b.N times. The benchmarking package executes and runs our `Sprintf` statement. During our test run, `b.N` is adjusted in the benchmark test until this function can be timed reliably. By default, a go benchmark test is run for 1 second in order to get a statistically significant result set.

There are a number of flags that are available during the invocation of the benchmarking utility. A few helpful flags for benchmarking can be found in the following table:

Flag	Use Case
`-benchtime t`	Run enough iterations of the test to take the defined t duration. Increasing this value will run more iterations of `b.N`.
`-count n`	Run each test n times.
`-benchmem`	Turn on memory profiling for your test.
`-cpu x,y,z`	Specify a list of GOMAXPROCS values for which the benchmarks should be executed.

The following is an example of benchmark execution. In our example execution, we are profiling our existing Hello benchmark twice. We're also using four GOMAXPROCS, viewing the memory profiling for our test, and performing these requests for 2 seconds instead of the default 1-second test invocation. We can invoke our `go test -bench` functionality like this:

```
$ go test -bench=. -benchtime 2s -count 2 -benchmem -cpu 4
```

A benchmark will run until the function returns, fails, or skips. The results of the benchmark are returned as a standard error once the test has completed. After the tests have completed and the results have been collated, we can make smart comparisons about the results of our benchmarks. Our following result shows an example test execution and the resulting output from the preceding `BenchmarkHello` function:

```
bob@blinky:~/git/HighPerformanceWithGo/2-data-structures-and-algorithms/hello          ×

File  Edit  View  Search  Terminal  Help
[bob@blinky hello]$ go test -bench=.
goos: linux
goarch: amd64
BenchmarkHello-8            10000000                    112 ns/op
PASS
ok      _/home/bob/git/HighPerformanceWithGo/2-data-structures-and-algorithms/he
llo     1.257s
[bob@blinky hello]$
```

In our output result, we can see a couple of different bits of data being returned:

- GOOS and GOARCH (which were discussed in the *Go toolset* section of Chapter 1, *Introduction to Performance in Go*)
- The name of the benchmark that was run, followed by the following:
  - **-8**: The number of GOMAXPROCS that were used to execute the tests.
  - **10000000**: The number of times our loop ran to gather the necessary data.
  - **112 ns/op**: The speed per loop during our test.
  - **PASS**: Indicates the end state of our benchmark run.
  - The final line of the test, with a compilation of the end state of our test run (**ok**), the path that we ran the test on, and the total time of our test run.

Real-world benchmarking

While you are running the benchmarks in this book, be sure to remember that benchmarks aren't the be-all and end-all for performance results. Benchmarking has both positives and drawbacks:

The positives of benchmarking are as follows:

- Surfaces potential problems before they become unwieldy
- Helps developers have a deeper understanding of their code
- Can identify potential bottlenecks in the design and data structures and algorithms stages

The drawbacks of benchmarking are as follows:

- Needs to be completed on a given cadence for meaningful results
- Data collation can be difficult
- Does not always yield a meaningful result for the problem at hand

Benchmarking is good for comparison. Benchmarking two things against one another on the same system can yield relatively consistent results. If you have the ability to run longer running benchmarks, it'll probably give you a much more indicative result of how a function is performing.

The Go benchstat (https://godoc.org/golang.org/x/perf/cmd/benchstat) package is a useful utility that helps you compare two benchmarks. Comparisons are very important in order to deduce whether or not the change you made to your function had a positive or negative impact on the system. You can install benchstat by using the go get utility:

```
go get golang.org/x/perf/cmd/benchstat
```

Consider the following comparison test. We are going to test the marshaling of a single JSON structure with three elements, compared to the marshaling of two JSON arrays with five elements. You can find the source for these at https://github.com/bobstrecansky/HighPerformanceWithGo/tree/master/2-data-structures-and-algorithms/Benchstat-comparison.

To get an example comparison operator, we execute our benchmarks against our tests, as shown in the following code snippet:

```
[bob@testhost single]$ go test -bench=. -count 5 -cpu 1,2,4 > ~/single.txt
[bob@testhost multi]$ go test -bench=. -count 5 -cpu 1,2,4 > ~/multi.txt
[bob@testhost ~]$ benchstat -html -sort -delta single.txt multi.txt >
out.html
```

This produces an HTML table that can be used to validate the largest delta at execution time. As shown in the following screenshot, adding even a small amount of complexity to our data structure and the number of elements we process makes a fairly substantial change to the execution time of the function:

	single.txt	multi.txt	delta	
	time/op		delta	
JSON-2	708ns ± 2%	1703ns ± 1%	+140.58%	(p=0.008 n=5+5)
JSON	709ns ± 0%	1711ns ± 1%	+141.19%	(p=0.008 n=5+5)
JSON-4	714ns ± 1%	1741ns ± 1%	+143.77%	(p=0.008 n=5+5)

Quickly identifying the performance pain points for your end users can help you determine the path to writing performant software.

In the next section, we will see what Big O notation is.

Introducing Big O notation

Big O notation is a good way to approximate the speed in which the algorithm you've chosen will change with the size of the data that's passed to your algorithm. Big O notation is often described as the growth behavior of a function, specifically its upper limit. Big O notation is broken down into classes. The most common classes that are described are O(1), O(log n), O(n), O(n log n), $O(n^2)$, and $O(2^n)$. Let's take a quick look at each of these algorithms, their definitions, and a practical example of them in Go.

A graph of these common classes is as follows. The source code for generating this plot can be found at `https://github.com/bobstrecansky/HighPerformanceWithGo/blob/master/2-data-structures-and-algorithms/plot/plot.go`:

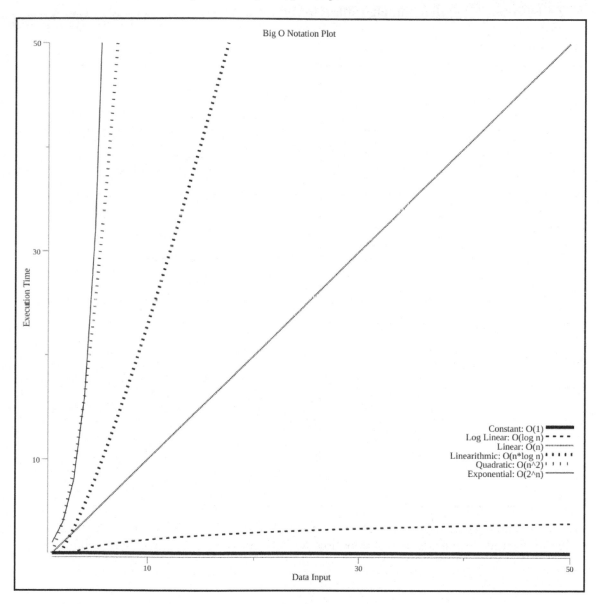

This Big O notation graph gives us a visual representation of the different algorithms that are commonly used in computer software.

Practical Big O notation example

If we take a sample dataset of 32 input values, we can quickly calculate the amount of time it's going to take for each of our algorithms to complete. You'll notice that the unit time to complete in the following table starts to grow very quickly. The practical Big O notation values are as follows:

Algorithm	Unit time to complete
O(1)	1
O(log n)	5
O(n)	32
O(n log n)	160
O(n^2)	1,024
O(2^n)	4,294,967,296

As the unit time to complete gets larger, our code becomes less performant. We should strive to use the simplest algorithm possible to solve the dataset that we have at hand.

Data structure operations and time complexity

The following diagram contains some of the common data structure operations and their time complexities. As we mentioned previously, data structures are a core piece of computer science performance. Understanding the difference between different data structures is important when writing performant code. Having this table readily accessible can help the developer choose the right data structure operation for the task at hand, while considering the impact that this operation is going to have on performance:

Common Data Structure Operations

Data Structure	Time Complexity								Space Complexity
	Average				Worst				Worst
	Access	Search	Insertion	Deletion	Access	Search	Insertion	Deletion	
Array	$\Theta(1)$	$\Theta(n)$	$\Theta(n)$	$\Theta(n)$	$O(1)$	$O(n)$	$O(n)$	$O(n)$	$O(n)$
Stack	$\Theta(n)$	$\Theta(n)$	$\Theta(1)$	$O(1)$	$O(n)$	$O(n)$	$O(1)$	$O(1)$	$O(n)$
Queue	$\Theta(n)$	$\Theta(n)$	$\Theta(1)$	$\Theta(1)$	$O(n)$	$O(n)$	$O(1)$	$O(1)$	$O(n)$
Singly-Linked List	$\Theta(n)$	$\Theta(n)$	$\Theta(1)$	$\Theta(1)$	$O(n)$	$O(n)$	$O(1)$	$O(1)$	$O(n)$
Doubly-Linked List	$\Theta(n)$	$\Theta(n)$	$\Theta(1)$	$\Theta(1)$	$O(n)$	$O(n)$	$O(1)$	$O(1)$	$O(n)$
Skip List	$\Theta(\log(n))$	$\Theta(\log(n))$	$\Theta(\log(n))$	$O(\log(n))$	$O(n)$	$O(n)$	$O(n)$	$O(n)$	$O(n\ \log(n))$
Hash Table	N/A	$\Theta(1)$	$\Theta(1)$	$\Theta(1)$	N/A	$O(n)$	$O(n)$	$O(n)$	$O(n)$
Binary Search Tree	$\Theta(\log(n))$	$\Theta(\log(n))$	$\Theta(\log(n))$	$\Theta(\log(n))$	$O(n)$	$O(n)$	$O(n)$	$O(n)$	$O(n)$
Cartesian Tree	N/A	$\Theta(\log(n))$	$\Theta(\log(n))$	$\Theta(\log(n))$	N/A	$O(n)$	$O(n)$	$O(n)$	$O(n)$
B-Tree	$\Theta(\log(n))$	$\Theta(\log(n))$	$\Theta(\log(n))$	$\Theta(\log(n))$	$O(\log(n))$	$O(\log(n))$	$O(\log(n))$	$O(\log(n))$	$O(n)$
Red-Black Tree	$\Theta(\log(n))$	$\Theta(\log(n))$	$\Theta(\log(n))$	$\Theta(\log(n))$	$O(\log(n))$	$O(\log(n))$	$O(\log(n))$	$O(\log(n))$	$O(n)$
Splay Tree	N/A	$\Theta(\log(n))$	$\Theta(\log(n))$	$\Theta(\log(n))$	N/A	$O(\log(n))$	$O(\log(n))$	$O(\log(n))$	$O(n)$
AVL Tree	$\Theta(\log(n))$	$\Theta(\log(n))$	$\Theta(\log(n))$	$\Theta(\log(n))$	$O(\log(n))$	$O(\log(n))$	$O(\log(n))$	$O(\log(n))$	$O(n)$
KD Tree	$\Theta(\log(n))$	$\Theta(\log(n))$	$\Theta(\log(n))$	$\Theta(\log(n))$	$O(n)$	$O(n)$	$O(n)$	$O(n)$	$O(n)$

Common data structure operations (from bigocheatsheet.com) – thanks to Eric Rowell

This table shows us time and space complexity given specific data structures. It is a valuable performance reference tool.

O(1) – constant time

Algorithms written in constant time have an upper bound that does not depend on the input size of the algorithm. Constant time is an upper bound by a constant value, and thus won't take longer than the upper bound of the dataset. This type of algorithm is usually okay to add to a function in practice – it doesn't add a lot of processing time to your function. Make sure to note the constant that occurs here. A single array lookup adds a negligible amount of time to a function. Looking up thousands of individual values in an array may add some overhead. Performance is always relative, and it is important to maintain cognizant of the additional load you're adding to your functions, even if they only perform a trivial amount of processing.

Examples of constant time are as follows:

- Accessing a single element in a map or an array
- Determining the modulus of a number
- Stack push or stack pop
- Deducing whether or not an integer is even or odd

An example of a constant time algorithm in Go would be accessing a single element within an array.

This would be written as follows in Go:

```
package main
import "fmt"
func main() {
    words := [3]string{"foo", "bar", "baz"}
    fmt.Println(words[1]) // This references the string in position 1 in the
array, "bar"
}
```

This function has a Big O notation of O(1) because we only have to look at the individual defined value of `words[1]` in order to find the value we are looking for, that is, `bar`. As our array size in this example grows, the time to refer to an object within the array will remain constant. The normalized timings for this algorithm should all be the same, as shown in the following table:

Number of items in the dataset	Resulting computation time
10	1 second
100	1 second
1,000	1 second

Some sample code for O(1) notation is as follows:

```
package oone

func ThreeWords() string {
  threewords := [3]string{"foo", "bar", "baz"}
  return threewords[1]
}

func TenWords() string {
  tenwords := [10]string{"foo", "bar", "baz", "qux", "grault", "waldo",
"plugh", "xyzzy", "thud", "spam"}
  return tenwords[6]
}
```

No matter how many items are in an array, the lookup for one element takes the same amount of time. In the following example output, we have arrays with three elements and 10 elements, respectively. Both take the same amount of time to execute and complete the same number of test iterations within their allotted time frame. This can be seen in the following screenshot:

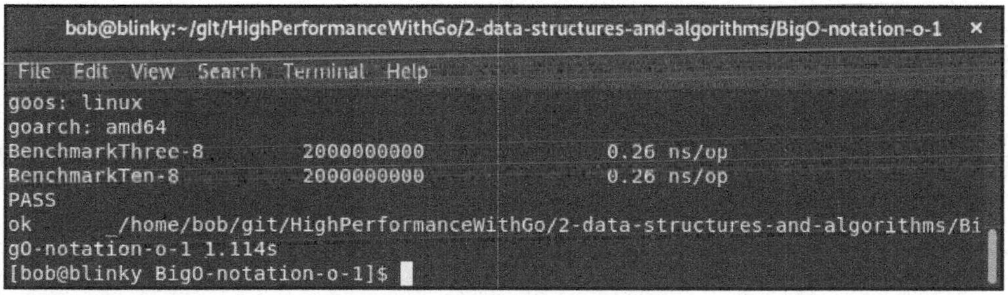

This benchmark performs as we would expect it to. Both the BenchmarkThree and BenchmarkTen benchmarks took **0.26 ns/op**, which should be consistent across array lookups.

O(log n) - logarithmic time

Logarithmic growth is often represented as a partial sum of the harmonic series. This can be represented as follows:

$$1 + \frac{1}{2} + \frac{1}{3} + \cdots + \frac{1}{n}$$

An algorithm written in logarithmic time has a number of operations that tend toward zero as the size of the input decreases. An O(log n) algorithm cannot be used in an algorithm when all of the elements in the array must be accessed. O(log n) is usually considered an efficient algorithm when it is used by itself. One important concept to think about with respect to performance in logarithmic time is that search algorithms are commonly used with sort algorithms, which adds to the complexity of finding the solution. Depending on the size and complexity of the dataset, it can often make sense to sort the data before the search algorithm is executed. Note the input and output ranges for this test – additional tests were added to show the logarithmic growth of the resulting computation time of the dataset.

Some examples of logarithmic time algorithms are as follows:

- Binary search
- Dictionary search

The following table shows the normalized timings for logarithmic time:

Number of items in the dataset	Resulting computation time
10	1 second
100	2 seconds
1,000	3 seconds

Go's standard library has a function called `sort.Search()`. It has been included in the following snippet for reference:

```
func Search(n int, f func(int) bool) int {
    // Define f(-1) == false and f(n) == true.
    // Invariant: f(i-1) == false, f(j) == true.
    i, j := 0, n
    for i < j {
        h := int(uint(i+j) >> 1) // avoid overflow when computing h
        // i ≤ h < j
        if !f(h) {
            i = h + 1 // preserves f(i-1) == false
        } else {
            j = h // preserves f(j) == true
        }
    }
    // i == j, f(i-1) == false, and f(j) (= f(i)) == true => answer is i.
    return i
}
```

This code sample can be found in the standard library at `https://golang.org/src/sort/search.go`. The code and benchmark for an O(log n) function can be found at `https://github.com/bobstrecansky/HighPerformanceWithGo/tree/master/2-data-structures-and-algorithms/BigO-notation-o-logn`.

The following screenshot shows a logarithmic time benchmark:

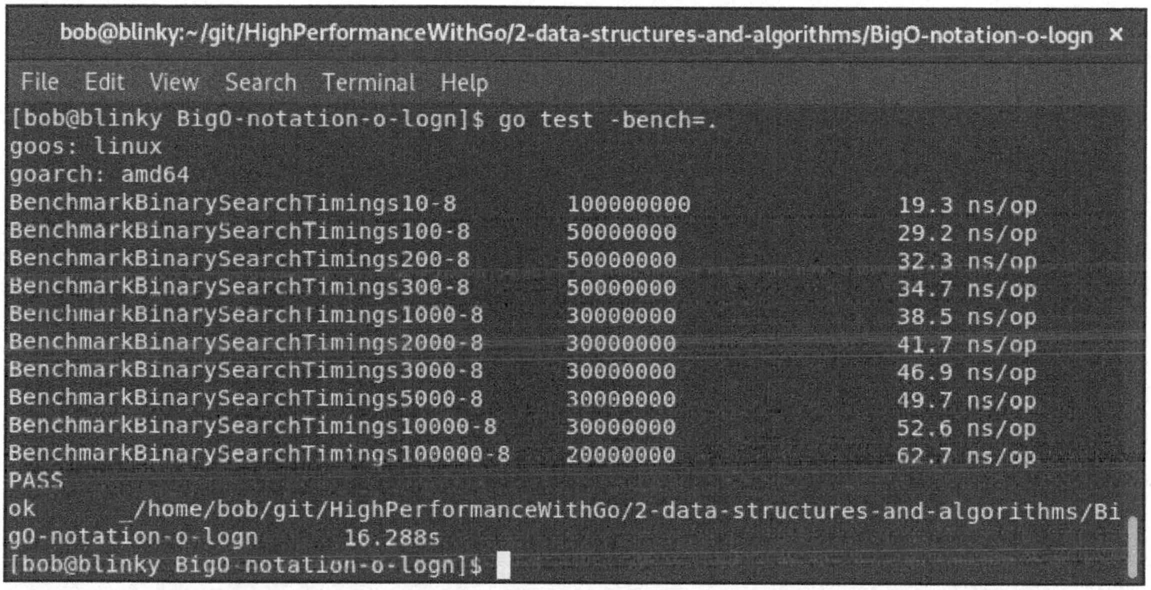

This test shows a logarithmic increase in timing based on the input we set. Algorithms with a logarithmic time response are very helpful in writing performant code.

O(n) – linear time

Algorithms written in linear time scale linearly with the size of their dataset. Linear time is the best possible time complexity when an entire dataset needs to be read sequentially. The amount of time an algorithm takes in linear time, scales on a 1:1 relationship with the number of items that are contained within the dataset.

Some examples of linear time are as follows:

- Simple loop
- Linear search

Normalized timings for linear time can be found in the following table:

Number of items in the dataset	Resulting computation time
10	10 seconds
100	100 seconds
1,000	1,000 seconds

Note that the result computation time increases linearly and correlates to the number of items that were found in our dataset (refer to the following screenshot). The code and benchmark of an O(n) function can be found at `https://github.com/bobstrecansky/HighPerformanceWithGo/tree/master/2-data-structures-and-algorithms/BigO-notation-o-n`:

An important point to remember is that Big O notation isn't necessarily a perfect indicator of response time growth; it just denotes an upper ceiling. While reviewing this benchmark, focus on the fact that the resulting computation time grows linearly with the number of items in the dataset. O(n) algorithms are typically not the big showstopper in computer science from a performance perspective. Computer scientists perform loops on iterators frequently, and it's a common pattern that's used to get computational work completed. Make sure that you're always cognizant of the size of your dataset!

O(n log n) – quasilinear time

Algorithms written in quasilinear (or log-linear) time are often used to order values within an array in Go.

Some examples of quasilinear time are as follows:

- The average case time complexity for Quicksort
- The average case time complexity for Mergesort
- The average case time complexity for Heapsort
- The average case time complexity for Timsort

The normalized timings for quasilinear time can be found in the following table:

Number of items in the dataset	Resulting computation time
10	10 seconds
100	200 seconds
1,000	3,000 seconds

You'll see a familiar pattern here. This algorithm follows a pattern that's similar to the O(log n) algorithm. The only thing that changes here is the n multiplier, so we can see similar results with a scaling factor (refer to the following screenshot). The code and benchmark of an O(n log n) function can be found at https://github.com/bobstrecansky/ HighPerformanceWithGo/tree/master/2 data-structures-and-algorithms/BigO-notation-o-nlogn:

```
bob@blinky:~/git/HighPerformanceWithGo/2-data-structures-and-algorithms/BigO-notation-o-nlogn   ×

File   Edit   View   Search   Terminal   Help
[bob@blinky BigO-notation-o-nlogn]$ go test -bench=.
goos: linux
goarch: amd64
BenchmarkOnlognLoop10-8          30000000              34.8 ns/op
BenchmarkOnlognLoop100-8          3000000               478 ns/op
BenchmarkOnlognLoop1000-8          200000              6973 ns/op
PASS
ok      _/home/bob/git/HighPerformanceWithGo/2-data-structures-and-algorithms/Bi
gO-notation-o-nlogn     4.481s
[bob@blinky BigO-notation-o-nlogn]$
```

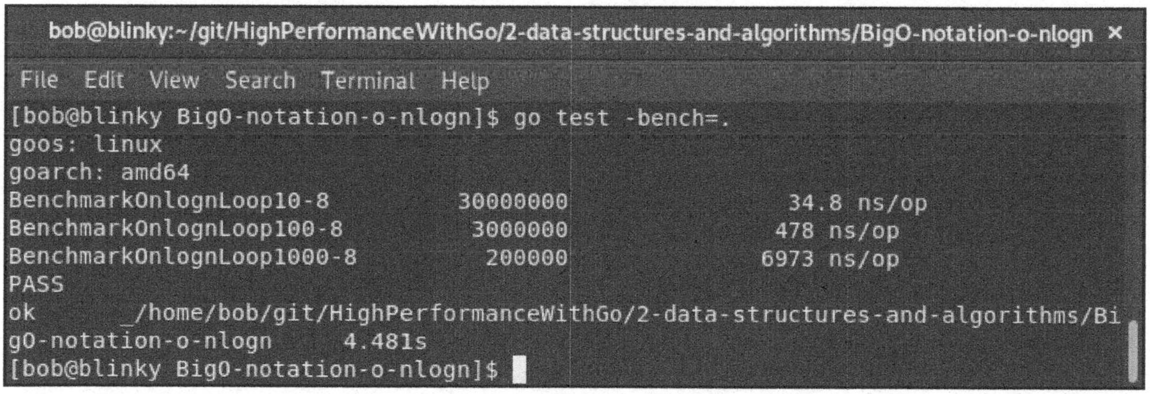

Sorting algorithms are still fairly fast and aren't the crux of ill-performing code. Frequently, sorting algorithms used in languages use a hybrid of multiple sorting algorithms based on size. Go's `quickSort` algorithm, the sort that's used in `sort.Sort()`, uses `ShellSort` and `insertionSort` if the slice contains less than 12 elements. This standard library algorithm for `quickSort` is as follows:

```
func quickSort(data Interface, a, b, maxDepth int) {
    for b-a > 12 { // Use ShellSort for slices <= 12 elements
```

```
    if maxDepth == 0 {
      heapSort(data, a, b)
      return
    }
    maxDepth--
    mlo, mhi := doPivot(data, a, b)
    // Avoiding recursion on the larger subproblem guarantees
    // a stack depth of at most lg(b-a).
    if mlo-a < b-mhi {
      quickSort(data, a, mlo, maxDepth)
      a = mhi // i.e., quickSort(data, mhi, b)
    } else {
      quickSort(data, mhi, b, maxDepth)
      b = mlo // i.e., quickSort(data, a, mlo)
    }
  }
  if b-a > 1 {
    // Do ShellSort pass with gap 6
    // It could be written in this simplified form cause b-a <= 12
    for i := a + 6; i < b; i++ {
      if data.Less(i, i-6) {
        data.Swap(i, i-6)
      }
    }
    insertionSort(data, a, b)
  }
}
```

The preceding code can be found in the standard library at https://golang.org/src/sort/ sort.go#L183. This quickSort algorithm is performant and is used constantly in the Go ecosystem.

O(n^2) – quadratic time

Algorithms written in quadratic time have an execution time that corresponds directly to the square of the input size. Nested loops are common quadratic time algorithms, which brings along sorting algorithms.

Some examples of quadratic time are as follows:

- Bubble Sort
- Insertion Sort
- Selection Sort

Normalized timings for quadratic time can be found in the following table:

Number of items in the dataset	Resulting computation time
10	100 seconds
100	10,000 seconds
1,000	1,000,000 seconds

You'll note from this table that as the input grows by a factor of 10, the resulting computation time grows quadratically.

Quadratic time algorithms should be avoided if possible. If you need to have a nested loop or a quadratic calculation, be sure to validate your inputs and attempt to constrain your input sizes.

The code and benchmark of an $O(n^2)$ function can be found at https://github.com/ bobstrecansky/HighPerformanceWithGo/tree/master/2-data-structures-and- algorithms/BigO-notation-o-n2. The following is the output of running this benchmark:

```
bob@blinky:~/git/HighPerformanceWithGo/2-data-structures-and-algorithms/BigO-notation-o-n2   ×
File  Edit  View  Search  Terminal  Help
[bob@blinky BigO-notation-o-n2]$ go test -bench=.
goos: linux
goarch: amd64
BenchmarkBubbleSort10-8              200000            9412 ns/op
BenchmarkBubbleSort100-8             50000           30602 ns/op
BenchmarkBubbleSort1000-8            1000          1605541 ns/op
BenchmarkBubbleSort10000-8          10        141126700 ns/op
BenchmarkBubbleSort100000-8          1      14104226133 ns/op
PASS
ok      _/home/bob/git/HighPerformanceWithGo/2-data-structures-and-algorithms/Bi
gO-notation-o-n2        21.268s
[bob@blinky BigO-notation-o-n2]$
```

Quadratic timing algorithms get very expensive very quickly. We can see this with our own benchmark.

$O(2^n)$ – exponential time

An exponential algorithm grows exponentially when data is added to the input set. These are usually used when there isn't an inclination of the input dataset and you must try every possible composite of the input set.

Some examples of exponential time are as follows:

- Poor recursion implementation of the Fibonacci sequence
- Towers of Hanoi
- Traveling salesman problem

Normalized timings for exponential time can be found in the following table:

Number of items in the dataset	Resulting computation time
10	1,024 seconds
100	$1.267 * 10^{30}$ seconds
1,000	$1.07 * 10^{301}$ seconds

As the number of items in the dataset grows, the resulting computation time grows exponentially.

Exponential time algorithms should only be used in dire situations with very narrowly scoped datasets. Usually, clarifying your underlying problem or dataset further can help you avoid using an exponential time algorithm.

The code for an $O(n^2)$ algorithm can be found at `https://github.com/bobstrecansky/HighPerformanceWithGo/tree/master/2-data-structures-and-algorithms/BigO-notation-o-n2`. Some example output for this benchmark can be seen in the following screenshot:

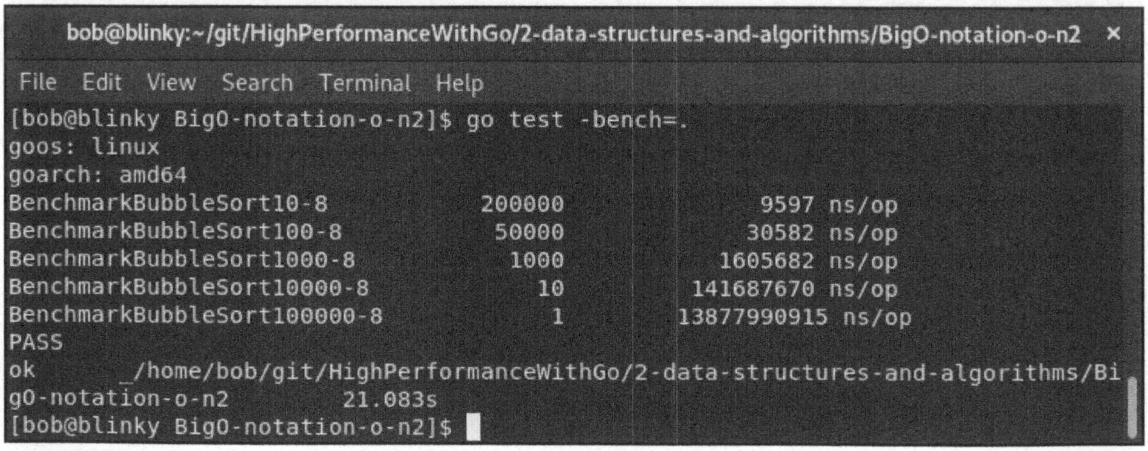

```
bob@blinky:~/git/HighPerformanceWithGo/2-data-structures-and-algorithms/BigO-notation-o-n2    ×

File   Edit   View   Search   Terminal   Help
[bob@blinky BigO-notation-o-n2]$ go test -bench=.
goos: linux
goarch: amd64
BenchmarkBubbleSort10-8          200000            9597 ns/op
BenchmarkBubbleSort100-8          50000           30582 ns/op
BenchmarkBubbleSort1000-8          1000         1605682 ns/op
BenchmarkBubbleSort10000-8           10       141687670 ns/op
BenchmarkBubbleSort100000-8           1     13877990915 ns/op
PASS
ok      _/home/bob/git/HighPerformanceWithGo/2-data-structures-and-algorithms/Bi
gO-notation-o-n2        21.083s
[bob@blinky BigO-notation-o-n2]$ 
```

Exponential time algorithm problems can often be broken down into smaller, more digestible pieces. This also allows for optimization.

In the next section, we will look at sort algorithms.

Understanding sort algorithms

Sorting algorithms are used to take individual elements in a dataset and put them in a specific order. Usually, sorting algorithms take a dataset and put them in either lexicographical or numerical order. Being able to sort efficiently is important in writing performant code, as many search algorithms require a sorted dataset. The common data structure operations can be seen in the following diagram:

Array Sorting Algorithms

Algorithm	Time Complexity			Space Complexity
	Best	Average	Worst	Worst
Quicksort	$\Omega(n \log(n))$	$\Theta(n \log(n))$	$O(n^2)$	$O(\log(n))$
Mergesort	$\Omega(n \log(n))$	$\Theta(n \log(n))$	$O(n \log(n))$	$O(n)$
Timsort	$\Omega(n)$	$\Theta(n \log(n))$	$O(n \log(n))$	$O(n)$
Heapsort	$\Omega(n \log(n))$	$\Theta(n \log(n))$	$O(n \log(n))$	$O(1)$
Bubble Sort	$\Omega(n)$	$\Theta(n^2)$	$O(n^2)$	$O(1)$
Insertion Sort	$\Omega(n)$	$\Theta(n^2)$	$O(n^2)$	$O(1)$
Selection Sort	$\Omega(n^2)$	$\Theta(n^2)$	$O(n^2)$	$O(1)$
Tree Sort	$\Omega(n \log(n))$	$\Theta(n \log(n))$	$O(n^2)$	$O(n)$
Shell Sort	$\Omega(n \log(n))$	$\Theta(n(\log(n))^2)$	$O(n(\log(n))^2)$	$O(1)$
Bucket Sort	$\Omega(n+k)$	$\Theta(n+k)$	$O(n^2)$	$O(n)$
Radix Sort	$\Omega(nk)$	$\Theta(nk)$	$O(nk)$	$O(n+k)$
Counting Sort	$\Omega(n+k)$	$\Theta(n+k)$	$O(n+k)$	$O(k)$
Cubesort	$\Omega(n)$	$\Theta(n \log(n))$	$O(n \log(n))$	$O(n)$

Common Data Structure Operations (from bigocheatsheet.com) - thanks to Eric Rowell

As you can see, array sorting algorithms can have vastly different Big O notation. Choosing the correct sort algorithm for your unordered list is important when it comes to providing an optimized solution.

Insertion sort

Insertion sort is a sorting algorithm that constructs an array one item at a time until it results in a sorted array. It's not very efficient, but it does have a simple implementation and is quick for very small datasets. The array is sorted in place, which can also help reduce the memory footprint of the function call.

This standard library algorithm for `insertionSort` can be found in the following code snippet. We can use the following code snippet to deduce that insertion sort is an average case of an $O(n^2)$ algorithm. This is due to the fact that we iterate through a 2D array and manipulate data:

```
func insertionSort(data Interface, a, b int) {
  for i := a + 1; i < b; i++ {
    for j := i; j > a && data.Less(j, j-1); j-- {
      data.Swap(j, j-1)
    }
  }
}
```

This code can be found in the standard library at `https://golang.org/src/sort/sort.go#L183`. A simple insertion sort is often valuable for small datasets because it is very easy to read and comprehend. Simplicity often outweighs everything else when it comes to writing performant code.

Heap sort

Go has a built-in `heapSort` in the standard library, as shown in the following code snippet. This code snippet helps us understand that `heapSort` is an $O(n \log n)$ sorting algorithm. This is better than our preceding insertion sort example, so for larger datasets, we are going to have more performant code when using our heap sort algorithm:

```
func heapSort(data Interface, a, b int) {
  first := a
  lo := 0
  hi := b - a
  // Build heap with greatest element at top.
  for i := (hi - 1) / 2; i >= 0; i-- {
    siftDown(data, i, hi, first)
  }
  // Pop elements, largest first, into end of data.
  for i := hi - 1; i >= 0; i-- {
    data.Swap(first, first+i)
    siftDown(data, lo, i, first)
```

```
      }
   }
```

This code can be found in the standard library at `https://golang.org/src/sort/sort.go#L53`. When our datasets become larger, it is important to start using efficient sort algorithms such as `heapSort`.

Merge sort

Merge sort is a sorting algorithm with an O(n log n) average time complexity. `MergeSort` is often used if the goal of the algorithm is to produce a stable sort. A stable sort ensures that two objects that share the same key in an input array appear in the resulting array in the same order. Stability is important if we want to make sure that a key-value order pair is organized within an array. An implementation of a stable sort can be found in the Go standard library. This can be seen in the following code snippet:

```
func stable(data Interface, n int) {
   blockSize := 20 // must be > 0
   a, b := 0, blockSize
   for b <- n {
      insertionSort(data, a, b)
      a = b
      b += blockSize
   }

   insertionSort(data, a, n)
   for blockSize < n {
      a, b = 0, 2*blockSize
      for b <= n {
         symMerge(data, a, a+blockSize, b)
         a = b
         b += 2 * blockSize
      }

      if m := a + blockSize; m < n {
         symMerge(data, a, m, n)
      }
      blockSize *= 2
   }
}
```

This code can be found in the standard library at `https://golang.org/src/sort/sort.go#L356`. Stable sorting algorithms are important when order needs to be maintained.

Quick sort

The Go standard library has a quick sort algorithm, as we saw in the *O(n log n) – quasilinear time* section. QuickSort was initially implemented in Unix as the default sort routine in the standard library. From there, it was built upon and used as qsort in the C programming language. Because of its familiarity and vast history, it is commonly used as a sorting algorithm in many computer science problems today. Using our algorithms table, we can deduce that a standard implementation of the `quickSort` algorithm has an average time complexity of O(n log n). It also has the added benefit of using, at worst, an O(log n) space complexity, making it ideal for in-place moves.

Now that we are done with sort algorithms, we will move on to search algorithms.

Understanding search algorithms

Search algorithms are typically used in order to retrieve an element from a dataset or to check for the presence of that element. Search algorithms are generally classified into two separate categories: linear search and interval search.

Linear search

In a linear search algorithm, every element in the slice or array is checked when the slice or array is traversed sequentially. This algorithm isn't the most efficient algorithm since it ranks in at an O(n) complexity because it can traverse every element on the list.

A linear search algorithm can be written simply as an iteration through a slice, as shown in the following code snippet:

```
func LinearSearch(data []int, searchVal int) bool {
for _, key := range data {
    if key == searchVal {
        return true
    }
  }
  return false
}
```

This function shows us that it'll get expensive quickly with larger datasets. With a dataset of 10 elements, this algorithm won't take very long as it will only iterate through 10 values at a maximum. If our dataset contained 1 million elements, this function would take much longer to return a value.

Binary search

A much more commonly used pattern (and the pattern that you'd most likely want to use for a performant search algorithm) is called binary search. An implementation of a binary search algorithm can be found in the Go standard library at `https://golang.org/src/sort/search.go` and was displayed in the sort search function earlier in this chapter. A binary search tree has an O(log n) search complexity compared to the O(n) complexity of the linear search function that we wrote previously. Binary search tends to get used frequently, especially when the dataset that needs to be searched gets to any sort of reasonable size. Binary search is also smart to implement early – if the dataset that you have grows without you being privy to the growth, at least the utilized algorithm will not increase in complexity. In the following code, we're using the `SearchInts` convenience wrapper for the Go search function. This allows us to iterate through an integer array with a binary search:

```go
package main

import (
    "fmt"
    "sort"
)

func main() {
    intArray := []int{0, 2, 3, 5, 11, 16, 34}
    searchNumber := 34
    sorted := sort.SearchInts(intArray, searchNumber)
    if sorted < len(intArray) {
        fmt.Printf("Found element %d at array position %d\n", searchNumber,
sorted)
    } else {
        fmt.Printf("Element %d not found in array %v\n", searchNumber,
intArray)
    }
}
```

The output from this function is as follows:

This shows us that the binary search library was able to find the number we were searching for (34) in the array that we were searching (`intArray`). It found the integer 34 in the 6th position in the array (which is correct; the array is 0 indexed).

The upcoming section deals with another data structure: trees.

Exploring trees

A tree is a non-linear data structure that is used in computer science to store information. It's commonly used to store data that maintains relationships, particularly if the relationships form a hierarchy. Trees are also simple to search (diagram for array sorting algorithms in the *Understanding sort algorithms* section) shows us that many trees have an O(log n) time complexity with operations in trees). For many problems, trees are the best solution because of how they reference hierarchical data. Trees are combinations of nodes that don't make a cycle.

Each tree is made up of elements called nodes. We start at the root node (the yellow box labeled root in the binary trees figure below). There is a left and a right reference pointer (numbers 2 and 7, in our case) and a data element (the number 1, in this case) within each node. As a tree grows, the depth of the node (the number of edges from the root to a given node) increases. Nodes 4, 5, 6, and 7 all have a depth of 3 in this diagram. The height of the node is the number of edges that occur from the node to the deepest leaf in the tree (as seen in the **height** 4 box in the following binary tree diagram). The height of the entire tree is equivalent to the height of the root node.

Binary trees

Binary trees are an important data structure in computer science. They are often used for search, priority queues, and databases. They are efficient because they are easy to traverse in a concurrent fashion. Go has great concurrency primitives (which we'll discuss in Chapter 3, *Understanding Concurrency*) that allow us to do this in a simple manner. Being able to use goroutines and channels to walk a binary tree can help speed up how we traverse a grouping of hierarchical data. A balanced binary tree can be seen in the following diagram:

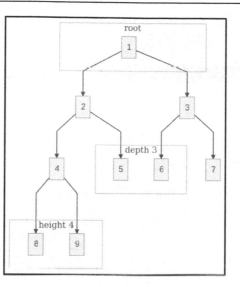

A couple of special binary trees are as follows:

- **Full binary tree**: Every node sans the leaf nodes has 2 child nodes.
- **Complete binary tree**: A tree that is completely filled, sans the bottom layer. The bottom layer must be filled from left to right.
- **Perfect binary tree**: A complete binary tree in which all the nodes have two children and all the leaves of the tree are at the same level.

Doubly linked list

Doubly linked lists are also part of the Go standard library. This is a relatively large package, so for convenience, the function signatures for this package can be found in the following code snippet:

```
func (e *Element) Next() *Element {
func (e *Element) Prev() *Element {
func (l *List) Init() *List {
func New() *List { return new(List).Init() }
func (l *List) Len() int { return l.len }
func (l *List) Front() *Element {
func (l *List) Back() *Element {
func (l *List) lazyInit() {
func (l *List) insert(e, at *Element) *Element {
func (l *List) insertValue(v interface{}, at *Element) *Element {
func (l *List) remove(e *Element) *Element {
func (l *List) move(e, at *Element) *Element {
```

```
func (l *List) Remove(e *Element) interface{} {
func (l *List) PushFront(v interface{}) *Element {
func (l *List) PushBack(v interface{}) *Element {
func (l *List) InsertBefore(v interface{}, mark *Element) *Element {
func (l *List) InsertAfter(v interface{}, mark *Element) *Element {
func (l *List) MoveToFront(e *Element) {
func (l *List) MoveToBack(e *Element) {
func (l *List) MoveBefore(e, mark *Element) {
func (l *List) MoveAfter(e, mark *Element) {
func (l *List) PushBackList(other *List) {
func (l *List) PushFrontList(other *List) {
```

These function signatures (and their corresponding methods) can be found in the Go standard library at `https://golang.org/src/container/list/list.go`.

Finally, we will look at queues.

Exploring queues

A queue is a pattern that is frequently used in computer science to implement a **first in first out** (**FIFO**) data buffer. The first thing to come into the queue is also the first thing to leave. This happens in an ordered fashion in order to process sorted data. Adding things to the queue is known as enqueueing the data into the queue, and removing it from the end of the queue is known as dequeuing. Queues are commonly used as a fixture in which data is stored and processed at another time.

Queues are beneficial because they don't have a fixed capacity. A new element can be added to the queue at any time, which makes a queue an ideal solution for asynchronous implementations such as a keyboard buffer or a printer queue. Queues are used in situations where tasks must be completed in the order that they were received, but when real-time occurs, it may not be possible based on extraneous factors.

Common queuing functions

Very frequently, other small queue operations are added in order to make a queue a little more useful:

- `isfull()` is commonly implemented to check whether or not a queue is full.
- `isempty()` is commonly implemented to check whether or not a queue is empty.
- `peek()` retrieves the element that is ready to be dequeued, but does not dequeue it.

These functions are useful because a normal enqueueing operation goes as follows:

1. Check to see if the queue is full and return an error if the queue is full
2. Increment the rear pointer; return the next empty space
3. Add the data element to the location in which the rear is being pointed at

After these steps are completed, we can enqueue the next item in our queue.

Dequeuing is also just as simple as doing the following:

1. Check to see if the queue is empty and return an error if the queue is empty
2. Access the data at the front of the queue
3. Increment the front pointer to the next available element

After these steps are completed, we have dequeued this item from our queue.

Common queuing patterns

Having an optimized queuing mechanism can be very helpful for writing performant Go code. Being able to push non-critical tasks to a queue allows you to complete the critical tasks faster. Another point to consider is that the queueing mechanism that you're using doesn't necessarily have to be a Go queue. You can push data to external mechanisms such as Kafka (https://kafka.apache.org/) or RabbitMQ (https://www.rabbitmq.com/) in a distributed system. Managing your own messaging queue can become very operationally expensive, so having a separate message queuing system is commonplace today. We will cover this in more detail in Chapter 14, *Clusters and Job Queues*, when we look at clustering and job queuing.

Summary

In this chapter, we learned about benchmarking Go programs. We learned about how Big O notation considerations can help you design impactful data structures and algorithms around your problem set. We also learned about search and sorting algorithms, trees, and queues in order to make our data structures and algorithms most impactful to the problem at hand.

In Chapter 3, *Understanding Concurrency*, we'll learn about some of the most important Go constructs and how they can impact performance. Closures, channels, and goroutines can help us make some powerful design decisions with respect to both parallelism and concurrency.

Understanding Concurrency

3

Iterators and generators are essential to Go. Utilizing channels and goroutines for parallelism and concurrency is idiomatic in Go and is one of the best ways to write high-performance, readable code in the language. We are going to first talk about some of the basic Go constructs in order to be able to understand how to use iterators and generators in the context of Go, followed by deep dives into the constructs of the available iterators and generators of the language.

In this chapter, we are going to cover the following topics:

- Closures
- Goroutines
- Channels
- Semaphores
- WaitGroups
- Iterators
- Generators

Being able to understand the basic constructs of the Go language and when and where to use the proper iterators and generators is essential to writing performant Go.

Understanding closures

One of the most important parts of Go is that it is a language that supports first-class functions. First-class functions are functions that have the ability to be passed to other functions as variables. They can also be returned from other functions. This is important to note because we can use them as closures.

Closures are helpful because they are a great way to keep your code DRY as well as helping to isolate your data. Keeping datasets small has been a core tenet of this book thus far, and that doesn't change in this chapter (nor any subsequent chapter). Being able to isolate the data that you wish to manipulate can help you to continue to write performant code.

Closures keep a local scope and have access to the outer function's scope and parameters, as well as global variables. Closures are functions that reference variables outside of their body. These functions have the ability to assign values to the referenced variables and access those values, so in turn, we can pass closures between functions.

Anonymous functions

The first step to understanding closures in Go is to understand anonymous functions. An anonymous function is created using a variable for the inception of the function. They are also functions that don't have a name or identifier, hence the name *anonymous functions*.

A normal function invocation to print `Hello Go` to the screen would be what is shown in the following code block:

```
func HelloGo(){
    fmt.Println("Hello Go")
}
```

Next, we could call `HelloGo()` and the function would print a `Hello Go` string.

If we wanted to instantiate our `HelloGo()` function as an anonymous function, we would invoke this as referenced in the following code block:

```
// Note the trailing () for this anonymous function invocation
func() {
    fmt.Println("Hello Go")
}()
```

Our preceding anonymous function and the `HelloGo()` function are lexically similar.

We could also store a function as a variable for use later on, as referenced in the following code block:

```
    fmt.Println("Hello Go from an Anonymous Function Assigned to a
Variable")
}
```

All three of these things – the `HelloGo()` function, our anonymous function, and the function assigned to the `hello` variable – are lexically similar.

After we've assigned this `hello` variable, we could then call this function using a simple invocation of `hello()`, where our preceding defined anonymous function would be called and `Hello Go` would be printed to the screen in the same fashion that it was printed in our previously called anonymous function.

We can see how each of these work in the following code block:

```
package main
import "fmt"
func helloGo() {
    fmt.Println("Hello Go from a Function")
}
func main() {
    helloGo()
    func() { fmt.Println("Hello Go from an Anonymous Function") }()
    var hello func() = func() { fmt.Println("Hello Go from an Anonymous
Function Variable") }
    hello()
}
```

The output from this program shows three print statements, all similar, with small differences in print to show how they were returned in the following screenshot:

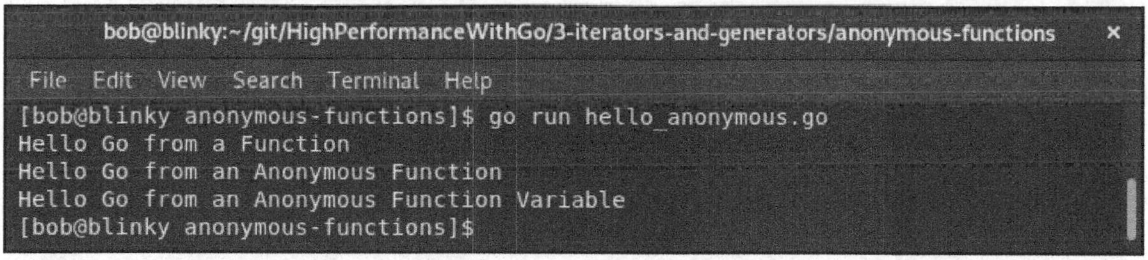

Anonymous functions are a powerful aspect of Go. As we continue this chapter, we'll see how we can build on them to make some very useful things.

Anonymous functions with respect to closures

You may be wondering at this point why it's prudent to have anonymous functions and how they pertain to closures. Once we have our anonymous function, we can then utilize a closure in order to reference variables that are declared outside of its own definition. We can see this in the code block that follows:

```
package main
import "fmt"
```

```
func incrementCounter() func() int {
 var initializedNumber = 0
 return func() int {
 initializedNumber++
 return initializedNumber
 }
}

func main() {
 n1 := incrementCounter()
 fmt.Println("n1 increment counter #1: ", n1()) // First invocation of n1
 fmt.Println("n1 increment counter #2: ", n1()) // Notice the second
invocation; n1 is called twice, so n1 == 2
 n2 := incrementCounter() // New instance of initializedNumber
 fmt.Println("n2 increment counter #1: ", n2()) // n2 is only called once,
so n2 == 1
 fmt.Println("n1 increment counter #3: ", n1()) // state of n1 is not
changed with the n2 calls
}
```

When we execute this code, we receive the following resulting output:

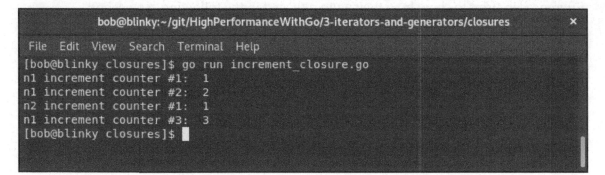

In this code sample, we can see how closures can help with data isolation. The n1 variable is initialized with the incrementCounter() function. This anonymous function sets initializedNumber to 0 and returns an integer that is an incremented count of the initializedNumber variable.

When we create the n2 variable, the same process occurs again. A new incrementCounter anonymous function is called and a new initializedNumber variable is returned. In our main function, we can note that n1 and n2 have separate maintained state. We can see that even after the n1() function call is invoked for the third time. Being able to persist this data between function calls while also isolating the data from another call is a powerful part of having anonymous functions.

Closures for nesting and deferring work

Closures are also often a good way to nest and defer work. In the following example, we can see a function closure that allows us to nest work:

```
package main
import (
 "fmt"
 "sort"
)

func main() {
 input := []string{"foo", "bar", "baz"}
 var result []string
 // closure callback
 func() {
 result = append(input, "abc") // Append to the array
 result = append(result, "dcf") // Append to the array again
 sort.Sort(sort.StringSlice(result)) // Sort the larger array
 }()
 fmt.Print(result)
}
```

In this example, we can see that we append to the string slice twice and sort the result. We will later see how we can nest an anonymous function in a goroutine to help improve performance.

HTTP handlers with closures

Closures are also commonly used as middleware in Go HTTP calls. You can wrap normal HTTP function calls around a closure in order to add additional information to your calls when you need to and reuse middleware for different functions.

In our example, we'll set up an HTTP server with four separate routes:

- /: This serves the following:
    - An HTTP response with an HTTP 418 status code (derived from the newStatusCode middleware).
    - A Foo:Bar header (derived from the addHeader middleware).
    - A Hello PerfGo! response (derived from the writeResponse middleware).
- /onlyHeader: Serves an HTTP response with only the Foo:Bar header added.
- /onlyStatus: Serves an HTTP response with only the status code changed.

- /admin: Checks for the presence of a user: admin header. If present, it prints the admin portal information alongside all the normal pertaining values. If not present, it returns an unauthorized response.

These examples have been used because they are easy to grok. Using closures for Go in HTTP handlers is also convenient because they can do the following:

- Isolate database information from DB calls
- Perform authorization requests
- Wrap other functions with isolated data (timing information, for example)
- Communicate with other third-party services transparently with acceptable timeouts

The Go *Writing Web Applications* document, located at [https://golang.org/doc/articles/wiki/], gives a bunch of other prime examples of setting up templating, being able to live-edit pages, validating user input, and more. Let's take a look at our example code that shows us closures within a HTTP handler in the following code blocks. First, we initialize our packages and create an adminCheck function, which helps us to determine whether or not a user is authorized to use the system:

```
package main

import (
 "fmt"
 "net/http"
)

// Checks for a "user:admin" header, proper credentials for the admin path
func adminCheck(h http.Handler) http.HandlerFunc {
 return http.HandlerFunc(func(w http.ResponseWriter, r *http.Request) {
 if r.Header.Get("user") != "admin" {
 http.Error(w, "Not Authorized", 401)
 return
 }
 fmt.Fprintln(w, "Admin Portal")
 h.ServeHTTP(w, r)
 })
}
```

We next set up some other examples, such as serving an HTTP 418 (the I'm a teapot status code) and adding a foo:bar HTTP header and setting a particular HTTP response:

```
// Sets a HTTP 418 (I'm a Teapot) status code for the response
func newStatusCode(h http.Handler) http.HandlerFunc {
 return http.HandlerFunc(func(w http.ResponseWriter, r *http.Request) {
```

```go
    w.WriteHeader(http.StatusTeapot)
    h.ServeHTTP(w, r)
    })
}

// Adds a header, Foo:Bar
func addHeader(h http.Handler) http.HandlerFunc {
    return http.HandlerFunc(func(w http.ResponseWriter, r *http.Request) {
    w.Header().Add("Foo", "Bar")
    h.ServeHTTP(w, r)
    })
}

// Writes a HTTP Response
func writeResponse(w http.ResponseWriter, r *http.Request) {
    fmt.Fprintln(w, "Hello PerfGo!")
}
```

Lastly, we wrap it all together with an HTTP handler:

```go
// Wrap the middleware together
func main() {
    handler := http.HandlerFunc(writeResponse)
    http.Handle("/", addHeader(newStatusCode(handler)))
    http.Handle("/onlyHeader", addHeader(handler))
    http.Handle("/onlyStatus", newStatusCode(handler))
    http.Handle("/admin", adminCheck(handler))
    http.ListenAndServe(":1234", nil)
}
```

Our router test examples follow. Here's the output with a header modification and HTTP status code modification:

```
bob@blinky:~/git/HighPerformanceWithGo/3-iterators-and-generators/closures

File  Edit  View  Search  Terminal  Help
[bob@blinky closures]$ curl -D - http://localhost:1234/
HTTP/1.1 418 I'm a teapot
Foo: Bar
Date: Tue, 16 Jul 2019 23:50:26 GMT
Content-Length: 14
Content-Type: text/plain; charset=utf-8

Hello PerfGo!
[bob@blinky closures]$
```

Here's the output with just the header modification:

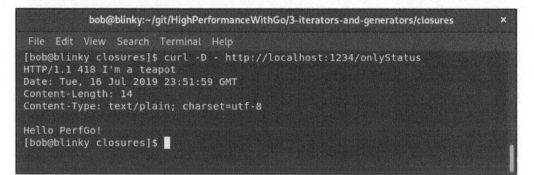

Here's the output with just the status modification:

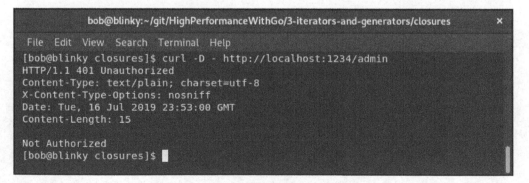

Here's the unauthorized admin output:

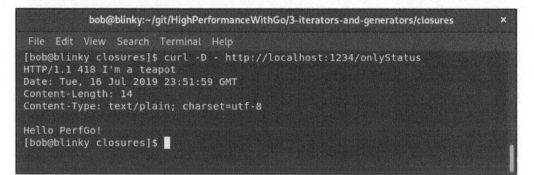

Here's the authorized admin output:

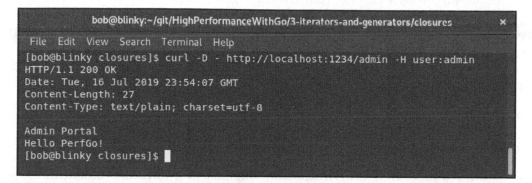

Being able to add middleware with anonymous functions can help to rapidly iterate while keeping code complexity low. In the next section, we'll explore goroutines.

Exploring goroutines

Go is a language designed with concurrency in mind. Concurrency is the ability to execute independent processes. Goroutines are a construct in Go that can help with concurrency. They are often referred to as *lightweight threads*—for good reason. In other languages, threads are handled by the OS. This, in turn, uses a larger-sized call stack and usually handles less concurrency with a given memory stack size. Goroutines are functions or methods that run within the Go runtime concurrently and don't connect to the underlying OS. The scheduler within the Go language manages goroutines' life cycles. The system's scheduler has a lot of overhead as well, so limiting the number of threads being utilized can help to improve performance.

The Go scheduler

There are a couple of different pieces involved in the management of goroutine life cycles by the Go runtime scheduler. The Go scheduler was changed in its second iteration, which was derived from a design document written by Dmitry Vyukov, released in Go 1.1. In this design doc, Vyukov discusses the initial Go scheduler and how to implement a work-sharing and work-stealing scheduler, as originally prescribed by Dr Robert D. Blumofe and Dr. Charles E. Leiserson in an MIT paper entitled, *Scheduling Multithreaded Computations by Work Stealing*. The fundamental concept behind this paper is to ensure dynamic, multithreaded computation in order to ensure that processors are utilized efficiently while maintaining memory requirements.

Goroutines only have a stack size of 2 KB on inception. This is one of the reasons why goroutines are preferred for a lot of concurrent programming—because it is much easier to have tens or hundreds of thousands of goroutines in one program. Threads in other languages can take up megabytes of space, making them a lot less flexible. If more memory is needed, Go's functions have the ability to allocate more memory in another place in available memory space to help the goroutine space grow. By default, the runtime gives the new stack twice the amount of memory.

Goroutines block a running thread only on system calls. When this occurs, the runtime takes another thread from the scheduler struct. These are used for other goroutines that are waiting to be executed.

Work sharing is a process in which a scheduler migrates new threads to other processors for work distribution. Work stealing performs a similar action, but in which the underutilized processors steal threads from other processors. Following the work-stealing pattern in Go has helped to make the Go scheduler much more efficient and, in turn, gives higher throughput to the goroutines that run on top of the kernel's scheduler. Lastly, Go's scheduler implements spinning threads. Spinning threads will utilize extra CPU cycles over preempting a thread. Threads spin in three different ways:

- When a thread is not attached to a processor.
- When making a goroutine ready will unblock an OS thread onto an idle processor.
- When a thread is running but no goroutines are attached to it. This idle thread will continue to search for runnable goroutines to execute.

Go scheduler goroutine internals

The Go scheduler has three key structures that handle the workload of goroutines: the M struct, the P struct, and the G struct. These three structs work together in order to process goroutines in a performant fashion. Let's take a look at each of these in more depth. If you'd like to take a look at the source code for these, it's available at `https://github.com/golang/go/blob/master/src/runtime/runtime2.go/`.

The M struct

The M struct is labeled **M** for **machine**. The M struct is a representation of an OS thread. It contains a pointer that points to the runnable goroutine global queue (defined by the P struct). M retrieves its work from the P struct. M contains the free and waiting goroutines that are ready to be executed. Some notable M struct parameters are the following:

- A goroutine that contains a scheduling stack (go)
- **Thread local storage (tls)**
- A P struct for executing Go code (p)

The P struct

This struct is labeled **P** for **processor**. The P struct represents a logical processor. This is set by GOMAXPROCS (which should be equivalent to the number of cores available after Go version 1.5). P maintains a queue of all of the goroutines (defined by the G struct). When you invoke a new goroutine using the Go executor, this new goroutine gets inserted into P's queue. If P doesn't have an associated M struct, it will allocate a new M. Some notable P struct parameters are the following:

- The P struct ID (id)
- A back link to an associated M struct if applicable (m)
- A pool of available defer structs (deferpool)
- The queue of runnable goroutines (runq)
- A struct of available Gs (gFree)

The G struct

This struct is labeled **G** for **goroutine**. The G struct represents the stack parameters of a single goroutine. It includes information on a couple of different parameters that are important for a goroutine. G structs get created for every new goroutine, as well as goroutines for the runtime. Some notable G struct parameters are the following:

- The current value of the stack pointers (stack.lo and stack.hi)
- The current value of the Go and C stack growth prologues (stackguard0 and stackguard1)
- The current value of the M struct (m)

Goroutines in action

Now that we have a basic understanding of the underlying principles of goroutines, we can check them out in action. In the following code block, we will see how to invoke a goroutine using the go call:

```
package main

import (
 "fmt"
 "time"
)

func printSleep(s string) {
 for index, stringVal := range s {
 fmt.Printf("%#U at index %d\n", stringVal, index)
 time.Sleep(1 * time.Millisecond) // printSleep sleep timer
 }
}

func main() {
 const t time.Duration = 9
 go printSleep("HELLO GOPHERS")
 time.Sleep(t * time.Millisecond) // Main sleep timer
 fmt.Println("sleep complete")
}
```

During the execution of this function, we only get a partial return of the printSleep() function wrapped in the goroutine call (printing HELLO GOPHERS) before the main sleep timer is complete. Why did this happen? If the main() goroutine completes, it is closed, the program is terminated, and leftover goroutines will not run. We were able to get the first nine characters returned because those goroutines completed before the main function finished executing. If we change our const t duration to 14, we will receive the entire HELLO GOPHERS string. The reason behind this is that the main function does not get completed before all of the goroutines that spawned around go printSleep() are executed. Goroutines are powerful only if used correctly.

Another Go built-in that helps with managing concurrent goroutines is Go channels, which is the topic we will cover in the next section.

Introducing channels

Channels are mechanisms that allow the sending and receiving of values. Channels are often used alongside goroutines in order to deliver transfer objects concurrently across goroutines. There are two main classifications of channels in Go: unbuffered channels and buffered channels.

Channel internals

Channels are invoked using the `make()` Golang built-in, where an `hchan` struct is created. The `hchan` struct contains a count of the data in the queue, the size of the queue, an array pointer for the buffer, send and receive indices and waiters, and a mutex lock. The following code block illustrates this:

```
type hchan struct {
    qcount   uint           // total data in the queue
    dataqsiz uint           // size of the circular queue
    buf      unsafe.Pointer // points to an array of dataqsiz elements
    elemsize uint16
    closed   uint32
    elemtype *_type // element type
    sendx    uint   // send index
    recvx    uint   // receive index
    recvq    waitq // list of recv waiters
    sendq    waitq // list of send waiters
    // lock protects all fields in hchan, as well as several
    // fields in sudogs blocked on this channel.
    //
    // Do not change another G's status while holding this lock
    // (in particular, do not ready a G), as this can deadlock
    // with stack shrinking.
    lock mutex
}
```

This code block is referenced from `https://golang.org/src/runtime/chan.go#L32`.

Buffered channels

Buffered channels are channels that have a bounded size. They are typically more performant than their unbounded counterparts. They are useful for retrieving values from an explicit number of goroutines that you've launched. Because they are **FIFO (first in first out)** queueing mechanisms, they can effectively be used as a fixed-size queueing mechanism, and we can process requests in the order in which they came in. Channels are created before they are used by invoking the `make()` function. Once a buffered channel is created, it is ready and available for use. Buffered channels don't block on incoming writes if there is still room in the channel. It's important to remember that data flows in the direction of the arrow within a channel. In our example (the following code block), we perform the following actions:

- Write `foo` and `bar` to our `buffered_channel`
- Check the length of the channel—the length is 2 because we've added two strings
- Pop `foo` and `bar` off the channel
- Check the length of the channel—the length is 0 because we've removed both strings
- Add `baz` to our channel
- Pop `baz` off the channel onto a variable, `out`
- Print the resulting `out` variable, which is `baz` (the last element we added to the channel)
- Close our buffered channel, indicating no more data is to pass across this channel

Let's have a look at the following code block:

```
package main
import "fmt"
 func main() {
 buffered_channel := make(chan string, 2)
 buffered_channel <- "foo"
 buffered_channel <- "bar"

 // Length of channel is 2 because both elements added to channel
 fmt.Println("Channel Length After Add: ", len(buffered_channel))

 // Pop foo and bar off the stack
 fmt.Println(<-buffered_channel)
 fmt.Println(<-buffered_channel)

 // Length of channel is 0 because both elements removed from channel
 fmt.Println("Channel Length After Pop: ", len(buffered_channel))
```

```
// Push baz to the stack
buffered_channel <- "baz"

// Store baz as a variable, out
out := <-buffered_channel
fmt.Println(out)
close(buffered_channel)
}
```

This code can be found at https://github.com/bobstrecansky/HighPerformanceWithGo/ blob/master/3-iterators-and-generators/channels/buffered_channel.go.

As we can see in our code block example, we are able to push data to the stack and pop data from the stack. It's also important to note that the `len()` built-in returns the number of elements that are unread (or queued) within the channel buffer. Alongside the `len()` built-in, we can also use the `cap()` built-in to deduce the total capacity of the buffer. These two built-ins used in conjunction can often be used to know the current state of your channel, especially if it's not acting the way you expect it to. It is also good to get in the habit of closing channels. When you close a channel, you are letting the Go scheduler know that there are no more values that will be sent across that channel. It's also important to note that if you attempt to write to a closed channel or a channel that has no room left in the queue, your program will panic.

The following program panics:

```
package main
 func main() {
 ch := make(chan string, 1)
 close(ch)
 ch <- "foo"
}
```

We'll get the error message shown in the following screenshot:

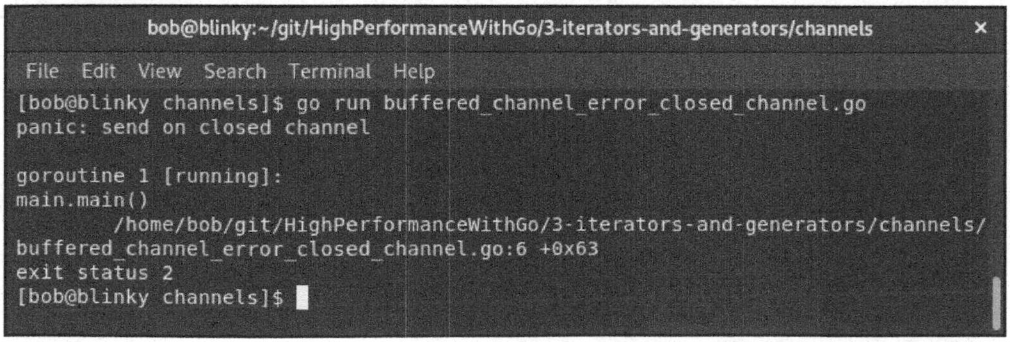

Understanding Concurrency

This is because we attempted to pass data (the `foo` string) to a channel (`ch`) that was already closed.

The following program also panics:

```
package main
 func main() {
 ch := make(chan string, 1)
ch <- "foo"
ch <- "bar"
 }
```

We'll see the following error message:

The program panics because the goroutine will block and wait. This error is then detected by the runtime and the program exits.

Ranges over channels

You may want to know all the values present in your buffered channel. We have the ability to do this by invoking a `range` built-in over the channel we'd like to check. Our example in the following code block adds three elements to the channel, closes the channel, and then writes all the elements from the channel using `fmt`:

```
package main
import "fmt"
func main() {
    bufferedChannel := make(chan int, 3)
    bufferedChannel <- 1
    bufferedChannel <- 3
    bufferedChannel <- 5
    close(bufferedChannel)
    for i := range bufferedChannel {
```

```
        fmt.Println(i)
    }
}
```

The resulting output shows us all of the values that live in our buffered channel:

A reminder—make sure you close the channel. If we remove the preceding close(bufferedChannel) function, we will get a deadlock.

Unbuffered channels

Unbuffered channels are the default channel configuration in Go. Unbuffered channels are flexible because they don't need to have a finite channel size definition. They are often best used when the receiver of the data from the channel is slower than the sender of the channel of the data. They also block on both read and write, as they are synchronous. The sender will block the channel until the receiver has received the value. They are often used in conjunction with goroutines to ensure that items are processed in the order that they are expected to be processed in.

In our following example code blocks, we perform the following actions:

- Create a Boolean channel to maintain state
- Create an unsorted slice
- Sort our slice with the sortInts() function
- Respond true to our channel so that we can move onto the next part of the function
- Search our slice for a given integer
- Respond true to our channel so that our transaction occurring over the channel is completed
- Return the channel value so that our Go function is completed

First, we import our packages and create a function that sorts integers across a channel:

```go
package main
import (
    "fmt"
    "sort"
)
func sortInts(intArray[] int, done chan bool) {
    sort.Ints(intArray)
    fmt.Printf("Sorted Array: %v\n", intArray)
    done < -true
}
```

Next, we create a searchInts function that searches integers across a channel:

```go
func searchInts(intArray []int, searchNumber int, done chan bool) {
    sorted := sort.SearchInts(intArray, searchNumber)
    if sorted < len(intArray) {
        fmt.Printf("Found element %d at array position %d\n", searchNumber,
sorted)
    } else {
        fmt.Printf("Element %d not found in array %v\n", searchNumber,
intArray)
    }
    done <- true
}
```

Lastly, we tie them all together in our main function:

```go
func main() {
    ch := make(chan bool)
    go func() {
        s := []int{2, 11, 3, 34, 5, 0, 16} // unsorted
        fmt.Println("Unsorted Array: ", s)
        searchNumber := 16
        sortInts(s, ch)
        searchInts(s, searchNumber, ch)
    }()
    <-ch
}
```

We can see our output from this program in the following screenshot:

```
bob@blinky:~/git/HighPerformanceWithGo/3-iterators-and-generators/channels        ×

 File  Edit  View  Search  Terminal  Help
[bob@blinky channels]$ go run unbuffered_channel_int.go
Unsorted Array:  [2 11 3 34 5 0 16]
Sorted Array: [0 2 3 5 11 16 34]
Found element 16 at array position 5
[bob@blinky channels]$
```

This is a great way to use channels to perform actions concurrently.

Selects

Selects are a construct that allow you to combine goroutines and channels in a meaningful way. We can multiplex Go functions in order to be able to execute a case that occurs when the goroutine is run. In our example, we create three separate channels: a `string` channel, a `bool` channel, and a `rune` channel. We next run some anonymous functions in the following code blocks in order to populate data in those channels, and use the select built-in to return values from the channels.

1. First, we initialize our package and set up three separate channels:

```
package main
import (
    "fmt"
    "time"
)
func main() {
    // Make 3 channels
    ch1 := make(chan string)
    ch2 := make(chan bool)
    ch3 := make(chan rune)
```

2. We next pass appropriate variables to each of our channels via anonymous functions:

```
// string anonymous function to ch1
go func() {
    ch1 <- "channels are fun"
}()
// bool anonymous function to ch2
go func() {
    ch2 <- true
}()
// rune anonymous function to ch3 with 1 second sleep
```

```
go func() {
    time.Sleep(1 * time.Second)
    ch3 <- 'r'
}()
```

3. Lastly, we pass these through with our `select` statement:

```
// select builtin to return values from channels
for i := 0; i < 3; i++ {
    select {
    case msg1 := <-ch1:
        fmt.Println("Channel 1 message: ", msg1)
    case msg2 := <-ch2:
        fmt.Println("Channel 2 message: ", msg2)
    case msg3 := <-ch3:
        fmt.Println("Channel 3 message: ", msg3)
    }
}
```

The resulting output from this program can be seen in the following screenshot:

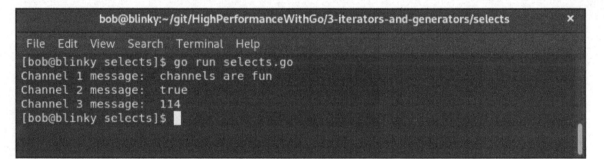

You'll notice that the `rune` anonymous function gets returned last here. This is due to the sleep that was inserted into that anonymous function. The `select` statements will return values that are passed into the channel randomly if multiples are ready, and sequentially when the goroutine results are ready.

In the next section, we will learn what semaphores are.

Introducing semaphores

Semaphores are another method for controlling how goroutines execute parallel tasks. Semaphores are convenient because they give us the ability to use a worker pool pattern, but we don't need to shut down workers after the work has been completed and the workers are idle. The idea of having a weighted semaphore in the Go language is relatively new; the sync package implementation of semaphores was implemented in early 2017, so it is one of the newest parallel task constructs.

If we take the example of a simple loop in the following code block, add 100 ms of latency to a request, and add an item to an array, we can quickly see that the amount of time it takes increases as these tasks are operating in a series:

```go
package main
import (
    "fmt"
    "time"
)
func main() {
    var out = make([]string, 5)
    for i := 0; i < 5; i++ {
        time.Sleep(100 * time.Millisecond)
        out[i] = "This loop is slow\n"
    }
    fmt.Println(out)
}
```

We can create a weighted semaphore implementation with the same constructs. We can see that in the following code block:

1. First, we initialize our program and set up our semaphore variables:

```go
package main

import (
  "context"
  "fmt"
  "runtime"
  "time"

  "golang.org/x/sync/semaphore"
)

func main() {
    ctx := context.Background()
    var (
```

```
            sem       =
    semaphore.NewWeighted(int64(runtime.GOMAXPROCS(0)))
            result = make([]string, 5)
        )
```

2. Then, we run through our semaphore code:

```
for i := range result {
    if err := sem.Acquire(ctx, 1); err != nil {
        break
    }
    go func(i int) {
        defer sem.Release(1)
        time.Sleep(100 * time.Millisecond)
        result[i] = "Semaphores are Cool \n"
    }(i)
}
if err := sem.Acquire(ctx, int64(runtime.GOMAXPROCS(0))); err != nil {
    fmt.Println("Error acquiring semaphore")
}
fmt.Println(result)
}
```

The difference in execution time between these two functions is quite noticeable and can be seen in the following outputs:

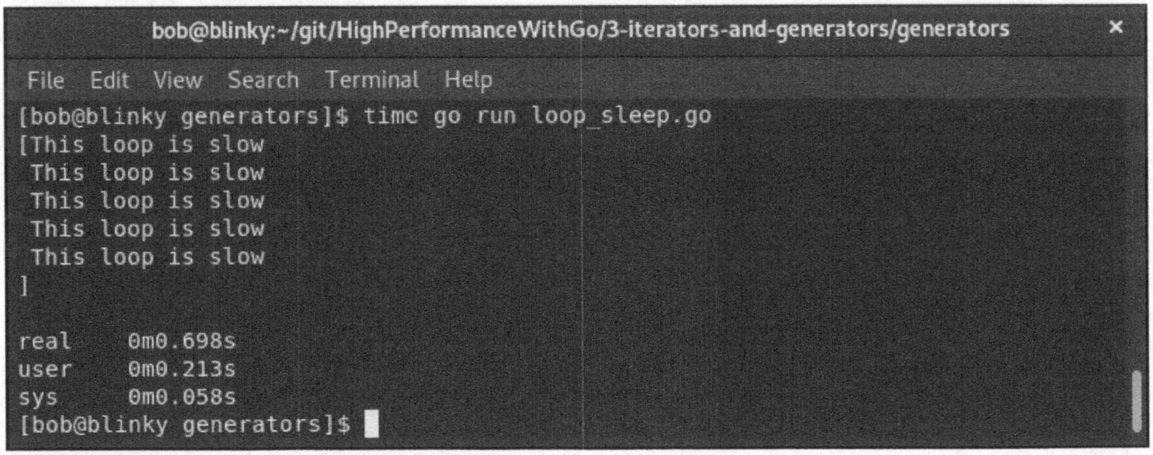

The semaphore implementation ran more than twice as fast which is shown in the following screenshot:

```
bob@blinky:~/git/HighPerformanceWithGo/3-iterators-and-generators/generators        ×

File  Edit  View  Search  Terminal  Help
[bob@blinky generators]$ time go run semaphore_sleep.go
[Semaphores are Cool
 Semaphores are Cool
 Semaphores are Cool
 Semaphores are Cool
 Semaphores are Cool
]

real    0m0.324s
user    0m0.243s
sys     0m0.076s
[bob@blinky generators]$
```

The semaphore implementation ran more than twice as fast. This is with only five 100 ms blocking sleeps. Being able to process things in parallel becomes more and more important as your scale continues to grow.

In the next section, we will discuss WaitGroups.

Understanding WaitGroups

WaitGroups are commonly used in order to validate the fact that multiple goroutines have completed. We do this in order to make sure we have completed all of the concurrent work that we expect to complete.

In the example in the following code block, we make requests to four websites with a WaitGroup. This WaitGroup will wait until all of our requests have been completed, and will only finish the main function after all of the WaitGroup values have been returned:

1. First, we initialize our packages and set up our retrieval function:

```
package main
import (
    "fmt"
    "net/http"
    "sync"
    "time"
)
func retrieve(url string, wg *sync.WaitGroup) {
    // WaitGroup Counter-- when goroutine is finished
    defer wg.Done()
```

```
        start := time.Now()
        res, err := http.Get(url)
        end := time.Since(start)
        if err != nil {
            panic(err)
        }
        // print the status code from the response
        fmt.Println(url, res.StatusCode, end)
    }
```

2. In our `main` function, we next use our retrieval function within a goroutine using WaitGroups:

```
func main() {
    var wg sync.WaitGroup
    var urls = []string{"https://godoc.org",
"https://www.packtpub.com", "https://kubernetes.io/"}
    for i := range urls {
        // WaitGroup Counter++ when new goroutine is called
        wg.Add(1)
        go retrieve(urls[i], &wg)
    }
    // Wait for the collection of goroutines to finish
    wg.Wait()
}
```

As you can see from the following output, we receive all the measurements for the web requests, their response code, and their respective timings:

```
bob@blinky:~/git/HighPerformanceWithGo/3-iterators-and-generators/workgroups      ×

  File  Edit  View  Search  Terminal  Help
[bob@blinky workgroups]$ go run workgroups.go
https://kubernetes.io/ 200 121.696845ms
https://www.packtpub.com 200 129.037232ms
https://godoc.org 200 233.128179ms
[bob@blinky workgroups]$
```

Very often, we expect all our goroutines to finish. WaitGroups can help us with this.

In the next section, we'll discuss the process of iteration.

Iterators and the process of iteration

Iteration is the method of looking through a group of data, usually a list, in order to retrieve information from said list. Go has a bunch of different iterator patterns, all with benefits and drawbacks:

Iterator	Benefit	Drawback
`for` loop	Simplest implementation	No default concurrency.
Iterator function with a callback	Simple implementation	Unconventional styling for Go; difficult to read.
Channels	Simple implementation	More expensive computationally than some other iterators (with a marginal cost difference). The only iterator that is naturally concurrent.
Stateful iterators	Difficult implementation	A nice caller interface. Useful for complex iterators (commonly used in the standard library).

It's important to benchmark all of these against one another in order to validate assumptions about how long each one takes. In the following tests, we take sums of 0 to n and run benchmarks against them.

The following code block has a simple `for` loop iterator:

```
package iterators

var sumLoops int
func simpleLoop(n int) int {
    for i: = 0; i < n; i++ {
        sumLoops += i
    }
    return sumLoops
}
```

The following code block has a callback iterator:

```
package iterators

var sumCallback int

func CallbackLoop(top int) {
    err: = callbackLoopIterator(top, func(n int) error {
        sumCallback += n
        return nil
    })
    if err != nil {
        panic(err)
    }
```

```
}

func callbackLoopIterator(top int, callback func(n int) error) error {
    for i: = 0; i < top; i++{
        err: = callback(i)
        if err != nil {
            return err
        }
    }
    return nil
}
```

The following code blocks will show the `Next()` incantation. Let's look at it step by step:

1. First, we initialize our package variables and structs. Next, we create a `CounterIterator`:

```
package iterators

var sumNext int

type CounterStruct struct {
    err error
    max int
    cur int
}

func NewCounterIterator(top int) * CounterStruct {
    var err error
    return &CounterStruct {
        err: err,
        max: top,
        cur: 0,
    }
}
```

2. This is followed by a `Next()` function, a `Value()` function, and a `NextLoop()` function:

```
func(i * CounterStruct) Next() bool {
    if i.err != nil {
        return false
    }
    i.cur++
        return i.cur <= i.max
}
func(i * CounterStruct) Value() int {
    if i.err != nil || i.cur > i.max {
```

```
            panic("Value is not valid after iterator finished")
        }
        return i.cur
    }
    func NextLoop(top int) {
        nextIterator: = NewCounterIterator(top)
        for nextIterator.Next() {
            fmt.Print(nextIterator.Value())
        }
    }
```

3. The next code block has a buffered channel implementation:

```
    package iterators

    var sumBufferedChan int

    func BufferedChanLoop(n int) int {

        ch: = make(chan int, n)

            go func() {
            defer close(ch)
            for i: = 0;
            i < n;
            i++{
                ch < -i
            }
        }()

        for j: = range ch {
            sumBufferedChan += j
        }
        return sumBufferedChan
    }
```

4. The next code block has an unbuffered channel implementation:

```
    package iterators

    var sumUnbufferedChan int

    func UnbufferedChanLoop(n int) int {
        ch: = make(chan int)

            go func() {
            defer close(ch)
            for i: = 0;
```

```
            i < n;
            i++{
                ch < -i
            }
    } ()

    for j: = range ch {
        sumUnbufferedChan += j
    }
    return sumUnbufferedChan
}
```

5. After we compile these all together, we can make a test benchmark. This benchmark can be found in the following code blocks. Let's look at it step by step again.

6. First, we initialize our package and set up a simple and callback loop benchmark:

```
package iterators

import "testing"

func benchmarkLoop(i int, b *testing.B) {
    for n := 0; n < b.N; n++ {
        simpleLoop(i)
    }
}

func benchmarkCallback(i int, b *testing.B) {
    b.ResetTimer()
    for n := 0; n < b.N; n++ {
        CallbackLoop(i)
    }
}
```

7. This is followed by a next and buffered channel benchmark:

```
func benchmarkNext(i int, b *testing.B) {
    b.ResetTimer()
    for n := 0; n < b.N; n++ {
        NextLoop(i)
    }
}

func benchmarkBufferedChan(i int, b *testing.B) {
    b.ResetTimer()
    for n := 0; n < b.N; n++ {
        BufferedChanLoop(i)
```

```
        }
    }
```

8. Lastly, we set up the unbuffered channel benchmark and create loop functions
   for each of the benchmarks:

```go
func benchmarkUnbufferedChan(i int, b *testing.B) {
    b.ResetTimer()
    for n := 0; n < b.N; n++ {
        UnbufferedChanLoop(i)
    }
}

func BenchmarkLoop10000000(b *testing.B)                {
benchmarkLoop(1000000, b)  }
func BenchmarkCallback10000000(b *testing.B)            {
benchmarkCallback(1000000, b)  }
func BenchmarkNext10000000(b *testing.B)                {
benchmarkNext(1000000, b)  }
func BenchmarkBufferedChan10000000(b *testing.B)    {
benchmarkBufferedChan(1000000, b)  }
func BenchmarkUnbufferedChan10000000(b *testing.B) {
benchmarkUnbufferedChan(1000000, b)  }
```

The result of the benchmark can be found in the following screenshot:

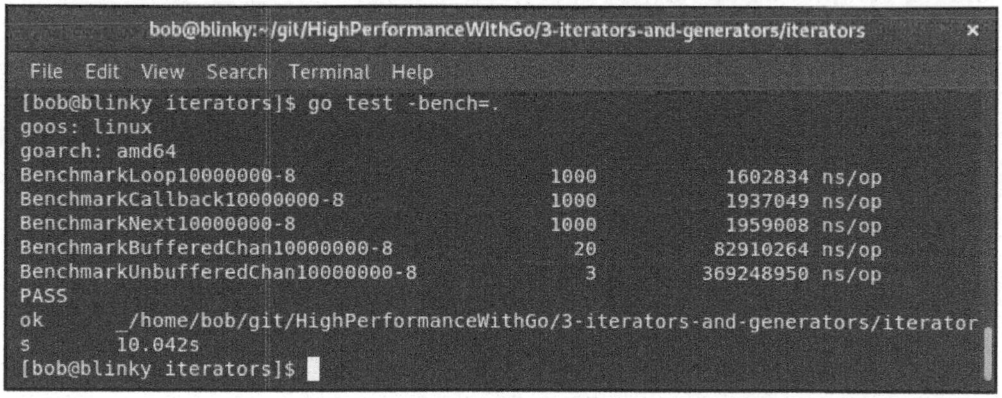

The context of these iterator tests is very important. Because we are doing simple addition
in these tests, a simple construct for iterating is key. If we were to add in latency within
each call, the concurrent channel iterators would perform much better. Concurrency is a
powerful thing, especially in the right context.

In the next section, we'll discuss generators.

Briefing on generators

A generator is a routine that returns the next sequential value within a loop construct. Generators are commonly used to implement iterators and bring in parallelism. Goroutines are utilized in Go in order to implement generators. To implement parallelism in Go, we can use generators that run in parallel with consumers to produce values. They are typically utilized within a looping construct. Generators can also be parallelized themselves. This is typically done when it's expensive to generate an output and the output can be generated in any order.

Summary

In this chapter, we have learned about many of the basic constructs that are used for iterators and generators in Go. Understanding anonymous functions and closures helped us to build foundational knowledge about how these functions work. We then learned how goroutines and channels work, and how to implement them fruitfully. We also learned about semaphores and WaitGroups, as well as how they play into the language. Understanding these skills will help us to parse through information in our computer programs in a more effective manner, allowing for more concurrent data manipulation. In Chapter 4, *STL Algorithm Equivalents in Go*, we'll learn about practical implementations of the **Standard Templating Library** (**STL**) in Go.

STL Algorithm Equivalents in Go

4

Many programmers coming from other high-performance programming languages, particularly C++, understand the concept of the **Standard Templating Library (STL)**. This library provides common programming data structures and functions access to a generalized library in order to rapidly iterate and write performant code at scale. Go does not have a built-in STL. This chapter will focus on how to utilize some of the most common STL practices within Go. The STL has four commonly referenced components:

- Algorithms
- Containers
- Functors
- Iterators

Being familiar with these topics will help you to write Go code more quickly and effectively, utilizing commonly implemented and optimized patterns. In this chapter, we are going to learn the following:

- How to use STL practices in Go
- How to utilize standard programming algorithms with respect to Go
- How containers store data
- How functions work in Go
- How to properly use iterators

Remember, all of these pieces are still part of our performance puzzle. Knowing when to use the right algorithm, container, or functor will help you to write better-performing code.

Understanding algorithms in the STL

Algorithms in the STL perform functions such as sorting and searching, as well as manipulating and counting data. These are called by the `<algorithm>` header in C++ and are used on ranges of elements. The groups of objects that are modified do not impact the structure of the container they are associated with. The patterns outlined in each of the subheadings here use Go's language structure to implement these algorithms. The following types of algorithm will be explained in this section of the chapter:

- Sort
- Reverse
- Min and max elements
- Binary search

Being able to understand how all of these algorithms work will help you to produce performant code when you need to use these techniques to manipulate data structures using algorithms.

Sort

The **sort** algorithm sorts an array into ascending order. Sort doesn't require new containers to be created, destroyed, or copied—the sort algorithm sorts all the elements within their container. We can do this in Go with the standard library sort. Go's standard library sort has helper functions for different data types (`IntsAreSorted`, `Float64sAreSorted`, and `StringsAreSorted`) for sorting their respective data types. We can implement the sorting algorithm as illustrated in the following code:

```
package main
import (
    "fmt"
    "sort"
)
func main() {
    intData := []int{3, 1, 2, 5, 6, 4}
    stringData := []string{"foo", "bar", "baz"}
    floatData := []float64{1.5, 3.6, 2.5, 10.6}
```

This code instantiates simple data structures with values. After this, we sort each of these data structures using the built-in `sort` functions, as follows:

```
sort.Ints(intData)
sort.Strings(stringData)
```

```
sort.Float64s(floatData)
fmt.Println("Sorted Integers: ", intData, "\nSorted Strings:
  ", stringData, "\nSorted Floats: ", floatData)
}
```

As we execute this, we can see that all of our slices have been sorted in order, as shown in the following screenshot:

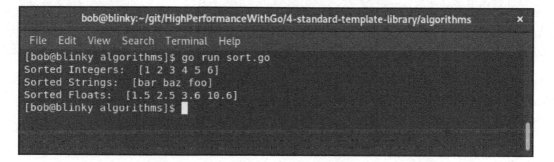

Integers are sorted low to high, strings are sorted alphabetically, and floats are sorted low to high. These are the default sorting methods within the `sort` package.

Reverse

The **reverse** algorithm takes a dataset and reverses the values of the set. The Go standard `sort` package does not have a built-in way to reverse slices. We can write a trivial `reverse` function in order to reverse the order of our dataset, like so:

```
package main

import (
  "fmt"
)

func reverse(s []string) []string {
  for x, y := 0, len(s)-1; x < y; x, y = x+1, y-1 {
    s[x], s[y] = s[y], s[x]
  }
  return s
}
func main() {
  s := []string{"foo", "bar", "baz", "go", "stop"}
  reversedS := reverse(s)
  fmt.Println(reversedS)
}
```

This function iterates through the slice, increments and decrements x and y until they converge, and swaps the elements in the slice, as we can see in the following screenshot:

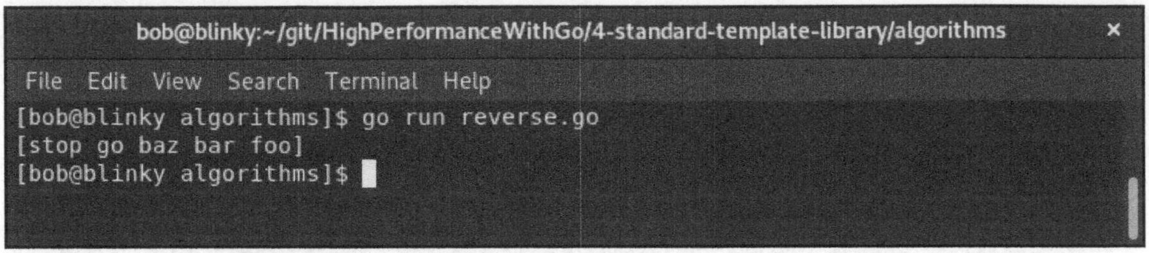

```
bob@blinky:~/git/HighPerformanceWithGo/4-standard-template-library/algorithms          ×

File   Edit   View   Search   Terminal   Help
[bob@blinky algorithms]$ go run reverse.go
[stop go baz bar foo]
[bob@blinky algorithms]$ ▮
```

As we can see, our slice is reversed using the reverse() function. Using the standard library makes a function that would be difficult to write by hand simple, concise, and reusable.

Min element and max element

We can find the smallest and largest values within a dataset using the min_element and max_element algorithms respectively. We can implement min_element and max_element in Go using a simple iterator:

1. First, we'll write a function to find the smallest integer in the slice:

```go
package main

import "fmt"

func findMinInt(a []int) int {
  var minInt int = a[0]
  for _, i := range a {
    if minInt > i {
      minInt = i
    }
  }
  return minInt

}
```

2. Next, we will follow the same process, but will attempt to find the largest integer in the slice:

```
func findMaxInt(b []int) int {
  var max int = b[0]
  for _, i := range b {
    if max < i {
      max = i
    }
  }
  return max
}
```

3. Lastly, we'll use these functions to print the resulting minimum and maximum values:

```
func main() {
  intData := []int{3, 1, 2, 5, 6, 4}
  minResult := findMinInt(intData)
  maxResult := findMaxInt(intData)
  fmt.Println("Minimum value in array: ", minResult)
  fmt.Println("Maximum value in array: ", maxResult)
}
```

These functions iterate through a slice of integers and find the minimum and maximum values within the slice, as shown in the following screenshot:

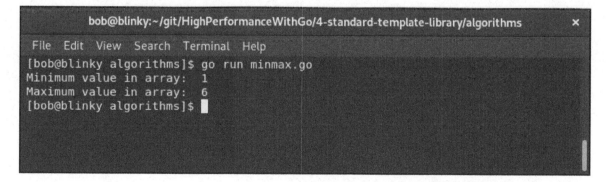

As you can see from our execution, the minimum and maximum values are found.

We also have `math.Min` and `math.Max` defined in the Go `math` package. These are only used for comparing `float64` data types. Float comparison is not an easy task, so the Go designers decided to make the default `Min` and `Max` signature; in the `math` library, you should use floats. If Go were to have generics, the main function we wrote above could potentially work for different types. This is part of the Go language design—keeping things simple and consolidated.

Binary search

Binary search is an algorithm that is used to find the location of a specific element in a sorted array. It starts by targeting the middle element in the array. If there is no match, the algorithm next takes the half of the array that could contain the item and uses the middle value to find the target. As we learned in Chapter 2, *Data Structures and Algorithms*, binary search is an efficient algorithm at $O(\log n)$. The Go standard library `sort` package has a built-in binary search function. We can use it like so:

```
package main

import (
  "fmt"
  "sort"
)

func main() {
  data := []int{1, 2, 3, 4, 5, 6}
  findInt := 2
  out := sort.Search(len(data), func(i int) bool { return data[i]
    >= findInt })
  fmt.Printf("Integer %d was found in %d at position %d\n",
    findInt, data, out)
}
```

The binary search algorithm correctly finds the value of the integer we are searching for, 2, in the position that it is expected to be in (position 1 in a zero-indexed slice). We can see the binary search execution in the following screenshot:

As a conclusion, the algorithms found in the STL all translate nicely to Go. Go's default functions and iterators make it easy to compose simple, reusable algorithms. In the next section, we will learn about containers.

Understanding containers

Containers fall under three separate categories in the STL:

- Sequence containers
- Sequence container adapters
- Associative containers

We are going to cover these three types of containers in the following sections.

Sequence containers

Sequence containers store data elements of a specific type. There are five current implementations of sequence containers: `array`, `vector`, `deque`, `list`, and `forward_list`. These sequence containers make it easy to reference data in a sequential manner. Being able to utilize these sequence containers is a great shortcut to writing effective code and reusing modular bits of the standard library. We will explore these in the following subsections.

Array

An **array** in Go is similar to that of an array in C++. Go's array structures are statically defined during compile time and are not resizable. Arrays are implemented in Go in the following manner:

```
arrayExample := [5]string{"foo", "bar", "baz", "go", "rules"}
```

This array holds the values of the strings defined in the `arrayExample` variable, which is defined as an array.

Vector

Go originally had a **vector** implementation, but this was removed very early on in the language development (October 11, 2011). It was deemed that slices are better (as was the title of the pull request) and slices became the de facto vector implementation in Go. We can implement a slice as follows:

```
sliceExample := []string{"slices", "are", "cool", "in", "go"}
```

Slices are beneficial because, like vectors in the STL, they can grow or shrink based on addition or deletion. In our example, we create a slice, append a value to the slice, and remove a value from the slice, as illustrated in the following code:

```
package main

import "fmt"

// Remove i indexed item in slice
func remove(s []string, i int) []string {
  copy(s[i:], s[i+1:])
  return s[:len(s)-1]
}

func main() {
  slice := []string{"foo", "bar", "baz"} // create a slice
  slice = append(slice, "tri") // append a slice
  fmt.Println("Appended Slice: ", slice) // print slice [foo, bar baz, tri]
  slice = remove(slice, 2) // remove slice item #2 (baz)
  fmt.Println("After Removed Item: ", slice) // print slice [foo, bar, tri]
}
```

As we execute our vector example, we can see our appending and removing in action, as shown in the following screenshot:

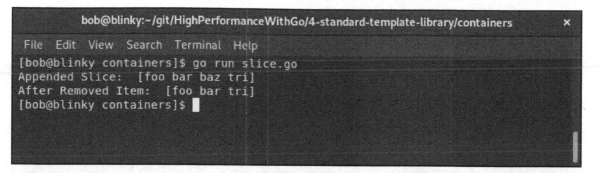

We can see that the `tri` element was appended to the end of our slice, and we can also see that the `baz` element (element number 3 in the slice) was removed based on our `remove()` function call.

Deque

A **deque**, or a double-ended queue, is a container that can be expanded. These expansions can occur in the front or the back of the container. Deques are often used when the top or the back of a queue needs to be referenced frequently. The following code block is a simple implementation of a deque:

```go
package main

import (
    "fmt"

    "gopkg.in/karalabe/cookiejar.v1/collections/deque"
)

func main() {
    d := deque.New()
    elements := []string{"foo", "bar", "baz"}
    for i := range elements {
        d.PushLeft(elements[i])
    }
    fmt.Println(d.PopLeft())  // queue => ["foo", "bar"]
    fmt.Println(d.PopRight()) // queue => ["bar"]
    fmt.Println(d.PopLeft())  // queue => empty
}
```

The `deque` package takes a slice of elements and pushes them onto the queue with the `PushLeft` function. Next, we can pop elements off of the left and the right of the deque, until our queue is empty. We can see the execution of our deque logic in the following screenshot:

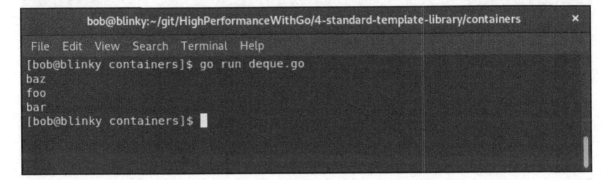

Our results show the output of the manipulation of the deque and how we can pull things from either end of the queue. Being able to pull things from either end of the queue is advantageous in data manipulation, and this is why a deque is a popular data structure choice.

List

A **list** is Go's implementation of a doubly linked list. This is built into the container/list package in the standard library. We can perform many actions using the implementation of a generic doubly linked list, as shown in the following code:

```
package main

import (
    "container/list"
    "fmt"
)

func main() {
    ll := list.New()
    three := ll.PushBack(3)              // stack representation -> [3]
    four := ll.InsertBefore(4, three)    // stack representation -> [4 3]
    ll.InsertBefore(2, three)            // stack representation ->
                                         // [4 2 3]
    ll.MoveToBack(four)                  // stack representation ->
                                         // [2 3 4]
    ll.PushFront(1)                      // stack representation ->
```

```
                              //  [1 2 3 4]
listLength := ll.Len()
fmt.Printf("ll type: %T\n", ll)
fmt.Println("ll length: :", listLength)
for e := ll.Front(); e != nil; e = e.Next() {
    fmt.Println(e.Value)
}
}
```

A doubly linked list is similar to the deque container, but it allows for insertion and removal from the middle of the stack if necessary. Doubly linked lists are used much more often in practice. We can see the execution of our doubly linked list code in the following screenshot:

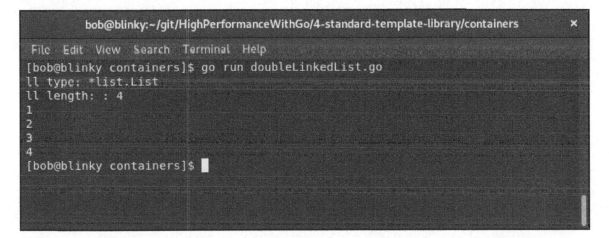

We can see that all the elements are in the order in which they were coordinated on the stack in the output from our program. Linked lists are quintessential to programming, as they are a fundamental algorithm that much of today's computer science is built on.

Forward list

A **forward list** is an implementation of a singly linked list. A singly linked list typically has a smaller memory footprint than a doubly linked list; however, iteration through a singly linked list isn't as good, particularly in the reverse direction. Let's see how to implement a forward list:

1. First, we initialize our program and define our structures:

```go
package main

import "fmt"

type SinglyLinkedList struct {
    head *LinkedListNode
}

type LinkedListNode struct {
    data string
    next *LinkedListNode
}
```

2. Then we create our `Append` function and apply it in our `main` function:

```go
func (ll *SinglyLinkedList) Append(node *LinkedListNode) {
    if ll.head == nil {
        ll.head = node
        return
    }

    currentNode := ll.head
    for currentNode.next != nil {
        currentNode = currentNode.next
    }
    currentNode.next = node
}

func main() {
    ll := &SinglyLinkedList{}
    ll.Append(&LinkedListNode{data: "hello"})
    ll.Append(&LinkedListNode{data: "high"})
    ll.Append(&LinkedListNode{data: "performance"})
    ll.Append(&LinkedListNode{data: "go"})

    for e := ll.head; e != nil; e = e.next {
        fmt.Println(e.data)
```

```
        }
    }
```

As we can see from the resulting output in the following screenshot, all of the pieces of data we appended to our singly linked list are accessible:

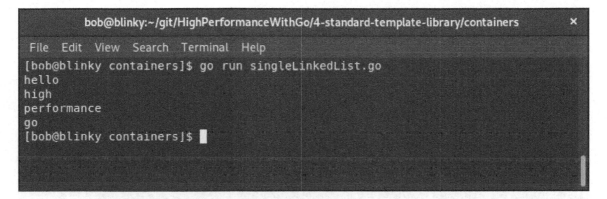

The initial elements of this data structure are put into the list in the order that they were added within the code block. This is expected, as singly linked lists are often used in order to keep the order of data within the data structure.

Container adapters

Container adapters take a sequential container and adapt the way it is used in order for the original sequential container to function in its intended manner. During the investigation of these container adapters, we will learn how all of them are created and how they are used from a practical standpoint.

Queue

Queues are containers that follow the **FIFO** queuing method, or **first in first out**. This means that we can add things to the container and pull them from the other end of the container. We can make the simplest form of a queue by appending and dequeueing from a slice, as shown in the following code:

```
package main

import "fmt"

func main() {
```

```
        var simpleQueue []string
        simpleQueue = append(simpleQueue, "Performance ")
        simpleQueue = append(simpleQueue, "Go")

        for len(simpleQueue) > 0 {
            fmt.Println(simpleQueue[0])    // First element
            simpleQueue = simpleQueue[1:] // Dequeue
        }
        fmt.Println(simpleQueue) //All items are dequeued so result should be
[]
    }
```

In our example, we append strings to our `simpleQueue` and then dequeue them by removing the first element of the slice:

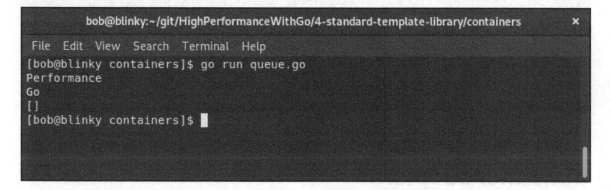

In our output, we can see that we correctly added elements to the queue and removed them.

Priority queue

A **priority queue** is a container that uses a heap to keep a prioritized list of the elements within the container. Priority queues are helpful because you can order the result set by priority. Priority queues are often used for many practical applications, from load balancing web requests to data compression, to Dijkstra's algorithm.

In our priority queue example, we create a new priority queue and insert a couple of different programming languages that have a given priority. We start with Java being the first priority and then Go becomes the first priority. PHP gets added and Java's priority gets pushed down to 3. The following code is an example of a priority queue. Here, we instantiate the necessary requirements, create a new priority queue, insert elements into the priority queue, change the priority of those items, and pop items from the stack:

```
package main

import (
    "fmt"

    pq "github.com/jupp0r/go-priority-queue"
)

func main() {
    priorityQueue := pq.New()
    priorityQueue.Insert("java", 1)
    priorityQueue.Insert("golang", 1)
    priorityQueue.Insert("php", 2)
    priorityQueue.UpdatePriority("java", 3)
    for priorityQueue.Len() > 0 {
        val, err := priorityQueue.Pop()
        if err != nil {
            panic(err)
        }
        fmt.Println(val)
    }
}
```

After our execution of this sample code, we can see a proper ordering of the languages based on the priority queue values that we have set, as we can see in the following code:

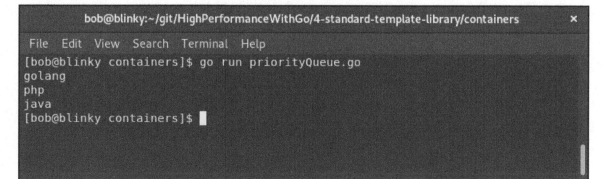

Priority queues are a commonly used, important data structure. They are used in order to process the most important elements within a data structure first, and being able to implement this with STL equivalents helps us to save time and effort while being able to prioritize incoming requests.

Stack

A **stack** serves the grouping of data using `push` and `pop` to add and remove elements from the container. Stacks usually have a **LIFO** (short for **last in first out**) order of operation, and the `Peek` operation usually lets you see what is on top of the stack without removing it from the stack. Stacks are very handy for things that have a bounded set of memory, as they can utilize the allocated memory effectively. The following code is a simple implementation of a stack:

```go
package main

import (
    "fmt"

    stack "github.com/golang-collections/collections/stack"
)

func main() {
    // Create a new stack
    fmt.Println("Creating New Stack")
    exstack := stack.New()
    fmt.Println("Pushing 1 to stack")
    exstack.Push(1) // push 1 to stack
    fmt.Println("Top of Stack is : ", exstack.Peek())
    fmt.Println("Popping 1 from stack")
    exstack.Pop() // remove 1 from stack
    fmt.Println("Stack length is : ", exstack.Len())
}
```

We can see the output from our program as follows:

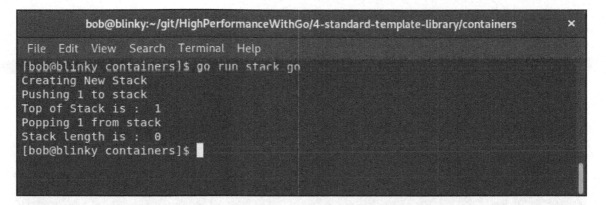

We can see that our stack operations were executed as expected. Being able to use stack manipulation is important in computer science as this is how many low-level programming techniques are executed.

Associative containers

Associative containers are containers that implement associative arrays. These arrays are ordered and differ only in the constraints placed by the algorithm on each of their elements. The STL references associative containers—namely set, map, multiset, and multimap. We will explore these in the following sections.

Set

A **set** is used to only store keys. Go doesn't have a set type, so a map of the type to a Boolean value is used frequently in order to build a set. The following code block is an implementation of an STL equivalent set:

```
package main

import "fmt"

func main() {
    s := make(map[int]bool)

    for i := 0; i < 5; i++ {
        s[i] = true
    }

    delete(s, 4)
```

```
    if s[2] {
        fmt.Println("s[2] is set")
    }
    if !s[4] {
        fmt.Println("s[4] was deleted")
    }
}
```

The resulting output shows that we were able to set and delete the values accordingly:

We can see from our output that our code can properly manipulate a set, which is crucial for common key–value pairings.

Multiset

Multisets are unordered sets with a count associated with each element. There are lots of convenient bits of manipulation that can be used with multisets, such as taking the difference, scaling the set, or checking the cardinality of a set.

In our example, we build a multiset x, scale it by 2 as a multiset y, validate that x is a subset of y, and check the cardinality of x. We can see an example implementation of a multiset in the following code:

```
package main

import (
    "fmt"

    "github.com/soniakeys/multiset"
)

func main() {
    x := multiset.Multiset{"foo": 1, "bar": 2, "baz": 3}
```

```
    fmt.Println("x: ", x)
    // Create a scaled version of x
    y := multiset.Scale(x, 2)
    fmt.Println("y: ", y)
    fmt.Print("x is a subset of y: ")
    fmt.Println(multiset.Subset(x, y))

    fmt.Print("Cardinality of x: ")
    fmt.Println(x.Cardinality())
}
```

As we execute this code, we can see x, the scaled version of x, y, the validation of x as a subset of y, and the cardinality calculation of x. The following is the output from the execution of our multiset code snippet:

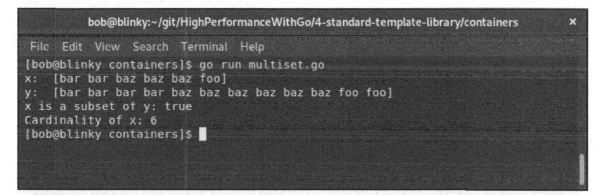

Multisets are useful for set manipulation and are convenient because there can be multiple instances of each element. A good practical example of a multiset would be a shopping cart—you can add many items to your shopping cart and you can have many counts of the same item in your shopping cart.

Map

A **map** is a kind of container that is used to store key–value pairs. Go's built-in `map` type uses a hash table to store keys and their associated values.

In Go, instantiating a map is simple, as shown in the following code:

```
package main

import "fmt"

func main() {
    m := make(map[int]string)
    m[1] = "car"
    m[2] = "train"
    m[3] = "plane"
    fmt.Println("Full Map:\t ", m)
    fmt.Println("m[3] value:\t ", m[3])
    fmt.Println("Length of map:\t ", len(m))
}
```

Now let's have a look at the output:

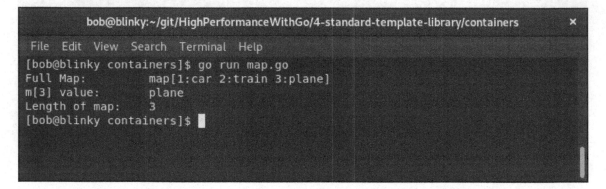

In the preceding execution result, we can see that we can create a map, reference a value in a map by using its key, and find the number of elements in our map using the `Len()` built-in type.

Multimap

A **multimap** is a map where one or more values can be returned with a key. A practical application of a multimap would be a web query string. Query strings can have multiple values assigned to the same key, as we can see with the following example URL: `https://www.example.com/?foo=bar&foo=baz&a=b`.

In our example, we are going to create a multimap of cars. Our `car` struct has a year and a style associated with each car. We'll be able to aggregate these different types together. The following code snippet is an implementation of a multimap:

```
package main

import (
    "fmt"

    "github.com/jwangsadinata/go-multimap/slicemultimap"
)

type cars []struct {
    year  int
    style string
}

func main() {

    newCars := cars{{2019, "convertible"}, {1966, "fastback"}, {2019,
"SUV"}, {1920, "truck"}}
    multimap := slicemultimap.New()

    for _, car := range newCars {
        multimap.Put(car.year, car.style)
    }

    for _, style := range multimap.KeySet() {
        color, _ := multimap.Get(style)
        fmt.Printf("%v: %v\n", style, color)
    }
}
```

We have multiple versions of cars with a 2019 model year (a convertible and SUV). In our resulting output, we can see these values aggregated together:

Multimaps are useful when you have a one-to-many association that you'd like to capture in a map. In the next section, we will look at function objects.

Understanding function objects

Function objects, also known as **functors**, are used for generating, testing, and operating on data. If you declare an object as a functor, you can use that object as one would use a function call. Oftentimes, the algorithms in the STL need a parameter to perform their designated tasks. Functors tend to be a useful way to assist in performing those tasks. In this section, we will learn about the following:

- Functors
- Internal and external iterators
- Generators
- Implicit iterators

Functors

A **functor** is a functional programming paradigm in which a transformation is performed on a structure while the structure is preserved.

In our example, we take an integer slice, `intSlice`, and lift the slice into a functor. `IntSliceFunctor` is an interface that includes the following:

- `fmt.Stringer`, which defines the string format for the value with its representation.
- `Map(fn func(int int) IntSliceFunctor` – this mapping applies `fn` to each element in our slice.
- A convenience function, `Ints() []int`, which allows you to get the `int` slice the functor holds.

After we have our lifted slice, we can perform operations on our newly created functor. In our example, we perform a square operation and a modulus three operation. The following is an example implementation of a functor:

```go
package main

import (
    "fmt"

    "github.com/go-functional/core/functor"
)

func main() {
    intSlice := []int{1, 3, 5, 7}
    fmt.Println("Int Slice:\t", intSlice)
    intFunctor := functor.LiftIntSlice(intSlice)
    fmt.Println("Lifted Slice:\t", intFunctor)

    // Apply a square to our given functor
    squareFunc := func(i int) int {
        return i * i
    }

    // Apply a mod 3 to our given functor
    modThreeFunc := func(i int) int {
        return i % 3
    }

    squared := intFunctor.Map(squareFunc)
    fmt.Println("Squared: \t", squared)

    modded := squared.Map(modThreeFunc)
    fmt.Println("Modded: \t", modded)
}
```

During the execution of this code, we can see that our function manipulation with functors worked as expected. We took our initial `intSlice`, lifted it into a functor, applied a square to each value with `squareFunc`, and applied `%3` to each value with `modThreeFunc`:

```
bob@blinky:~/git/HighPerformanceWithGo/4-standard-template-library/functions          ×

File  Edit  View  Search  Terminal  Help
[bob@blinky functions]$ go run functor.go
Int Slice:      [1 3 5 7]
Lifted Slice:   []int{1, 3, 5, 7}
Squared:        []int{1, 9, 25, 49}
Modded:         []int{1, 0, 1, 1}
[bob@blinky functions]$
```

Functors are a very powerful language construct. A functor abstracts a container in a way that is easily modifiable. It also allows for a separation of concerns—for instance, you can separate iteration logic from calculation logic, functors can be parameterized more simply, and functors can also be stateful.

Iterators

We discussed iterators in `Chapter 3`, *Understanding Concurrency*. Iterators are objects that allow the traversal of lists and other containers. Iterators are often implemented as part of a container's interface, which is an important method for a programmer. These are often split into the following categories:

- Internal iterators
- External iterators
- Generators
- Implicit iterators

We will cover what these categories are in more detail in the following sections.

Internal iterators

Internal iterators are represented as higher-order functions (often utilizing anonymous functions, as we saw in `Chapter 3`, *Understanding Concurrency*). Higher-order functions take functions as arguments and return functions as outputs. Anonymous functions are functions that aren't bound to identifiers.

Internal iterators often map themselves to applying a function to every element in a container. This can be represented by a variable identifier or it can be represented anonymously. The authors of the language have mentioned that apply/reduce are possible in Go, but shouldn't be used (this is because `for` loops tend to be preferred in Go). This pattern follows along with Go's motto of *simple is better than clever*.

External iterators

External iterators are used in order to access elements within an object and point to the next element in the object (known as element access and traversal, respectively). Go uses the `for` loop iterator heavily. The `for` loop is Go's only natural looping construct, and greatly simplifies program construction. A `for` loop is as simple as the following:

```
package main

import "fmt"

func main() {
    for i := 0; i < 5; i++ {
        fmt.Println("Hi Gophers!")
    }
}
```

We can see our output as follows:

Our `for` loop iterator is simple, but it proves a strong point—sometimes, simplicity works as expected for difficult problem sets.

Generators

Generators return the subsequent value in a sequence when a function is called. As you can see in the following code block, anonymous functions can be used to implement the generator iterator pattern in Go:

```
package main

import "fmt"

func incrementCounter() func() int {
    initializedNumber := 0
    return func() int {
        initializedNumber++
        return initializedNumber
    }
}

func main() {
    n1 := incrementCounter()
    fmt.Println("n1 increment counter #1: ", n1())
    fmt.Println("n1 increment counter #2: ", n1())
    n2 := incrementCounter()
    fmt.Println("n2 increment counter #1: ", n2())
    fmt.Println("n1 increment counter #3: ", n1())
}
```

When `incrementCounter()` is called, the integer represented in the function is incremented. Being able to use anonymous functions concurrently in this manner is a big draw for a lot of programmers coming to Go from other languages. It gives a succinct method for drawing on the concurrency of the language.

Implicit Iterators

An **implicit iterator** gives the programmer an easy way to iterate through the elements that are stored within a container. This is often created with a built-in range in Go. The built-in range allows you to iterate through your container. The following is a code snippet implementing an implicit iterator:

```
package main

import "fmt"

func main() {
    stringExample := []string{"foo", "bar", "baz"}
```

```
    for i, out := range stringExample {
        fmt.Println(i, out)
    }
}
```

We can see the resulting output as follows:

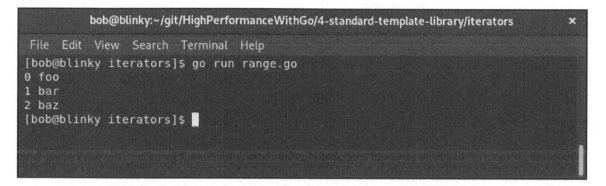

This output shows our iteration through the range of our `stringExample` variable. The `range` function is a very powerful construct that is concise and easy to read.

Summary

In this chapter, we learned how to use STL practices in Go. We also learned how to utilize standard programming algorithms with respect to Go, learned about how containers store data, learned how functions work in Go, and looked at how to use iterators properly. As we continue on our Go performance journey, we should always keep these algorithms, containers, functors, and iterators at the forefront of our choices for writing code. Doing so will help us to write idiomatic Go quickly and concisely. Choosing the proper combination of these STL idioms will help us to manipulate the data that we have in our hands faster and more effectively. In the next chapter, we will learn how to compute vectors and matrices in Go.

Matrix and Vector Computation in Go

5

Matrix and vector computation are important in computer science. Vectors can hold a group of objects in a dynamic array. They use contiguous storage and can be manipulated to accommodate growth. Matrices build on vectors, creating a two-dimensional set of vectors. In this chapter, we are going to discuss matrices and vectors along with how these two data structures can be used practically to perform much of the data manipulation that happens in computer science today. Vectors and matrices are building blocks that are commonly used for linear algebra, which is important in today's computer science. Processes such as image processing, computer vision, and web search all utilize linear algebra to perform their respective actions.

In this chapter, you will learn about the following topics:

- **Basic Linear Algebra Subprograms (BLAS)**
- Vectors
- Matrices
- Vector and matrix manipulation

Once we are able to tie all of these things together, you will learn how these different facets of matrix and vector computation can help drive forward the effective manipulation of large groupings of data.

Introducing Gonum and the Sparse library

One of the most popular libraries in Go for scientific algorithms is the Gonum package. The Gonum package (`https://github.com/gonum`) provides utilities that assist us in writing effective numerical algorithms using Go. This package focuses on creating performant algorithms for use in many different applications, and vectors and matrices are core tenets of this package. This library was created with performance in mind – the creators saw a problem with fighting vectorization in C, so they built this library in order to be able to manipulate vectors and matrices more easily in Go. The Sparse library (`https://github.com/james-bowman/sparse`) was built on top of the Gonum library in order to handle some of the normal sparse matrix operations that happen in machine learning and other parts of scientific computing. Using these libraries together is a performant way to manage vectors and matrices in Go.

In the next section, we'll look at what BLAS is.

Introducing BLAS

A specification called BLAS is commonly used in order to perform linear algebra operations. This library was originally created as a FORTRAN library in 1979 and has been maintained since then. BLAS has many optimizations for performant manipulation of matrices. Because of the depth and breadth of this specification, many languages have chosen to use this specification as part of their linear algebra libraries within their domain. The Go Sparse library uses a BLAS implementation for its linear algebra manipulation. The BLAS specification is composed of three separate routines:

- Level 1: Vector operations
- Level 2: Matrix-vector operations
- Level 3: Matrix-matrix operations

Having these leveled routines helps with the implementation and testing of this specification. BLAS has been used in many implementations, from Accelerate (macOS and iOS framework) to the Intel **Math Kernel Library** (**MKL**), and has been an integral part of linear algebra in applied computer science.

Now, it's time to learn about vectors.

Introducing vectors

A vector is a one-dimensional array that is often used for storing data. Go originally had a container/vector implementation, but this was removed on 18 October 2011, as slices were deemed more idiomatic for vector use in Go. The functionality provided by the built-in slice gives plenty of vector manipulation help. A slice would be a row vector, or 1 × m matrix, implementation. A simple row vector looks as follows:

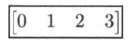

As you can see, we have a 1 × m matrix. To implement a simple row vector in Go, we can use a slice representation, like so:

```
v := []int{0, 1, 2, 3}
```

This is an easy way to portray a simple row vector using Go's built-in functionality.

Vector computations

A column vector is an m × 1 matrix, also known as the transpose of a row vector. A matrix transposition is when a matrix is flipped over its diagonal, often denoted with a superscript T. We can see an example of a column vector in the following image:

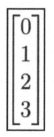

If we want to implement a column vector in Go, we can use the Gonum vector package to initialize this vector, as shown in the following code block:

```
package main

import (
    "fmt"
    "gonum.org/v1/gonum/mat"
)
```

```go
func main() {
    v := mat.NewVecDense(4, []float64{0, 1, 2, 3})
    matPrint(v)
}

func matrixPrint(m mat.Matrix) {
    formattedMatrix := mat.Formatted(m, mat.Prefix(""), mat.Squeeze())
    fmt.Printf("%v\n", formattedMatrix)
}
```

This will print out a column vector like the one shown in the preceding image.

We can also do some neat vector manipulation with the Gonum package. For example, in the following code block, we can see how simple it is to double the values within a vector. We can add two vectors together using the `AddVec` function, thus creating a doubled vector. We also have the `prettyPrintMatrix` convenience function to make our matrix easier to read:

```go
package main

import (
    "fmt"
    "gonum.org/v1/gonum/mat"
)

func main() {
    v := mat.NewVecDense(5, []float64{1, 2, 3, 4, 5})
    d := mat.NewVecDense(5, nil)
    d.AddVec(v, v)
    fmt.Println(d)
}

func prettyPrintMatrix(m mat.Matrix) {
    formattedM := mat.Formatted(m, mat.Prefix(""), mat.Squeeze())
    fmt.Printf("%v\n", formattedM)
}
```

The result of this function, that is, a doubled vector, is as follows:

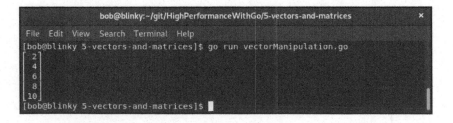

The `gonum/mat` package also gives us many other neat helper functions for vectors, including the following:

- `Cap()` gives you the capacity of the vector
- `Len()` gives you the number of columns within the vector
- `IsZero()` validates whether or not a vector is zero-sized
- `MulVec()` multiplies vectors *a* and *b* and serves the result
- `AtVec()` returns the value within the vector at a given position

The vector manipulation functions within the `gonum/mat` package help us to easily manipulate vectors into the datasets that we need.

Now that we are done with vectors, let's look at matrices.

Introducing matrices

Matrices are two-dimensional arrays, categorized by rows and columns. They are important in graphics manipulation and AI; namely, image recognition. Matrices are commonly used for graphics since the rows and columns that reside within a matrix can correspond to the row and column arrangement of pixels on a screen, as well as because we can have the matrix values correspond to a particular color. Matrices are also frequently used for digital sound processing as digital audio signals are filtered and compressed using Fourier transforms, and matrices help with performing these actions.

Matrices are usually denoted with an *M* × *N* naming scheme, where *M* is the number of rows in the matrix and *N* is the number of columns in the matrix, as shown in the following image:

$$\begin{bmatrix} 0 & 1 & 2 \\ 3 & 4 & 5 \\ 6 & 7 & 8 \end{bmatrix}$$

The preceding image, for example, is a 3 x 3 matrix. An *M* x *N* matrix is one of the core tenants of linear algebra, so it's important to see its relationship here.

Now, let's see how matrices operate.

Matrix operations

Matrices are a good way to store a large amount of information in an efficient manner, but the manipulation of matrices is where the real value of matrices is derived from. The most commonly used matrix manipulation techniques are as follows:

- Matrix addition
- Matrix scalar multiplication
- Matrix transposition
- Matrix multiplication

Being able to perform these actions on matrices is important as they can help with real-world data manipulation at scale. We will take a look at some of these operations, as well as practical applications of them, in the following sections.

Matrix addition

Matrix addition is the method in which we add two matrices together. Perhaps we want to find the resulting value of the summation of two 2D sets. If we have two matrices of the same size, we can add them together, like so:

$$\begin{bmatrix} 1 & 2 & 3 \\ 4 & 5 & 6 \\ 7 & 8 & 9 \end{bmatrix} + \begin{bmatrix} 1 & 2 & 3 \\ 4 & 5 & 6 \\ 7 & 8 & 9 \end{bmatrix} = \begin{bmatrix} 2 & 4 & 6 \\ 8 & 10 & 12 \\ 14 & 16 & 18 \end{bmatrix}$$

We can also represent this in Go code, as shown in the following code block:

```
package main

import (
    "fmt"
    "gonum.org/v1/gonum/mat"
)

func main() {
    a := mat.NewDense(3, 3, []float64{1, 2, 3, 4, 5, 6, 7, 8, 9})
    a.Add(a, a) // add a and a together
    matrixPrint(a)
}

func matrixPrint(m mat.Matrix) {
```

```
    formattedMatrix := mat.Formatted(m, mat.Prefix(""), mat.Squeeze())
    fmt.Printf("%v\n", formattedMatrix)
}
```

The result of executing this function is as follows:

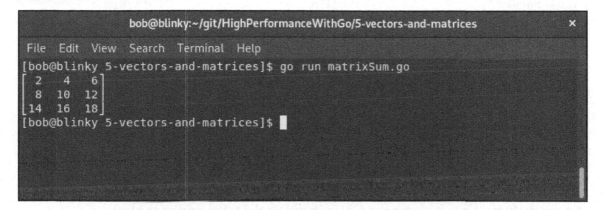

The result is a depiction of the matrix summation from our code block.

In the next section, we will discuss a practical example of matrix manipulation. To demonstrate this example, we will use matrix subtraction.

A practical example (matrix subtraction)

Suppose you own two restaurants, one in **New York, NY** and one in **Atlanta, GA**. You want to figure out what items are selling the best in your restaurants each month in order to make sure that you stock the right ingredients in the upcoming months. We can utilize matrix subtraction to find the net total number of unit sales we had for each restaurant. We need to have the raw data for unit sales for each restaurant, as shown in the following tables:

May unit sales:

	New York, NY	Atlanta, GA
Lobster Bisque	1,345	823
House Salad	346	234
Ribeye Steak	843	945
Ice Cream Sundae	442	692

June unit sales:

	New York, NY	Atlanta, GA
Lobster Bisque	920	776
House Salad	498	439
Ribeye Steak	902	1,023
Ice Cream Sundae	663	843

Now, we can find the difference in unit sales between these two months using the following matrix subtraction:

$$\begin{bmatrix} 920 & 776 \\ 298 & 439 \\ 902 & 1023 \\ 663 & 843 \end{bmatrix} - \begin{bmatrix} 1345 & 823 \\ 346 & 234 \\ 843 & 945 \\ 442 & 692 \end{bmatrix} = \begin{bmatrix} -425 & -47 \\ 152 & 205 \\ 59 & 78 \\ 221 & 151 \end{bmatrix}$$

We can perform this same action in Go, as shown in the following code block:

```
package main

import (
  "fmt"

  "gonum.org/v1/gonum/mat"
)

func main() {
  a := mat.NewDense(4, 2, []float64{1345, 823, 346, 234, 843, 945, 442,
692})
  b := mat.NewDense(4, 2, []float64{920, 776, 498, 439, 902, 1023, 663,
843})
  var c mat.Dense
  c.Sub(b, a)
  result := mat.Formatted(&c, mat.Prefix(""), mat.Squeeze())
 fmt.Println(result)
}
```

Our resulting output gives us the difference in sales for both restaurants between May and June, as follows:

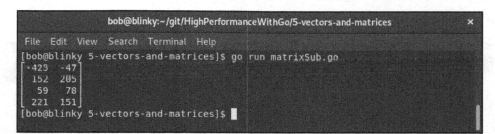

The result in the preceding screenshot is shown as an *N* x *M* matrix, depicting the sales differences.

As we gain more restaurants and add more items to our restaurant menu, utilizing matrix subtraction will help us to keep a note of which items we need to keep in stock.

Scalar multiplication

While manipulating matrices, we may want to multiply all of the values within a matrix by a scalar value.

We can represent this in Go with the following code:

```
package main

import (
  "fmt"

  "gonum.org/v1/gonum/mat"
)

func main() {
  a := mat.NewDense(3, 3, []float64{1, 2, 3, 4, 5, 6, 7, 8, 9})
  a.Scale(4, a) // Scale matrix by 4
  matrixPrint(a)
}

func matrixPrint(m mat.Matrix) {
  formattedMatrix := mat.Formatted(m, mat.Prefix(""), mat.Squeeze())
  fmt.Printf("%v\n", formattedMatrix)
}
```

This code produces the following results:

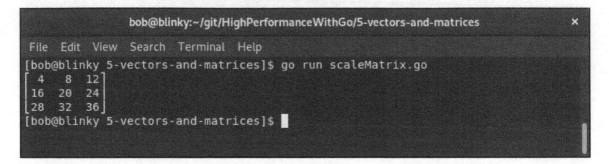

Here, we can see that each element in our matrix has been scaled by 4, thus providing an executed example of matrix scaling.

Scalar multiplication practical example

Let's say we own a hardware store and we have a catalog of products that have a **United States Dollar (USD)** value associated with them. Our company has decided to start selling our products in Canada, as well as the US. At the time of writing this book, $1 USD is equivalent to $1.34 **Canadian Dollars (CAD)**. We can look at our matrix of prices for screws, nuts, and bolts based on volume count, as shown in the following table:

	Individual USD	100ct USD	1000ct USD
Screws	$0.10	$0.05	$0.03
Nuts	$0.06	$0.04	$0.02
Bolts	$0.03	$0.02	$0.01

If we use matrix scalar multiplication to find the resulting cost in CAD, we'll end up with the following matrix computation:

$$1.34 * \begin{bmatrix} 0.1 & 0.05 & 0.03 \\ 0.06 & 0.04 & 0.02 \\ 0.03 & 0.02 & 0.01 \end{bmatrix} = \begin{bmatrix} 0.134 & 0.067 & 0.040 \\ 0.080 & 0.054 & 0.027 \\ 0.040 & 0.027 & 0.013 \end{bmatrix}$$

We can validate this with our Go scalar multiplication functionality, as shown in the following code snippet:

```
package main
import (
```

```
    "fmt"
    "gonum.org/v1/gonum/mat"
)
func main() {
    usd := mat.NewDense(3, 3, []float64{0.1, 0.05, 0.03, 0.06, 0.04, 0.02,
0.03, 0.02, 0.01})
    var cad mat.Dense
    cad.Scale(1.34, usd)
    result := mat.Formatted(&cad, mat.Prefix(""), mat.Squeeze())
    fmt.Println(result)
}
```

We receive a resulting matrix that contains the values for each of our items in CAD:

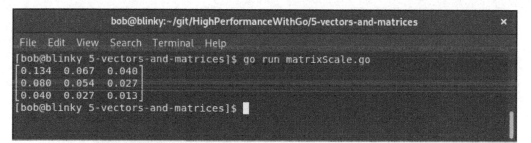

The output shows us the scaled resulting matrix.

As we get more and more products and have more different currencies that we'd like to account for, our scalar matrix manipulation will come in very handy as it will reduce the amount of work we have to do to manipulate these large sets of data.

Matrix multiplication

We may also want to multiply two matrices together. Multiplying two matrices together gives you a product of the two matrices. This can be very helpful when we want to multiply many numbers together at once in a concurrent fashion. We can take matrix A, an $N \times M$ matrix, alongside B, an $M \times P$ matrix. The resulting set is called AB, which is an $N \times P$ matrix, as follows:

$$\begin{bmatrix} 1 & 2 \\ 3 & 4 \end{bmatrix} * \begin{bmatrix} 1 & 2 & 3 \\ 4 & 5 & 6 \end{bmatrix} = \begin{bmatrix} 9 & 12 & 15 \\ 19 & 26 & 33 \end{bmatrix}$$

We can represent this in Go with the following code:

```
package main

import (
    "fmt"
    "gonum.org/v1/gonum/mat"
)

func main() {
    a := mat.NewDense(2, 2, []float64{1, 2, 3, 4})
    b := mat.NewDense(2, 3, []float64{1, 2, 3, 4, 5, 6})
    var c mat.Dense
    c.Mul(a, b)
    result := mat.Formatted(&c, mat.Prefix(""), mat.Squeeze())
    fmt.Println(result)
}
```

After execution, we receive the following result:

This is how we can multiply matrices together using the gonum/mat package. Matrix multiplication is a common matrix function, and understanding how to perform this action will help you manipulate matrices effectively.

Matrix multiplication practical example

Let's talk about a practical example of matrix multiplication so that we can tie our theoretical work into a workable example. Two separate electronic vendors are vying for your business to make widgets for your company. Vendor A and vendor B both design offerings for the widget and give you a parts list for what they'll need. Both vendor A and vendor B use the same component supplier. In this example, we can use matrix multiplication to find out which vendor creates a less expensive widget. The parts list that each vendor gave you is as follows:

- **Vendor A**:
  Resistors: 5
  Transistors: 10
  Capacitors: 2

- **Vendor B**:
  Resistors: 8
  Transistors: 6
  Capacitors: 3

You know from the component's supplier catalog that the pricing for each of these components is as follows:

- Resistors cost: $0.10
- Transistors cost: $0.42
- Capacitors cost: $0.37

We can represent each of these inputs with matrices, as we learned previously. This is done as follows:

1. We create a matrix composed of the cost of the components, as follows:

$$\begin{bmatrix} 0.10 & 0.42 & 0.37 \end{bmatrix}$$

We create a matrix composed of the number of components from each vendor:

$$\begin{bmatrix} 5 & 8 \\ 10 & 6 \\ 2 & 3 \end{bmatrix}$$

3. Then, we use matrix multiplication to find some neat results:

$$\begin{bmatrix} 0.10 & 0.42 & 0.37 \end{bmatrix} * \begin{bmatrix} 5 & 8 \\ 10 & 6 \\ 2 & 3 \end{bmatrix} = \begin{bmatrix} 5.44 & 4.43 \end{bmatrix}$$

This result tells us that vendor A's solution costs $5.44 for parts, whereas vendor B's solution costs $4.43 for parts. Vendor B's solution is less expensive from a raw materials perspective.

This can be calculated in Go with the following code:

```
package main

import (
    "fmt"
    "gonum.org/v1/gonum/mat"
)

func main() {
    a := mat.NewDense(1, 3, []float64{0.10, 0.42, 0.37})
    b := mat.NewDense(3, 2, []float64{5, 8, 10, 6, 2, 3})
    var c mat.Dense
    c.Mul(a, b)
    result := mat.Formatted(&c, mat.Prefix("    "), mat.Squeeze())
    fmt.Println(result)
}
```

The resulting output confirms the calculations we did in the preceding program:

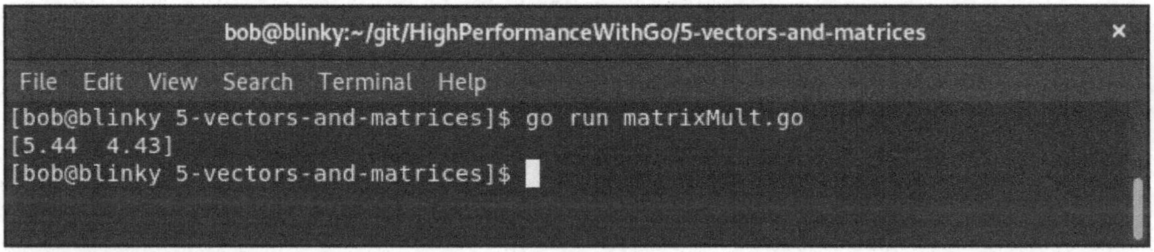

```
bob@blinky:~/git/HighPerformanceWithGo/5-vectors-and-matrices          ×

File   Edit   View   Search   Terminal   Help
[bob@blinky 5-vectors-and-matrices]$ go run matrixMult.go
[5.44  4.43]
[bob@blinky 5-vectors-and-matrices]$
```

As we see from our result, our formatted matrix lines up with the math that we performed earlier. Having a practical example can be very helpful in solidifying our understanding of theoretical concepts.

Matrix transposition

Transposing a matrix flips a matrix diagonally, swapping rows and column indices. The following image shows an example transposition of a matrix:

$$\begin{bmatrix} 0 & 1 & 2 \\ 3 & 4 & 5 \end{bmatrix}^{\mathsf{T}} = \begin{bmatrix} 0 & 3 \\ 1 & 4 \\ 2 & 5 \end{bmatrix}$$

We can represent a matrix transposition in Go using the following code:

```go
package main

import (
    "fmt"
    "gonum.org/v1/gonum/mat"
)

func main() {
    a := mat.NewDense(3, 3, []float64{5, 3, 10, 1, 6, 4, 8, 7, 2})
    matrixPrint(a)
    matrixPrint(a.T())
}

func matrixPrint(m mat.Matrix) {
    formattedMatrix := mat.Formatted(m, mat.Prefix(""), mat.Squeeze())
    fmt.Printf("%v\n", formattedMatrix)
}
```

The result of this matrix transposition can be seen in the following image:

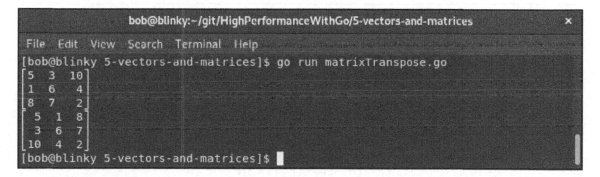

In the preceding output, we can see the regular matrix and the transposed version. Matrix transposition is often used in computer science to do things such as improve memory locality by transposing a matrix while still in memory.

Matrix transposition practical example

Transposing matrices is fun, but it may be helpful for you to have a practical example of when matrix transposition might be used. Let's say that we have three engineers: **Bob**, **Tom**, and **Alice**. These three engineers push Git commits daily. We want to keep track of these Git commits in a meaningful way so that we can make sure the engineers have all the resources they need to continue writing code. Let's take a count of our engineers' code commits for 3 days:

User	Day	Commits
Bob	1	5
Bob	2	3
Bob	3	10
Tom	1	1
Tom	2	6
Tom	3	4
Alice	1	8
Alice	2	7
Alice	3	2

After we have our data points, we can represent them in a 2D array:

$$\begin{bmatrix} BD_1 & BD_2 & BD_3 \\ TD_1 & TD_2 & TD_3 \\ AD_1 & AD_2 & AD_3 \end{bmatrix} = \begin{bmatrix} 5 & 3 & 10 \\ 1 & 6 & 4 \\ 8 & 7 & 2 \end{bmatrix}$$

Now that we have this array, we can take the transposition of the array:

$$\begin{bmatrix} BD_1 & BD_2 & BD_3 \\ TD_1 & TD_2 & TD_3 \\ AD_1 & AD_2 & AD_3 \end{bmatrix}^T = \begin{bmatrix} 5 & 1 & 8 \\ 3 & 6 & 7 \\ 10 & 4 & 2 \end{bmatrix}$$

Now that we've performed this transposition, we can see that the rows of the transposed array correspond to the day of commits rather than the individual end users' commits. Let's look at the first row:

$$\begin{bmatrix} 5 & 1 & 8 \end{bmatrix}$$

This now represents **BD1**, **TD1**, and **AD1** – the day 1 commits for each of the developers.

Now that we are done with the operations part, it's high time we had a look at matrix structures.

Understanding matrix structures

Matrices are usually classified into two different structures: dense matrices and sparse matrices. A dense matrix is composed of mostly non-zero elements. A sparse matrix is a matrix that is mostly composed of elements with a 0 value. The sparsity of a matrix is calculated as the number of elements with a zero value divided by the total count of elements.

If the result of this equation is greater than 0.5, the matrix is sparse. This distinction is important as it helps us to determine the best method for matrix manipulation. If a matrix is sparse, we may be able to use some optimizations to make the matrix manipulation more efficient. Inversely, if we have a dense matrix, we know that we will most likely be performing actions on the whole matrix.

It is important to remember that operations on matrices are most likely going to be memory bound with today's computer hardware. The size of the matrix is an important thing to remember. When you're calculating when to use a sparse matrix or a dense matrix, a dense matrix will have the value of one int64, which, according to the size and alignment for numeric types in Go, is 8 bytes. A sparse matrix will have that value, plus an int for the column index of the entry. Keep these sizes in mind as you're choosing which data structure to use for your data.

Dense matrices

When you create a dense matrix, all of the values of the matrix are stored. There are times when this is unavoidable – when we care about all of the values associated with a table and the table is mostly full. Using 2D slices or arrays for dense matrix storage can often be the best choice, but if you'd like to manipulate matrices, using the Gonum package can offer data manipulation in an effective manner. In practice, most matrices do not fall into the dense matrix category.

Sparse matrices

Sparse matrices come up frequently in real-world datasets. Whether or not someone has viewed a video in a movie catalog, listened to the number of songs on a playlist, or completed an item in their to-do list are all good examples of times it's possible to use a sparse matrix. Many of the values within these tables are zero, so it doesn't make sense to store these matrices as dense matrices. This would take up a lot of room in memory and would be expensive to manipulate.

We can use the Go sparse library in order to create and manipulate sparse matrices. The Sparse library uses idioms from BLAS routines in order to perform a lot of common matrix manipulation. The Go Sparse library is fully compatible with the Gonum matrix package, so it can be used interchangeably with this package. In this example, we're going to create a new sparse **Dictionary of Keys (DOK)**. After we create this, we'll set particular *M x N* values for sets in the array. Lastly, we will use the `gonum/mat` package in order to print the sparse matrix that we have created.

In the following code, we're creating a sparse matrix using the Sparse package. The `ToCSR()` and `ToCSC()` matrix functions create CSR and CSC matrices, respectively:

```go
package main

import (
    "fmt"
    "github.com/james-bowman/sparse"
    "gonum.org/v1/gonum/mat"
)

func main() {
    sparseMatrix := sparse.NewDOK(3, 3)
    sparseMatrix.Set(0, 0, 5)
    sparseMatrix.Set(1, 1, 1)
    sparseMatrix.Set(2, 1, -3)
    fmt.Println(mat.Formatted(sparseMatrix))
    csrMatrix := sparseMatrix.ToCSR()
    fmt.Println(mat.Formatted(csrMatrix))
    cscMatrix := sparseMatrix.ToCSC()
    fmt.Println(mat.Formatted(cscMatrix))
}
```

After we execute this code, we can see that the sparse matrix has been returned:

This output shows us the resulting sparse matrix.

Sparse matrices can be grouped into three separate formats:

- Formats that are utilized for the efficient creation and modification of a matrix
- Formats that are utilized for efficient access and matrix operations
- Specialized formats

The formats that are utilized for the efficient creation and modification of a matrix are as follows:

- **Dictionary of Keys (DOK)**
- **List of Lists (LIL)**
- **Coordinate Lists (COO)**

These formats will be defined in the following sections.

DOK matrix

A DOK matrix is a map in Go. This map links row and column pairs to their associated value. If no value has been defined for a particular coordinate in the matrix, it is assumed to be zero. Usually, a hashmap is used as the underlying data structure, which affords O(1) for random access, but iterating over elements ends up being a little bit slower. A DOK is useful for matrix construction or updating, but it is a non-performant choice for arithmetic operations. A DOK matrix can also be simply converted into a COO matrix once it's been created.

LIL matrix

An LIL matrix stores a list per row that contains the column index and the value, usually sorted by column, as this decreases lookup time. LIL matrices are useful for incrementally composing sparse matrices. They are also useful when we don't know the sparsity pattern for our incoming dataset.

COO matrix

A COO matrix (also frequently referred to as a triplet format matrix) stores lists of tuples containing rows, columns, and values, sorted by row and column index. A COO matrix is simple to append to with an O(1) timing. Random reads from a COO matrix are relatively slow (O(n)). COO matrices are a good choice for matrix initialization and conversion into CSR. COO matrices are a poor choice for arithmetic operations. We can improve the performance of a sequential iteration on a COO matrix by sorting the vectors within the matrix.

The formats that are utilized for efficient access and matrix operations are as follows:

- **Compressed Sparse Row (CSR)**
- **Compressed Sparse Column (CSC)**

These formats will be defined in the following sections.

CSR matrix

CSR matrices use three one-dimensional arrays to represent a matrix. The CSR format uses these three arrays:

- A: Values present within the array.
- IA: The index in which each of these values is present. These are defined as follows:
    - The value of IA at the 0 index, IA[0] = 0
    - The value of IA at the i index, IA[i] = IA[i – 1] + (number of non-zero elements on the i-1th row in the original matrix)
- JA: Stores the column indices of the elements.

The following image shows an example of a 4 x 4 matrix. This is the matrix that we are going to use in our following code sample:

$$\begin{bmatrix} 0 & 0 & 1 & 0 \\ 2 & 0 & 0 & 0 \\ 0 & 0 & 0 & 3 \\ 0 & 4 & 0 & 0 \end{bmatrix}$$

We can calculate these values as follows:

- A = [1 2 3 4]

- IA = [0 1 2 3 4]
- JA = [2 0 3 1]

We can validate this using the `sparse` package, as shown in the following code snippet:

```
package main

import (
    "fmt"
    "github.com/james-bowman/sparse"
    "gonum.org/v1/gonum/mat"
)

func main() {
    sparseMatrix := sparse.NewDOK(4, 4)
    sparseMatrix.Set(0, 2, 1)
    sparseMatrix.Set(1, 0, 2)
    sparseMatrix.Set(2, 3, 3)
    sparseMatrix.Set(3, 1, 4)
    fmt.Print("DOK Matrix:\n", mat.Formatted(sparseMatrix), "\n\n") //
Dictionary of Keys
    fmt.Print("CSR Matrix:\n", sparseMatrix.ToCSR(), "\n\n")         //
Print CSR version of the matrix
}
```

The result shows us the reconverted values of the DOK representation of the matrix that we created, as well as its corresponding CSR matrix:

The output from this code shows us a CSR matrix that prints the IA, JA, and A values, respectively. As the matrix grows, being able to calculate a CSR matrix makes matrix manipulation more and more efficient. Computer science often manipulates matrices with millions of rows and columns, so being able to do so in an efficient manner makes your code much more performant.

CSC matrix

A CSC matrix has an identical format to CSR matrices, but with one small difference. The column index slice is the element that is compressed, rather than the row index slice, as we saw within the CSR matrix. This means CSC matrices store their values in column-major order, instead of row-major order. This can also be viewed as a natural transposition of a CSR matrix. We can manipulate the example that we used in the previous section to look at how a CSC matrix is created, as shown in the following code block:

```
package main

import (
    "fmt"

    "github.com/james-bowman/sparse"
    "gonum.org/v1/gonum/mat"
)

func main() {
    sparseMatrix := sparse.NewDOK(4, 4)
    sparseMatrix.Set(0, 2, 1)
    sparseMatrix.Set(1, 0, 2)
    sparseMatrix.Set(2, 3, 3)
    sparseMatrix.Set(3, 1, 4)
    fmt.Print("DOK Matrix:\n", mat.Formatted(sparseMatrix), "\n\n") //
Dictionary of Keys
    fmt.Print("CSC Matrix:\n", sparseMatrix.ToCSC(), "\n\n")          //
Print CSC version
}
```

The result shows us the reconverted values of the DOK representation of the matrix that we created, as well as its corresponding CSC matrix:

```
bob@blinky:~/git/HighPerformanceWithGo/5-vectors-and-matrices        ×

 File  Edit  View  Search  Terminal  Help
[bob@blinky 5-vectors-and-matrices]$ go run cscMatrix.go
DOK Matrix:
⎡0  0  1  0⎤
⎢2  0  0  0⎥
⎢0  0  0  3⎥
⎣0  4  0  0⎦

CSC Matrix:
&{{4 4 [0 1 2 3 4] [1 3 0 2] [2 4 1 3]}}

[bob@blinky 5-vectors-and-matrices]$
```

The output from the preceding code block shows us the DOK matrix as well as the CSC matrix. Knowing how to represent CSR and CSC matrices is vital in the process of matrix manipulation. These two different types of matrices have different distinguishing characteristics. For example, DOK matrices have an O(1) access pattern, while CSC matrices use column-oriented operations for efficiency.

Summary

In this chapter, we discussed matrices and vectors, alongside how these two data structures are used practically to perform much of the data manipulation that happens in computer science today. Also, we learned about BLAS, vectors, matrices, and vector/matrix manipulation. Vectors and matrices are building blocks that are commonly used for linear algebra, and we saw hard examples of where this can take place.

The examples we have discussed in this chapter will help us a lot in situations pertinent to real-world data manipulation. In Chapter 6, *Composing Readable Go Code*, we are going to talk about composing readable Go code. Being able to write readable Go code will help keep topics and ideas clear and succinct for easy collaboration across code contributors.

2
Section 2: Applying Performance Concepts in Go

In this section, you'll learn why performance concepts are important in Go. They allow you to serve concurrent requests effectively. Go was written with performance in mind, and understanding the performance idioms associated with writing Go code will help you to write code that will help in many situations.

This section contains the following chapters:

- Chapter 6, *Composing Readable Go Code*
- Chapter 7, *Template Programming in Go*
- Chapter 8, *Memory Management in Go*
- Chapter 9, *GPU Parallelization in Go*
- Chapter 10, *Compile Time Evaluations in Go*

Composing Readable Go Code

6

Learning how to write readable Go code is an essential part of the language. Language developers used their previous experience while writing other languages to create a language that they felt was clear and concise. A commonly used phrase in describing the proper way to write with this language is *idiomatic Go*. This phrase is used to describe the *correct* way to program in Go. Style is often subjective, but the Go team has worked hard in order to write the language in an opinionated way and facilitate developer velocity, readability, and collaboration. In this chapter, we are going to talk about how to maintain some core tenets of the language:

- Simplicity
- Readability
- Packaging
- Naming
- Formatting
- Interfaces
- Methods
- Inheritance
- Reflection

Understanding these patterns and idioms will help you to write Go code that is more easily readable and operable between teams. Being able to write idiomatic Go will help raise the level of your code quality and help your project maintain velocity.

Maintaining simplicity in Go

Out of the box, Go doesn't follow specific patterns that other programming languages use. The writers chose different idioms for some of these following language constructs in order to keep the language simple and clear. Keeping the simplicity of the language has been a difficult task for language developers. Having tooling, libraries, fast execution, and fast compilation, all while maintaining simplicity, has been at the forefront of the language's development. Go's language developers have kept on track with these decisions with a design-by-consensus model—having a general consensus on adding things to a language ensures they are added in a way that is important to the development of the language.

Language maintainers are active on the GitHub issues page and are very happy to review pull requests if you have them. Getting feedback from others who write with the language allows language maintainers to make informed decisions about adding new features and functionality to the language while maintaining readability and simplicity.

The following section will show us the next fundamental aspect of the Go language: readability.

Maintaining readability in Go

Readability is another core tenet of Go. Being able to quickly grok a new code base and understand some of its nuances is an important part of any programming language. As distributed systems continue to grow, with vendored libraries and APIs becoming more commonplace, being able to easily read the code that is included and be able to make sense of it is helpful for forward momentum. This also makes broken code easier to fix.

Having concrete data types, interfaces, packages, concurrency, functions, and methods has helped Go to continue moving forward. Readability is one of the most important parameters of being able to maintain a large code base over an extended period of time, and this is one of the most important things that sets Go apart from its competitors. The language was constructed with readability as a first class citizen.

Go has a lot of complex looking underlying internal parts of the language, but these are really not complex at all. Things such as simply defined constants, interfaces, packages, garbage collection, and easy to implement concurrency are all complex under the hood, but transparent to the end user. Having these constructs available has helped to make Go thrive as a language.

Let's see what packaging in Go means in the next section.

Exploring packaging in Go

Packaging is a fundamental part of the Go language. Every single Go program is required to have a package definition on the first line of the program. This helps readability, maintainability, referencing, and organization.

The `main` package in a Go program uses the main declaration. This main declaration calls the `main` function of the program. After this occurs, we have other imports within the `main` function that can be used to import other packages within the program. We should try and keep the main package small in order to modularize all dependencies within our programs. We will talk about package naming next.

Package naming

While naming packages, developers should adhere to the following rules:

- Packages shouldn't have underscores, hyphens, or mixedCaps
- Packages shouldn't be named with generic naming schemes, such as common, util, base, or helper
- Package naming should be related to the function that the package is performing
- Packages should retain a decent-sized scope; all the elements in a package should have similar goals and objectives
- Utilizing internal packages can help while you're vetting new packages before they are aligned with your public API

Packaging layout

When we discuss the layout of a Go program, we have a couple of different processes that we should follow. A common convention is to keep your main programs in a folder named `cmd`. Your other packages that you build to be executed from the `main` function should live in a `pkg` directory. This separation helps to encourage the reuse of packages. In the following example, if we want to reuse the notification package for both the CLI and web main programs, we have the ability to do that easily with one import. The following a screenshot shows this separation:

```
bob@blinky:~/git/HighPerformanceWithGo/6-composing-readable-go-code            ×

File  Edit  View  Search  Terminal  Help
[bob@blinky 6-composing-readable-go-code]$ tree exampleProgram/
exampleProgram/
├── cmd
│   ├── examplecli
│   │   └── main.go
│   └── exampleweb
│       └── main.go
├── Dockerfile
├── go.mod
├── go.sum
├── Jenkinsfile
├── pkg
│   ├── api
│   │   ├── api.go
│   │   └── api_test.go
│   ├── integration
│   │   ├── integration.go
│   │   └── integration_test.go
│   └── notification
│       ├── notification.go
│       └── notification_test.go
└── README.md

7 directories, 13 files
[bob@blinky 6-composing-readable-go-code]$ 
```

An anti-pattern for Go is to have a one-to-one file for package mapping. We should be writing Go with the idea of driving common use cases together within a specific directory structure. For example, we could create a single directory per file and test it as follows:

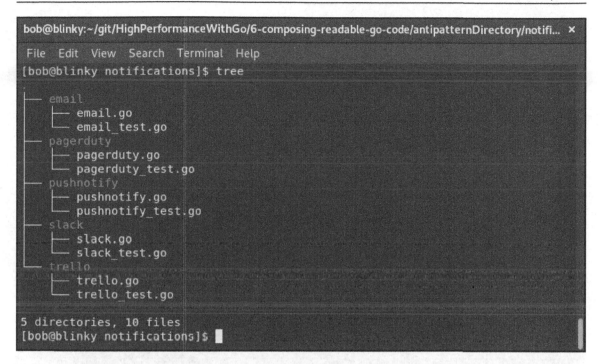

Instead, however, we should create our packages as follows:

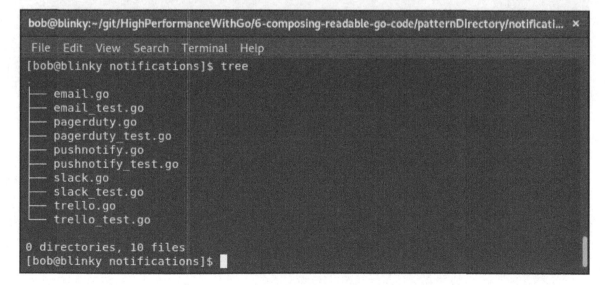

All of these different notification strategies share a common practice. We should attempt to keep similar functionality coupled in the same package. This will help others to understand any context in which the notifications package has similar functionality.

Internal packaging

Many Go programs use the concept of an internal package in order to signify an API that is not ready for external consumption. The idea of internal packages was first introduced in Go 1.4, to add boundaries around components within your program. These internal packages cannot be imported from outside the subtree in which they are stored. This is useful if you want to maintain your internal packages and not expose them to the rest of the program. Once you've vetted internal packages in the manner you deem fit, you can change the folder name and expose the previously internal package.

Let's see an example:

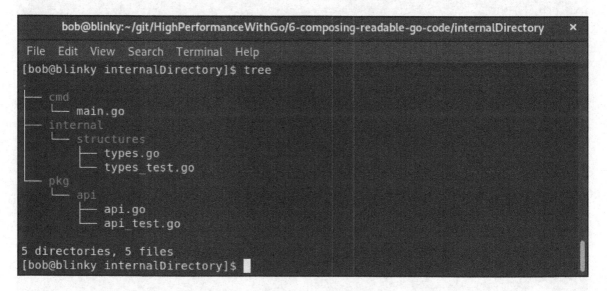

In the preceding example, we can see that we have an internal directory. This is only accessible from within this project. The `pkg` and `cmd` directories, however, will be accessible from other projects. This is important as we continue to develop new products and features that should not yet be available for import in other projects.

Vendor directory

The idea of a vendor directory originated with the release of Go 1.5. The `vendor` folder is a place to store a compiled grouping of external and internal sources into a directory within the project. This means that the code composer no longer has to copy in dependent packages to the source tree. The `vendor` folder is searched for when the `GOPATH` looks for dependencies. This is good for a number of reasons:

- We can keep local copies of external dependencies on our projects. This can be helpful if we want to execute our programs on networks that have limited or no external network connectivity.
- This makes compilation of our Go programs faster. Storing all of these vendored dependencies locally means that we don't need to pull down our dependencies at build time.
- If you'd like to use third-party code but have tweaked it for your particular use case, you can vendor that code and change it for internal release.

Go modules

Go modules were introduced in Go 1.11. They afford the ability to keep track of versioned dependencies within a Go code base. They are a collection of Go packages that are stored as a cohesive unit in a `go.mod` file within a project directory.

We will perform the following steps to initialize a new module:

1. We first execute `go mod init repository`:

```
go mod init github.com/bobstrecansky/HighPerformanceWithGo
go: creating new go.mod: module
github.com/bobstrecansky/HighPerformanceWithGo
```

2. After you've initialized this new module, you can build your Go package and execute it as you normally would. You'll have any imported modules from within your project saved in a `go.mod` file within your project's directory.

   As an example, if we want to be able to create a simple web server using the Gin framework [https://github.com/gin-gonic/gin], we would create a directory for this in our project structure as follows:
   `/home/bob/git/HighPerformanceWithGo/6-composing-readable-go-code/goModulesExample`.

3. We next create a simple web server that returns a response with `bar` to a `/foo` request:

```
package main
import "github.com/gin-gonic/gin"
func main() {
  server := gin.Default()
  server.GET("/foo", func(c *gin.Context) {
    c.JSON(200, gin.H{
      "response": "bar",
    })
  })
  server.Run()
}
```

4. After this, we can create a new Go module in our newly created directory:

```
bob@blinky:~/git/HighPerformanceWithGo/6-composing-readable-go-code/goModulesExample          ✕

 File   Edit   View   Search   Terminal   Help
[bob@blinky goModulesExample]$ go mod init github.com/bobstrecansky/HighPerforma
nceWithGo/6-composing-readable-go-code/goModulesExample
go: creating new go.mod: module github.com/bobstrecansky/HighPerformanceWithGo/6
-composing-readable-go-code/goModulesExample
[bob@blinky goModulesExample]$ go mod vendor
[bob@blinky goModulesExample]$ ls vendor/
github.com  golang.org  gopkg.in   modules.txt
[bob@blinky goModulesExample]$
```

5. Next, we can execute our Go program; the proper dependencies will be pulled in as necessary:

```
bob@blinky:~/git/HighPerformanceWithGo/6-composing-readable-go-code/goModulesExample    ×

 File  Edit  View  Search  Terminal  Help
[bob@blinky goModulesExample]$ go run main.go
[GIN-debug] [WARNING] Creating an Engine instance with the Logger and Recovery m
iddleware already attached.

[GIN-debug] [WARNING] Running in "debug" mode. Switch to "release" mode in produ
ction.
 - using env:    export GIN_MODE=release
 - using code:   gin.SetMode(gin.ReleaseMode)

[GIN-debug] GET    /foo                      --> main.main.func1 (3 handlers)
[GIN-debug] Environment variable PORT is undefined. Using port :8080 by default
[GIN-debug] Listening and serving HTTP on :8080
```

We can now see that we have our dependencies for our simple web server stored in the
go.sum file within our directory (I've used the head command to truncate the list to the top
10 entries):

```
bob@blinky:~/git/HighPerformanceWithGo/6-composing-readable-go-code/goModulesExample    ×

 File  Edit  View  Search  Terminal  Help
[bob@blinky goModulesExample]$ head -10 go.sum
github.com/davecgh/go-spew v1.1.0/go.mod h1:J7Y8YcW2NihsgmVo/mv3lAwl/skON4iLHjSs
I+c5H38=
github.com/gin-contrib/sse v0.0.0-20190301062529-5545eab6dad3 h1:t8FVkw33L+wilf2
QiWkw0UV77qRpcH/JHPKGpKa2E8g=
github.com/gin-contrib/sse v0.0.0-20190301062529-5545eab6dad3/go.mod h1:VJ0WA2NB
N22VlZ2dKZQPAPnyWw5XTlK1KymzLKsr59s=
github.com/gin-gonic/gin v1.4.0 h1:3tMoCCfM7ppqsR0ptz/wi1impNpT7/9wQtMZ8lr1mCQ=
github.com/gin-gonic/gin v1.4.0/go.mod h1:OW2EZn3DO8Ln9oIKOvM++LBO+5UPHJJDH72/q/
3rZdM=
github.com/golang/protobuf v1.3.1 h1:YF8+flBXS5eO826T4nzqPrxfhQThhXl0YzfuUPu4SBg
=
github.com/golang/protobuf v1.3.1/go.mod h1:6lQm79b+lXiMfvg/cZm0SGofjICqVBUtrP5y
JMmIC1U=
github.com/json-iterator/go v1.1.6 h1:MrUvLMLTMxbqFJ9kzlvat/rYZqZnW3u4wkLzWTaFwK
s=
github.com/json-iterator/go v1.1.6/go.mod h1:+SdeFBvtyEkXs7REEP0seUULqWtbJapLOCV
DaaPEHmU=
github.com/mattn/go-isatty v0.0.7 h1:UvyT9uN+3r7yLEYSlJsbQGdsaB/a0DlgWP3pql6iwOc
=
[bob@blinky goModulesExample]$ 
```

Go modules help keep vendored items within a Go repository clean and consistent. We can also use a vendored repository if we want to keep all of our dependencies local to our project.

Opinions on vendoring dependencies within your repository often vary greatly. Some like to use a vendored repository because it decreases build time and limits the risk of not being able to pull packages from an external repository. Others feel that vendoring can be a hindrance to package updates and security patches. Whether you choose to use a vendored directory in your program is up to you, but the fact that Go modules include this functionality in the language is convenient. The following output illustrates this:

```
bob@blinky:~/git/HighPerformanceWithGo/6-composing-readable-go-code/goModulesExample    ×

File  Edit  View  Search  Terminal  Help
[bob@blinky goModulesExample]$ go mod init github.com/bobstrecansky/HighPerforma
nceWithGo/6-composing-readable-go-code/goModulesExample
go: creating new go.mod: module github.com/bobstrecansky/HighPerformanceWithGo/6
-composing-readable-go-code/goModulesExample
[bob@blinky goModulesExample]$ go mod vendor
[bob@blinky goModulesExample]$ ls vendor/
github.com  golang.org  gopkg.in  modules.txt
[bob@blinky goModulesExample]$ 
```

Being able to vendor directories with the built-in compilation tools makes it easy to set up and configure.

In the next section, we will discuss naming things in Go.

Understanding naming in Go

There are a lot of consistent behaviors that Go programmers like to retain in order to keep readable, maintainable code. Go naming schemes tend to be consistent, accurate, and short. We want to create names with the following idioms in mind:

- Local variables for iterators should be short and simple:
  - i for an iterator; i and j if you have a two-dimensional iterator
  - r for a reader
  - w for a writer
  - ch for channels

- Global variable names should be short and descriptive:
  - `RateLimit`
  - `Log`
  - `Pool`

- Acronyms should follow the convention of using all capitals:
  - `FooJSON`
  - `FooHTTP`

- Avoid stuttering with the package name:
  - `log.Error()` instead of `log.LogError()`

- Interfaces with one method should follow the method name plus the `-er` suffix:
  - `Stringer`
  - `Reader`
  - `Writer`
  - `Logger`

- Names in Go should follow a Pascal or mixedCaps case method:
  - `var ThingOne`
  - `var thingTwo`

 It's important to remember that, if a name has an initial capital letter, it is exported and can be used in other functions. Remember this whilst coming up with your own naming schemes for things.

Following some of these naming conventions can you to have readable, consumable, reusable code. Another good practice is to use consistent naming styles. If you're instantiating the same type of parameter, make sure that it follows a consistent naming convention. This makes it easier for new consumers to follow along with the code that you have written.

In the next section, we will discuss formatting Go code.

Understanding formatting in Go

As mentioned in Chapter 1, *Introduction to Performance in Go*, gofmt is an opinionated formatter for Go code. It indents and aligns your code the way the language maintainers intended for it to be read. Many of the most popular code editors today can execute gofmt when a file is saved. Doing this, as well as having your continuous integration software verification, saves you having to focus on the formatting of the code that you're writing since the language will be prescriptive in output. Using this tool will make Go code easier to read, write, and maintain with multiple contributors. It also removes quite a bit of controversy within the language, since spaces, tabs, and braces are positioned automatically.

We can also add a pre-commit hook to our Git repository (in .git/hooks/pre-commit) in order to corroborate the fact that all of the code that is being committed to a repository is formatted as expected. The following code block illustrates this:

```bash
#!/bin/bash
FILES=$(/usr/bin/git diff --cached --name-only --diff-filter=dr | grep
'\.go$')
[ -z "$FILES" ] && exit 0
FORMAT=$(gofmt -l $FILES)
[ -z "$FORMAT" ] && exit 0

echo >&2 "gofmt should be used on your source code. Please execute:"
  for gofile in $FORMAT; do
      echo >&2 " gofmt -w $PWD/$gofile"
  done
  exit 1
```

After we add this pre-commit hook, we can confirm that things are working as expected by adding some erroneous spacing to a file within our repository. After we do so and git commit our code, we will see a warning message as follows:

```
git commit -m "test"
//gofmt should be used on your source code. Please execute:
gofmt -w /home/bob/go/example/badformat.go
```

gofmt also has a lesser known but vastly helpful simplify method, which will perform source transformations where possible. This will take some of the composite, slice and range composite literals, and shorten them. The simplify formatting command will take the following code:

```
package main
import "fmt"
func main() {
    var tmp = []int{1, 2, 3}
    b := tmp[1:len(tmp)]
    fmt.Println(b)
    for i, _ := range tmp {
        fmt.Println(tmp[i])
    }
}
```

This will simplify to the following code: gofmt -s gofmtSimplify.go.

The output of this gofmt code snippet is as follows:

```
package main
import "fmt"
func main() {
    var tmp = []int{1, 2, 3}
    b := tmp[1:]
    fmt.Println(b)
    for i := range tmp {
        fmt.Println(tmp[i])
    }
}
```

Note that the variable b in the preceding code snippet has a simple definition and that the empty variable in the range definition has been removed by the gofmt tool. This tool can help you to have more cleanly defined code in your repository. It can also be used as a mechanism for writing code in such way that the writer can think through the problem, but the resulting code from gofmt can be stored in the shared repository in a tightly knit fashion.

In the next section, we will discuss interfaces in Go.

Briefing on interfaces in Go

Go's interfacing system is different from the interfacing systems in other languages. They are named collections of methods. Interfaces are important in composing readable Go code because they make the code scalable and flexible. Interfaces also give us the ability to have polymorphism (providing a single interface to items with different types) in Go. Another positive aspect of interfaces is that they are implicitly implemented—the compiler checks that a specific type implements a specific interface.

We can define an interface as follows:

```
type example interface {
foo() int
bar() float64
}
```

If we want to implement an interface, all we need to do is implement the methods that are referenced in the interface. The compiler validates your interface's methods so that you don't have to perform this action.

We can also define an empty interface, which is an interface that has zero methods, represented by `interface{}`. Empty interfaces are valuable and practical in Go, as we can pass arbitrary values to them, as shown in the following code block:

```
package main
import "fmt"
func main() {
    var x interface{}
    x - "hello Go"
    fmt.Printf("(%v, %T)\n", x, x)
    x = 123
    fmt.Printf("(%v, %T)\n", x, x)
    x = true
    fmt.Printf("(%v, %T)\n", x, x)
}
```

As we execute our empty interface example, we can see that the type and value of the x interface change as we change the definition of the (initially) empty interface:

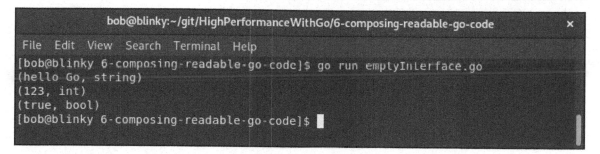

```
bob@blinky:~/git/HighPerformanceWithGo/6-composing-readable-go-code          ×

File  Edit  View  Search  Terminal  Help
[bob@blinky 6-composing-readable-go-code]$ go run emptyInterface.go
(hello Go, string)
(123, int)
(true, bool)
[bob@blinky 6-composing-readable-go-code]$
```

Empty, mutable interfaces are convenient because they give us the flexibility to manipulate our data in a way that makes sense to the code composer.

In the next section, we will discuss comprehending methods in Go.

Comprehending methods in Go

Methods in Go are functions that have a special type, called a `receiver`, that sits between the `function` keyword and the method name associated with the keyword. Go doesn't have classes in the same manner that other programming languages do . Structs are often used in conjunction with methods in order to bundle data and its corresponding methods in a similar fashion to how classes are constructed in other languages. As we instantiate a new method, we can add struct values in order to enrich the function call.

We can instantiate a structure and a method as follows:

```
package main
import "fmt"
type User struct {
    uid int
    name string
    email string
    phone string
}

func (u User) displayEmail() {
    fmt.Printf("User %d Email: %s\n", u.uid, u.email)
}
```

After this has been done, we can then use this struct and method to display information about a user as follows:

```
func main() {
    userExample := User{
        uid: 1,
        name: "bob",
        email: "bob@example.com",
        phone: "123-456-7890",
    }
    userExample.displayEmail()
}
```

This will return the result from `userExample.displayEmail()`, which prints the pertinent part of the structs as part of the method call as follows:

As we have larger structs of data, we have the ability to reference the data that is stored within these structs easily and effectively. If we decided that we wanted to write a method to find the end user's phone number, it would be simple to use our existing data type and write a method similar to the `displayEmail` method in order to return the end user's phone number.

The methods we have looked at so far only have value receivers. Methods can also have pointer receivers. Pointer receivers are helpful when you would like to update the data in place and have the results available to the caller function.

Consider our previous example with a couple of modifications. We are going to have two methods that will allow us to update our user's email address and phone number. The email address update is going to use a value receiver, whereas the phone update is going to use a pointer receiver.

We create these functions in the following code block in order to be able to update the end user's information easily:

```
package main
import "fmt"

type User struct {
    uid int
    name string
    email string
    phone string
}

func (u User) updateEmail(newEmail string) {
    u.email = newEmail
}

func (u *User) updatePhone(newPhone string) {
    u.phone = newPhone
}
```

We next create our example end user in `main`, as shown in the following code block:

```
func main() {
    userExample := User{
        uid: 1,
        name: "bob",
        email: "bob@example.com",
        phone: "123-456-7890",
    }
```

We then update the email and phone number of our end user in the following code block:

```
    userExample.updateEmail("bob.strecansky@example.com")
    (userExample).updatePhone("000-000-0000")
    fmt.Println("Updated User Email: ", userExample.email)
    fmt.Println("Updated User Phone: ", userExample.phone)
}
```

In our resulting output, we can see that the user email has not been updated from the perspective of the receiver, but that the user's phone number has:

This is important to remember when attempting to mutate state from within method calls. Methods are very helpful in manipulating data in Go programs.

It's now time to see what inheritance in Go is all about.

Comprehending inheritance in Go

Go does not have inheritance. Composition is used in order to embed items (mostly structs) in one another. This is convenient when you have a baseline struct that is used for many different functions, with other structs that build on top of the initial struct.

We can describe some of the items in my kitchen to show how inheritance works.

We can initialize our program as shown in the following code block. In this block, we create two structs:

Utensils: For the utensils I have in my drawers in my kitchen

Appliances: For the appliances I have in my kitchen

```
package main
import "fmt"

func main() {
    type Utensils struct {
        fork string
        spoon string
        knife string
    }

    type Appliances struct {
```

```
        stove string
        dishwasher string
        oven string
    }
```

I can next use Go's nested structuring to create a `Kitchen` struct that contains all of the utensils and appliances as follows:

```
type Kitchen struct {
    Utensils
    Appliances
}
```

I can then fill my kitchen with the utensils and appliances that I have:

```
bobKitchen := new(Kitchen)
bobKitchen.Utensils.fork = "3 prong"
bobKitchen.Utensils.knife = "dull"
bobKitchen.Utensils.spoon = "deep"
bobKitchen.Appliances.stove = "6 burner"
bobKitchen.Appliances.dishwasher = "3 rack"
bobKitchen.Appliances.oven = "self cleaning"
fmt.Printf("%+v\n", bobKitchen)
}
```

Once all of these things are in, we can see the resulting output where my kitchen items (the `Utensils` and `Appliances`) are organized in my `Kitchen` struct. My `Kitchen` struct is then easily referenced later in other methods.

Having nested structs can be very practical for future extension. If I decided that I'd like to add other elements in my house to this structure, I could make a `House` struct and nest my `Kitchen` struct within the `House` struct. I could also compose structs for other rooms in my house and add them to the house struct as well.

In the next section, we will explore reflection in Go.

Exploring reflection in Go

Reflection in Go is a form of metaprogramming. Using reflection in Go lets the program understand its own structure. There are times when you want to use a variable at runtime that doesn't exist when the program was composed. We use reflection to check the key and value pair that is stored within an interface variable. Reflection is not often clear, so be wary of using it—it should be used in special cases when necessary. It only has runtime checks (not compile checks), so we need to use reflection with common sense.

It's important to remember that Go's variables are statically typed. There are many different variable types that we can use in Go—`rune`, `int`, `string`, and so on. We can declare a specific type as follows:

```
Type foo int
var x int
var y foo
```

Both variables, `x` and `y`, will be int typed variables.

There are three important pieces of reflection that are used in order to find out information:

- Types
- Kinds
- Values

These three different pieces all work together to deduce the information you might need to know in relation to an interface. Let's take a look at each one individually and see how they mesh together.

Types

Being able to tell the type of a variable is important in Go. In our example, we can validate the fact that a string type is, in fact, a string, as shown in the following code block:

```
package main

import (
    "fmt"
    "reflect"
)

func main() {
    var foo string = "Hi Go!"
```

```
    fooType := reflect.TypeOf(foo)
    fmt.Println("Foo type: ", fooType)
}
```

The output from our program will show us that the reflection type will accurately derive the foo string type:

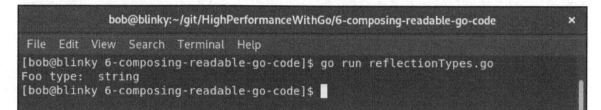

Although this example is simple, it's important to understand the underlying principle: if, instead of validating the string, we are looking at an incoming network call or the return from an external library call, or trying to build a program that can handle different types, the reflection library's TypeOf definition can help us to identify these types correctly.

Kinds

A kind is used as a placeholder to define the kind of type that a specific type represents. It is used to denote what the type is made of. This is very useful in determining what sort of structure has been defined. Let's look at an example:

```
package main
import (
    "fmt"
    "reflect"
)

func main() {
    i := []string{"foo", "bar", "baz"}
    ti := reflect.TypeOf(i)
    fmt.Println(ti.Kind())
}
```

In our example, we can see that we have created a slice of strings – `foo`, `bar`, and `baz`. From there, we can use reflection to find the type of `i`, and we can use the `Kind()` function to determine what the type is made of—in our case, a slice as follows:

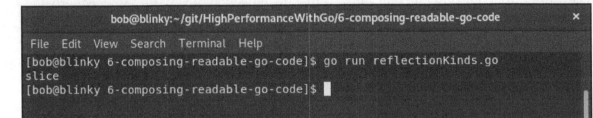

This can be useful if we want to deduce the type of a particular interface.

Values

Values in reflection help to read, set, and store results on particular variables. In the following example, we can see that we set an example variable, `foo`, and, using the reflection package, we can deduce the value of our example variable in the resulting print statement as follows:

```
package main
import (
    "fmt"
    "reflect"
)

func main() {
    example := "foo"
    exampleVal := reflect.ValueOf(example)
    fmt.Println(exampleVal)
}
```

In our output, we can see that the value of the example variable, `foo`, gets returned:

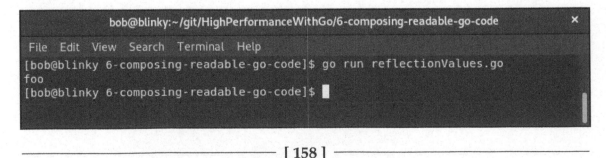

These three different functions within the reflect system help us to deduce types that we can use within our code base.

Summary

In this chapter, we learned how to use some core tenets of the language to write readable Go code. We learned how simplicity and readability are important, and how packaging, naming, and formatting are vital to writing readable Go. Also, we learned how interfaces, methods, inheritance, and reflection can all be used to write code that others can understand. Being able to use these core Go concepts effectively will help you produce more efficient code.

In the next chapter, we are going to learn about memory management in Go and how to optimize for the memory resources that we have at hand.

Template Programming in Go 7

Template programming in Go allows the end user to write Go templates that produce, manipulate, and run Go programs. Go has clear, static dependencies, which assist with metaprogramming. Template programming in Go, including generated binaries, CLI tooling, and templating libraries, are all core tenets of the language that help us write maintainable, scalable, performant Go code.

In this chapter, we'll cover the following topics:

- Go generate
- Protobuf code generation
- Linking toolchains
- Configuration metaprogramming using Cobra and Viper
- Text and HTML templating
- Sprig for Go templating

All of these topics will help you write Go code faster and more effectively. In the next section, we'll talk about Go generate and how it is useful in the Go programming language.

Understanding Go generate

As of Go version 1.4, the language contains a tool that helps with code generation, called Go generate. Go generate scans source code for general commands to run. This operates independently of `go build`, and thus must be run before code is built. Go generate is run by the code author, not by users of the compiled binary. This tool runs similarly to how Makefiles and shell scripts are typically used, but it is packaged with the Go tool and we don't need to include any other dependencies.

Go generate will search the code base for lines with the following pattern: `//go:generate command argument`.

A generated source file should have a line such as the following, in order to convey that the code was generated:

```
^// Code generated .* DO NOT EDIT\.$
```

Go generate utilizes a group of variables when the generator is run:

- `$GOARCH`: The architecture of the executing platform
- `$GOOS`: The operating system of the executing platform
- `$GOFILE`: The filename
- `$GOLINE`: The source file's line number that contains the directive
- `$GOPACKAGE`: The package name in which the file containing the directive lives
- `$DOLLAR`: A literal $

We can use this Go generate command for all sorts of different use cases in Go. They can be thought of as built-in build mechanisms for Go. The operations that are performed with Go generate can be done with other build toolings, such as Makefiles, but having Go generate available means that you don't need any other dependencies in your build environment. This means that all of your build artifacts live within Go files to maintain consistency across your projects.

Generated code for protobufs

One practical use case for generating code in Go is generating protocol buffers using gRPC. Protocol buffers are a new method that is used to serialize structured data. It's commonly used to pass data between services in distributed systems, as it tends to be much more efficient than its JSON or XML counterparts. Protocol buffers are also extensible across multiple languages on multiple platforms. They come with a structured data definition; once you have your data structured, source code is generated that can be read from, and written to, data sources.

First, we need to grab the latest version of the protocol buffers: `https://github.com/protocolbuffers/protobuf/releases`.

At the time of writing, the stable version of this software is 3.8.0. After installing this package, we need to make sure that we pull the required Go dependencies using the `go get github.com/golang/protobuf/protoc-gen-go` command. Next, we can generate a very generic protocol definition:

```
syntax = "proto3";
package userinfo;
  service UserInfo {
  rpc PrintUserInfo (UserInfoRequest) returns (UserInfoResponse) {}

}

message UserInfoRequest {
  string user = 1;
  string email = 2;
}

message UserInfoResponse {
  string response = 1;
}
```

After this, we can generate our protofile by using Go generate. Create a file in the same directory as your `.proto` file that contains the following contents:

```
package userinfo
//go:generate protoc -I ../userinfo --go_out=plugins=grpc:../userinfo
../userinfo/userinfo.proto
```

This allows us to generate a protobuf definition just by using Go generate. After we execute Go generate in this directory, we get a file, `userinfo.pb.go`, that contains all of our protobuf definitions in the Go format. We can use this information when we are generating our client and server architecture with gRPC.

Next, we can create a server to use the gRPC definitions that we added earlier:

```
package main
import (
    "context"
    "log"
    "net"
    pb "github.com/HighPerformanceWithGo/7-metaprogramming-in-
go/grpcExample/userinfo/userinfo"
    "google.golang.org/grpc"
)
type userInfoServer struct{}
func (s *userInfoServer) PrintUserInfo(ctx context.Context, in
*pb.UserInfoRequest) (*pb.UserInfoResponse, error) {
```

```
      log.Printf("%s %s", in.User, in.Email)
      return &pb.UserInfoResponse{Response: "User Info: User Name: " +
in.User + " User Email: " + in.Email}, nil
}
```

After we initialize our server struct and have a function for returning user information, we can set up our gRPC server to listen on our standard port and register our server:

```go
func main() {
  l, err := net.Listen("tcp", ":50051")
  if err != nil {
    log.Fatalf("Failed to listen %v", err)
  }
  s := grpc.NewServer()
  pb.RegisterUserInfoServer(s, &userInfoServer{})
  if err := s.Serve(l); err != nil {
    log.Fatalf("Couldn't create Server: %v", err)
  }
}
```

Once we have our server definition set up, we can focus on the client. Our client has all of our normal imports, as well as a couple of default constant declarations, as follows:

```go
package main

import (
  "context"
  "log"
  "time"

  pb "github.com/HighPerformanceWithGo/7-metaprogramming-in-
go/grpcExample/userinfo/userinfo"
  "google.golang.org/grpc"
)

const (
  defaultGrpcAddress = "localhost:50051"
  defaultUser = "Gopher"
  defaultEmail = "Gopher@example.com"
)
```

After we have our imports and constants set up, we can use these in our main function to send these values to our server. We set up a context with a default timeout of 1 second, we make a `PrintUserInfo` protobuf request, and we get a response and log it. The following is our protobuf example:

```go
func main() {
  conn, err := grpc.Dial(defaultGrpcAddress, grpc.WithInsecure())
```

```
if err != nil {
  log.Fatalf("did not connect: %v", err)
}
defer conn.Close()
c := pb.NewUserInfoClient(conn)

user := defaultUser
email := defaultEmail
ctx, cancel := context.WithTimeout(context.Background(), time.Second)
defer cancel()
r, err := c.PrintUserInfo(ctx, &pb.UserInfoRequest{User: user, Email:
email})
  if err != nil {
    log.Fatalf("could not greet: %v", err)
  }
  log.Printf("%s", r.Response)
}
```

We can see our protobuf example in action here. Protobufs are a powerful way to send messages across a distributed system. Google has often mentioned how important protobufs are to their stability at scale. We'll talk about the results from our protobuf code in the next section.

Protobuf code results

Once we have our protocol definition, our server, and our client, we can execute them together to see our work in action. First, we start the server:

Next, we execute the client code. We can see the default user name and email address that we created in our client code:

On the server-side, we can see the log for the request that we made:

```
bob@blinky:~/git/HighPerformanceWithGo/7-metaprogramming-in-go/grpcExample        ×

File   Edit   View   Search   Terminal   Help
[bob@blinky grpcExample]$ go run server/main.go
go: finding github.com/HighPerformanceWithGo/7-metaprogramming-in-go/grpcExample
/userinfo/userinfo v0.0.0
2019/07/09 18:17:03 Gopher Gopher@example.com
```

gRPC is a very efficient protocol: it uses HTTP/2 and protocol buffers in order to rapidly serialize data. Multiple calls can make use of a single connection from the client to the server, which in turn reduces latency and increases throughput.

In the next section, we will talk about the link toolchain.

The link toolchain

Go has a bunch of handy tools in its link tool that allow us to pass pertinent data to an executable function. With this tool, the programmer has the ability to set a value for a string with a particular name and value pair. Using the `cmd/link` package in Go allows you to pass in information to the Go program at hand at link time. The way to pass this information from the toolchain to the executable is to utilize the build parameter:

```
go build -ldflags '-X importpath.name=value'
```

For example, if we were trying to take in a serial number for our program from the command line, we could do something like the following:

```go
package main

import (
  "fmt"
)

var SerialNumber = "unlicensed"

func main() {
  if SerialNumber == "ABC123" {
    fmt.Println("Valid Serial Number!")
  } else {
    fmt.Println("Invalid Serial Number")
  }
}
```

As shown in the preceding output, if we attempt to execute this program while not passing in a serial number, the program will tell us that our serial number is invalid:

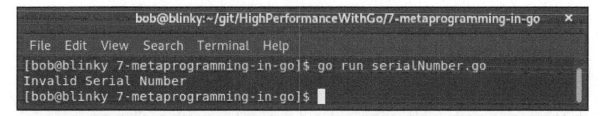

If we pass in an incorrect serial number, we will get the same result:

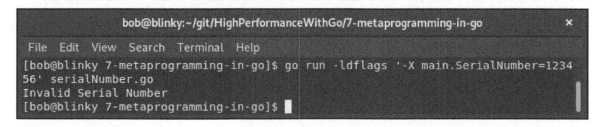

If we pass in the correct serial number, our program will tell us that we have a valid serial number:

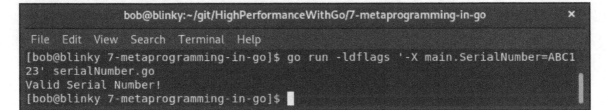

Having the ability to pass data into your program at link time can be useful when troubleshooting a large code base. It can also be useful when, though you have a compiled binary that you need to deploy, later a common value may need to be updated in a non-deterministic fashion.

In the next section, we will discuss two tools—Cobra and Viper—that are commonly used for configuration programming.

Introducing Cobra and Viper for configuration programming

Two commonly used Go libraries, `spf13/cobra` and `spf13/viper`, are used for configuration programming. Together, these two libraries can be used to create CLI binaries that have many configurable options. Cobra allows you to generate applications and command files, while Viper helps to read and maintain complete configuration solutions for 12-factor Go applications. Cobra and Viper are used in some of the most commonly used Go projects, including Kubernetes and Docker.

To use these two libraries together to make a `cmd` library, we need to make sure we nest our project directory, as follows:

```
bob@blinky:~/git/HighPerformanceWithGo/7-metaprogramming-in-go/clitooling    ×

File  Edit  View  Search  Terminal  Help
[bob@blinky clitooling]$ tree
.
├── cmd
│   ├── date.go
│   └── go.mod
├── go.mod
├── go.sum
└── main.go

1 directory, 5 files
[bob@blinky clitooling]$ █
```

Once we have created our nested directory structure, we can start setting up our main program. In our `main.go` file, we have defined our date command—the `main.go` function for Cobra and Viper us deliberately simple so that we can invoke functions written in the `cmd` directory (this is a common Go idiom). Our `main` package is as follows:

```
package main
import (
    "fmt"
    "os"
    "github.com/HighPerformanceWithGo/7-metaprogramming-in-
go/clitooling/cmd"
)
func main() {
    if err := cmd.DateCommand.Execute(); err != nil {
        fmt.Println(err)
        os.Exit(1)
    }
}
```

Once we have our `main` function defined, we can start setting up the rest of our command tooling. We start by importing our requirements:

```
package cmd
import (
    "fmt"
    "time"
    "github.com/spf13/cobra"
    "github.com/spf13/viper"
)
var verbose bool
```

Next, we can set up our root `date` command:

```
var DateCommand = &cobra.Command{
    Use: "date",
    Aliases: []string{"time"},
    Short: "Return the current date",
    Long: "Returns the current date in a YYYY-MM-DD HH:MM:SS format",
    Run: func(cmd *cobra.Command, args []string) {
        fmt.Println("Current Date :\t", time.Now().Format("2006.01.02
15:04:05"))
        if viper.GetBool("verbose") {
            fmt.Println("Author :\t", viper.GetString("author"))
            fmt.Println("Version :\t", viper.GetString("version"))
        }
    },
}
```

Once we have this set up, we can also set up a subcommand to display our licensing information, as shown in the following code sample. A subcommand is a second argument for the CLI tool in order to give `cli` more information:

```
var LicenseCommand = &cobra.Command{
    Use: "license",
    Short: "Print the License",
    Long: "Print the License of this Command",
    Run: func(cmd *cobra.Command, args []string) {
        fmt.Println("License: Apache-2.0")
    },
}
```

Lastly, we can set up our `init()` function. The `init()` function in Go is used for a couple of things:

- Initial information displayed to the user
- Initial variable declaration
- Initializing connections to outside parties (a DB connection pool or message broker initialization)

We can leverage our new `init()` function knowledge in the last bit of this code to initialize the `viper` and `cobra` commands we defined previously:

```
func init() {
    DateCommand.AddCommand(LicenseCommand)
    viper.SetDefault("Author", "bob")
    viper.SetDefault("Version", "0.0.1")
    viper.SetDefault("license", "Apache-2.0")
```

```
DateCommand.PersistentFlags().BoolP("verbose", "v", false, "Date
  Command Verbose")
DateCommand.PersistentFlags().StringP("author", "a", "bob", "Date
  Command Author")
viper.BindPFlag("author",
  DateCommand.PersistentFlags().Lookup("author"))
viper.BindPFlag("verbose",
  DateCommand.PersistentFlags().Lookup("verbose"))
}
```

The preceding code snippet shows us some default, persistent, and binding flags that are commonly used in Viper.

Cobra/Viper resulting sets

Now that we have instantiated all of our functionality, we can see our new code in action.

If we invoke our new `main.go` without any optional parameters, we will just see the date return that we defined in our initial `DateCommand` run block, as shown in the following code output:

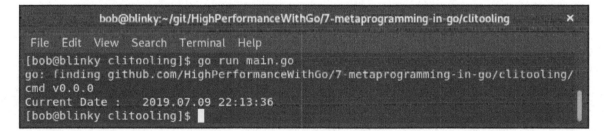

If we add additional flags to our input, we can gather verbose information and change the **Author** of the package using command-line flags, as follows:

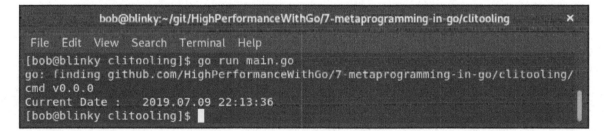

We can also view the subcommand that we created for licensing by adding it as a parameter, as follows:

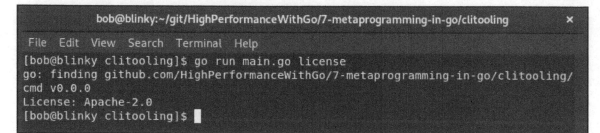

We have seen a small fraction of the functionality of the spf13 Cobra and Viper packages, but it is important to understand their root principle – they are used in order to facilitate extensible CLI tooling within Go. In the next section, we'll talk about text templating.

Text templating

Go has a built-in templating language, text/template, that implements templates with data and generates a text-based output. We use structs in order to define the data that we want to use within our templates. As with all things, Go input text is defined as UTF-8 and can be passed in as any format. We use double braces {{}} to denote actions that we want to perform on our data. A cursor, represented by ., allows us to add data to our template. These things combined create a powerful templating language that will allow us to reuse templates for many bits of code.

First, we are going to initialize our package, import our necessary dependencies, and define our struct for the data that we would like to pass into our template:

```go
package main

import (
  "fmt"
  "os"
  "text/template"
)

func main() {
  type ToField struct {
    Date string
    Name string
    Email string
```

```
    InOffice bool
}
```

Now, we can set up our template and our input structure using the text/template definitions we mentioned previously:

```
    const note = `
{{/* we can trim whitespace with a {- or a -} respectively */}}
Date: {{- .Date}}
To: {{- .Email | printf "%s"}}
{{.Name}},
{{if .InOffice }}
Thank you for your input yesterday at our meeting.  We are going to go
ahead with what you've suggested.
{{- else }}
We were able to get results in our meeting yesterday.  I've emailed them to
you.  Enjoy the rest of your time Out of Office!
{{- end}}
Thanks,
Bob
`
    var tofield = []ToField{
        {"07-19-2019", "Mx. Boss", "boss@example.com", true},
        {"07-19-2019", "Mx. Coworker", "coworker@example.com", false},
    }
```

Lastly, we can execute our template and print it. Our example prints to Stdout, but we could print to a file, write to a buffer, or send an email automatically:

```
    t := template.Must(template.New("Email Body").Parse(note))
    for _, k := range tofield {
        err := t.Execute(os.Stdout, k)
        if err != nil {
            fmt.Print(err)
        }
    }
}
```

Utilizing the Go text templating system allows us to reuse these templates to produce consistent quality content. Since we have new inputs, we can adjust our templates and derive a result accordingly. In the next section, we will discuss HTML templating.

HTML templating

We can also use HTML templating, akin to how we performed text tempting, in order to generate dynamic results for HTML pages in Go. In order to do this, we need to initialize our package, import the proper dependencies, and set up a data structure to hold the values that we are planning to use in our HTML templates, like so:

```
package main

import (
    "html/template"
    "net/http"
)

type UserFields struct {
    Name string
    URL string
    Email string
}
```

Next, we create the `userResponse` HTML template:

```
var userResponse = `
<html>
<head></head>
<body>
<h1>Hello {{.Name}}</h1>
<p>You visited {{.URL}}</p>
<p>Hope you're enjoying this book!</p>
<p>We have your email recorded as {{.Email}}</p>
</body>
</html>
`
```

Then, we create an HTTP request handler:

```
func rootHandler(w http.ResponseWriter, r *http.Request) {
    requestedURL := string(r.URL.Path)
    userfields := UserFields{"Bob", requestedURL, "bob@example.com"}
    t := template.Must(template.New("HTML Body").Parse(userResponse))
    t.Execute(w, userfields)
    log.Printf("User " + userfields.Name + " Visited : " + requestedURL)
}
```

After that, we initialize the HTTP server:

```
func main() {
 s := http.Server{
 Addr: "127.0.0.1:8080",
 }
 http.HandleFunc("/", rootHandler)
 s.ListenAndServe()
}
```

Then, we invoke our web server using `go run htmlTemplate.go`. When we request a page on this domain, we will see the following result:

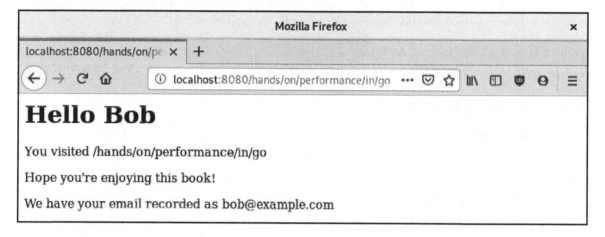

The preceding output comes from the templated code from our HTML template. This example could be extended to include parsing for an incoming IP address request via an X-Forwarded-For header, the end user's browser information based on the user agent string, or any other particular request parameter that could be used in order to give a rich response back to the client. In the next section, we'll discuss Sprig, a library for Go templating functions.

Exploring Sprig

Sprig is a library that is used to define Go templating functions. The library includes many functions that extend the functionality of Go's templating language. The Sprig library has a few principles that help determine which functions are available to drive enhanced templates:

- Only allows simple math
- Only deals with data that is passed to templates; never retrieves data from an external source
- Utilizes functions from the template library to build the resulting layout
- Never overrides the Go core template functionality

In the following subsections, we'll take a closer look at Sprig's functionality.

String functions

Sprig has a grouping of string functions that are capable of manipulating strings within a template.

In our example, we are going to take the "   -   bob smith" string (note the spaces and dashes). From there, we are going to do the following:

- Trim white space using the `trim()` utility
- Replace the instance of the word `smith` with the word `strecansky`
- Trim the – prefix
- Change the string to title case, that is, from `bob strecansky` to `Bob Strecansky`
- Repeat the string 10 times
- Create a word wrap of 14 characters (the width of my name) and separate each with a new line

The Sprig library can do this in one line, akin to how bash shells can pipe functions to one another.

We start by initializing our package and importing the necessary dependencies:

```
package main
import (
    "fmt"
    "os"
```

```
    "text/template"
    "github.com/Masterminds/sprig"
)
```

Next, we set our string map to `interface`, perform our transformations, and render our template to standard output:

```
func main() {
  inStr := map[string]interface{}{"Name": " - bob smith"}
  transform :- `{{.Name | trim | replace "smith" "strecansky" | trimPrefix
"-" | title | repeat 10 | wrapWith 14 "\n"}}`

  functionMap := sprig.TxtFuncMap()
  t := template.Must(template.New("Name
Transformation").Funcs(functionMap).Parse(transform))

  err := t.Execute(os.Stdout, inStr)
  if err != nil {
    fmt.Printf("Couldn't create template: %s", err)
    return
  }
}
```

After we execute our program, we will see string manipulations occurring the way we expected:

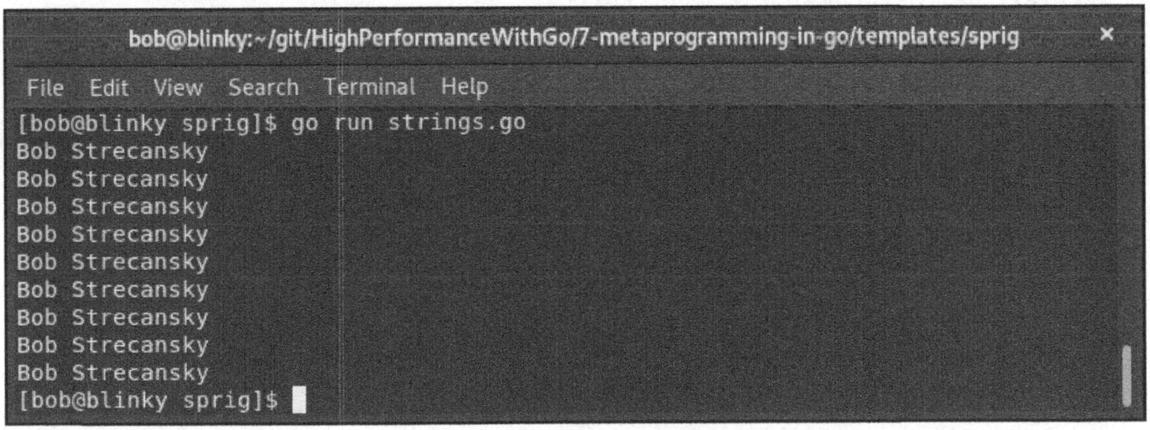

Being able to manipulate strings in templates like in our example helps us to quickly rectify any issues we may have with incoming templates and manipulate them on the fly.

String slice functions

Being able to manipulate slices of strings is helpful, as we have seen in previous chapters. The Sprig library helps us perform some string slice manipulation actions. In our example, we'll split a string based on the . character.

First, we import the necessary libraries:

```
package main
import (
    "fmt"
    "os"
    "text/template"
    "github.com/Masterminds/sprig"
)
func main() {
```

Next, we split our templated string using the . delimiter:

```
tpl := `{{$v := "Hands.On.High.Performance.In.Go" | splitn "."
5}}{{$v._3}}`
functionMap := sprig.TxtFuncMap()
t := template.Must(template.New("String
  Split").Funcs(functionMap).Parse(tpl))
fmt.Print("String Split into Dict (word 3): ")
err := t.Execute(os.Stdout, tpl)
if err != nil {
    fmt.Printf("Couldn't create template: %s", err)
    return
}
```

We also have the ability to sort a templated list into alphabetical order using the sortAlpha function, as follows:

```
alphaSort := `{{ list "Foo" "Bar" "Baz" | sortAlpha}}`
s := template.Must(template.New("sortAlpha").
  Funcs(functionMap).Parse(alphaSort))
fmt.Print("\nAlpha Tuple: ")
alphaErr := s.Execute(os.Stdout, tpl)
if alphaErr != nil {
    fmt.Printf("Couldn't create template: %s", err)
    return
}
fmt.Print("\nString Slice Functions Completed\n")
}
```

These string manipulations can help us organize lists of strings that are included in templated functions.

Default functions

Sprig's default functions return default values for templated functions. We can check the default values for particular data structures and whether or not they are *empty*. Empty is defined for each data type:

Numeric	0
String	" " (empty string)
Lists	[] (empty list)
Dicts	{} (empty dict)
Boolean	false
And always	Nil (also referred to as null)
Structs	No definition for empty; will never return the default

We start with our imports:

```
package main
import (
    "fmt"
    "os"
    "text/template"
    "github.com/Masterminds/sprig"
)
```

Next, we set up our empty and non-empty template variables:

```
func main() {
    emptyTemplate := map[string]interface{}{"Name": ""}
    fullTemplate := map[string]interface{}{"Name": "Bob"}
    tpl := `{{empty .Name}}`
    functionMap := sprig.TxtFuncMap()
    t := template.Must(template.New("Empty
      String").Funcs(functionMap).Parse(tpl))
```

Then, we validate our empty and non-empty templates:

```
    fmt.Print("empty template: ")
    emptyErr := t.Execute(os.Stdout, emptyTemplate)
    if emptyErr != nil {
        fmt.Printf("Couldn't create template: %s", emptyErr)
```

```
            return
        }
    fmt.Print("\nfull template: ")
    fullErr := t.Execute(os.Stdout, fullTemplate)
    if emptyErr != nil {
        fmt.Printf("Couldn't create template: %s", fullErr)
        return
    }
    fmt.Print("\nEmpty Check Completed\n")
}
```

This is useful when we have template inputs where we need to verify the input is not empty. Our resulting output shows us what we expect: the empty template is marked as true, while the full template is marked as false:

We can also encode JSON literals as JSON strings and pretty-print them. This is especially helpful if you are taking an HTML-created template that needs to return a JSON array to an end user:

```
package main
import (
    "fmt"
    "os"
    "text/template"
    "github.com/Masterminds/sprig"
)
func main() {
    jsonDict := map[string]interface{}{"JSONExamples":
map[string]interface{}{"foo": "bar", "bool": false, "integer": 7}}
    tpl := `{{.JSONExamples | toPrettyJson}}`
    functionMap := sprig.TxtFuncMap()
    t := template.Must(template.New("String
Split").Funcs(functionMap).Parse(tpl))
    err := t.Execute(os.Stdout, jsonDict)
    if err != nil {
        fmt.Printf("Couldn't create template: %s", err)
        return
```

```
        }
    }
```

In our resulting output, we can see a pretty-printed JSON blob based on our jsonDict input:

This is extremely useful when used with the HTML/template builtin and an added content-encoding:json HTTP header.

The Sprig library has quite a few functionalities, some of which we will discuss within this section of the book.

A full list of the functionality that's available via Sprig can be found at http:// masterminds.github.io/sprig/.

Summary

In this chapter, we discussed generating Go code. We talked about how to do so for one of the most commonly generated pieces of go code, gRPC protobufs. Then, we talked about the using link toolchain to add command-line arguments and spf13/cobra and spf13/viper to create metaprogrammed CLI tooling. Lastly, we talked about templated programming using the text/template, HTML/template, and Sprig libraries. Using all of these packages will help us make readable, reusable, performant Go code. These templates will also save us a lot of work in the long run as they tend to be reusable and scalable.

In the next chapter, we'll discuss how to optimize for memory resource management.

Memory Management in Go

8

Memory management is paramount to system performance. Being able to utilize a computer's memory footprint to the fullest allows you to keep highly functioning programs in memory so that you don't often have to take the large performance hit of swapping to disk. Being able to manage memory effectively is a core tenet of writing performant Go code. In this chapter, we will learn about the following topics:

- Computer memory
- How memory is allocated
- How Go utilizes memory effectively
- How objects are allocated in memory
- Strategies for computing devices with limited memory

Understanding how memory is utilized can help you learn to utilize memory effectively in your programs. Memory is one of the fastest places in the computer to store and manipulate data, so being able to manage it performantly will have a lasting impact on your code quality.

Understanding Modern Computer Memory - A Primer

Modern computers have **Random Access Memory (RAM)**, which is utilized in machine code and data storage. RAM is used alongside the CPU and hard disks in order to store and retrieve information. Utilizing the CPU, RAM, and disks has performance trade-offs. In a modern computer at the time of writing, we have the following generic, rounded timings for some common operations in computers:

Data Storage Type	Timing
L1 (Processor Cache) Reference	1 ns
L2 (Processor Cache) Reference	4 ns
Main Memory Reference	100 ns

SSD Random Read	16 µs
7200 RPM HDD Disk Seek	2 ms

As you'll notice from the table, the different storage types have wildly differing timings for different portions of a modern computer's architecture. New computers have KBs of L1 cache, MBs of L2 cache, GBs of main memory, and TBs of SSD/HDD. As we recognize that these different types of data storage vary significantly in terms of cost and performance, we need to learn how to use each of them effectively in order to write performant code.

Allocating memory

The main memory that a computer has is used for many things. The **Memory Management Unit** (**MMU**) is a piece of computer hardware that translates between physical and virtual memory addresses. When a CPU performs an instruction that uses a memory address, the MMU takes that logical memory address and translates it to a physical memory address. These are handled in groupings of physical memory addresses called pages. Pages are usually handled in 4 kB segments, using a table called a page table. The MMU also has other functionality, including using buffers, such as the **Translation Lookaside Buffer** (**TLB**), to hold recently accessed translations.

Virtual memory is helpful because it does the following:

- Allows hardware device memory to be mapped to an address space
- Allows access permissions (rwx) for particular memory regions
- Allows processes to have separate memory mappings
- Allows memory to be more easily moved
- Allows memory to be more easily swapped to disk
- Allows for shared memory, where physical ram is mapped to many processes simultaneously

When the virtual memory is allocated in a modern Linux OS, both the kernel and user space processes use virtual addresses. These virtual addresses are often split into two pieces—the upper portion of memory in a virtual address space is used for the kernel and kernel processes, and the lower portion of the memory is used for user space programs.

The OS utilizes this memory. It moves processes between memory and disk to optimize the use of the resources that we have available in our computer. Computer languages use **virtual memory space (VMS)** in the underlying OS that they run on. Go is no exception to that rule. If you've programmed in C, you'll know the malloc and free idioms. In Go, we don't have a `malloc` function. Go is also a garbage-collected language, so we don't have to consider freeing memory allocation.

We have two different primary measures of memory within the user space: VSZ and RSS.

Introducing VSZ and RSS

VSZ, the **virtual memory size**, references all of the memory that an individual process can access, including swapped memory. This is the memory size that is allocated during the initial execution of the program. VSZ is reported in KiB.

RSS, the **resident set size**, references how much memory a particular process has allocated in RAM, not including swapped memory. RSS includes shared library memory as long as that memory is currently available. RSS also includes stack and heap memory. RSS memory can be larger than the total memory available in the system based on the fact that these memory references are often shared. RSS is reported in kilobytes.

When we start up a simple HTTP server, we can see the VSZ and RSS that are allocated to our individual processes as follows:

```
package main
import (
    "io"
    "net/http"
)

func main() {
    Handler := func(w http.ResponseWriter, req *http.Request) {
        io.WriteString(w, "Memory Management Test")
    }
    http.HandleFunc("/", Handler)
    http.ListenAndServe(":1234", nil)
}
```

We can then take a look at the process ID that is spawned when the server is invoked, as can be seen in the following output:

```
                    bob@blinky:~/git/HighPerformanceWithGo/8-memory-management            ×

   File  Edit  View  Search  Terminal  Help
   [bob@blinky 8-memory-management]$ ps aux | grep '[s]impleServer.go'
   bob        21249  0.3  0.1 1222312 17168 pts/2    Sl+   11:36    0:00 go run simpleSe
   rver.go
   [bob@blinky 8-memory-management]$ ps -u --pid 21249
   USER        PID %CPU %MEM    VSZ    RSS TTY      STAT START    TIME COMMAND
   bob        21249  0.3  0.1 1222312 17168 pts/2    Sl+   11:36    0:00 go run simpleSe
   [bob@blinky 8-memory-management]$ ▮
```

Here, we can see the VSZ and RSS values for the `server.go` process that we've invoked.

If we want to reduce the Go binary build size, we can build our binary without libc libraries using a `build` flag as follows:

```
go build -ldflags '-libgcc=none' simpleServer.go
```

If we build our binary without including the libc libraries, we will have a much smaller memory footprint for our example server, as shown in the following output:

```
                    bob@blinky:~/git/HighPerformanceWithGo/8-memory-management            ×

   File  Edit  View  Search  Terminal  Help
   [bob@blinky 8-memory-management]$ ps aux | grep '[s]impleServer'
   bob        22938  0.0  0.0 477032  5468 pts/2    Sl+   11:41    0:00 ./simpleServer
   [bob@blinky 8-memory-management]$ ps -u --pid 22938
   USER        PID %CPU %MEM    VSZ    RSS TTY      STAT START    TIME COMMAND
   bob        22938  0.0  0.0 477032  5468 pts/2    Sl+   11:41    0:00 ./simpleServer
   [bob@blinky 8-memory-management]$ ▮
```

As we can see, both our VSZ and RSS memory utilization were reduced considerably. In practice, memory is inexpensive and we can leave the libc libraries in our Golang binaries. Libc is utilized for a lot of standard library bits, including user and group resolution as well as bits of host resolution, and this is why it's dynamically linked at build time.

After we build our Go binaries, they are stored in a container format. Linux machines store this particular binary in a format known as **ELF** (short for **Executable** and **Linkable Format**). Go's standard library has a methodology for reading ELF files. We can examine the `simpleServer` binary that we have generated previously:

```
package main
import (
    "debug/elf"
    "fmt"
    "log"
```

```
        "os"
    )
    func main() {
        if len(os.Args) != 2 {
            fmt.Println("Usage: ./elfReader elf_file")
            os.Exit(1)
        }
        elfFile, err := elf.Open(os.Args[1])
        if err != nil {
            log.Fatal(err)
        }
        for _, section := range elfFile.Sections {
            fmt.Println(section)
        }
    }
}
```

The resulting output from our `simpleServer` example is as follows:

```
bob@blinky:~/git/HighPerformanceWithGo/8-memory-management                                    ×
File Edit View Search Terminal Help
[bob@blinky 8-memory-management]$ go run elfReader.go simpleServer
&{{ SHT_NULL 0x0 0 0 0 0 0 0 0} 0xc000090420 0xc000090420 0 0}
&{{.text SHT_PROGBITS SHF_ALLOC+SHF_EXECINSTR 4198400 4096 2211473 0 0 16 0 2211473} 0xc000090450 0xc000090450 0 0}
&{{.plt SHT_PROGBITS SHF_ALLOC+SHF_EXECINSTR 6409888 2215584 528 0 0 16 16 528} 0xc000090480 0xc000090480 0 0}
&{{.rodata SHT_PROGBITS SHF_ALLOC 6414336 2220032 917295 0 0 32 0 917295} 0xc0000904b0 0xc0000904b0 0 0}
&{{.rela SHT_RELA SHF_ALLOC 7331632 3137320 24 11 0 0 24 24} 0xc0000904e0 0xc0000904e0 0 0}
&{{.rela.plt SHT_RELA SHF_ALLOC 7331656 3137352 768 11 2 8 24 768} 0xc000090510 0xc000090510 0 0}
&{{.gnu.version SHT_GNU_VERSYM SHF_ALLOC 7332448 3138144 74 11 0 2 2 74} 0xc000090540 0xc000090540 0 0}
&{{.gnu.version_r SHT_GNU_VERNEED SHF_ALLOC 7332544 3138240 80 10 2 8 0 80} 0xc000090570 0xc000090570 0 0}
&{{.hash SHT_HASH SHF_ALLOC 7332640 3138336 184 11 0 8 4 184} 0xc0000905a0 0xc0000905a0 0 0}
&{{.shstrtab SHT_STRTAB 0x0 0 3138528 511 0 0 1 0 511} 0xc0000905d0 0xc0000905d0 0 0}
&{{.dynstr SHT_STRTAB SHF_ALLOC 7333344 3138040 531 0 0 1 0 531} 0xc000090600 0xc000090600 0 0}
&{{.dynsym SHT_DYNSYM SHF_ALLOC 7333888 3139584 888 10 0 8 24 888} 0xc000090630 0xc000090630 0 0}
&{{.typelink SHT_PROGBITS SHF_ALLOC 7334784 3140480 8416 0 0 32 0 8416} 0xc000090660 0xc000090660 0 0}
&{{.itablink SHT_PROGBITS SHF_ALLOC 7343200 3148896 2136 0 0 8 0 2136} 0xc000090690 0xc000090690 0 0}
&{{.gosymtab SHT_PROGBITS SHF_ALLOC 7345336 3151032 0 0 0 1 0 0} 0xc0000906c0 0xc0000906c0 0 0}
&{{.gopclntab SHT_PROGBITS SHF_ALLOC 7345344 3151040 1488876 0 0 32 0 1488876} 0xc0000906f0 0xc0000906f0 0 0}
&{{.got.plt SHT_PROGBITS SHF_WRITE+SHF_ALLOC 8835072 4640768 280 0 0 8 8 280} 0xc000090720 0xc000090720 0 0}
&{{.dynamic SHT_DYNAMIC SHF_WRITE+SHF_ALLOC 8835360 4641056 304 10 0 8 16 304} 0xc000090750 0xc000090750 0 0}
&{{.got SHT_PROGBITS SHF_WRITE+SHF_ALLOC 8835664 4641360 8 0 0 8 8 8} 0xc000090780 0xc000090780 0 0}
&{{.noptrdata SHT_PROGBITS SHF_WRITE+SHF_ALLOC 8835680 4641376 173921 0 0 32 0 173921} 0xc0000907b0 0xc0000907b0 0 0}
&{{.data SHT_PROGBITS SHF_WRITE+SHF_ALLOC 9009632 4815328 44304 0 0 32 0 44304} 0xc0000907e0 0xc0000907e0 0 0}
&{{.bss SHT_NOBITS SHF_WRITE+SHF_ALLOC 9053952 4859648 126640 0 0 32 0 126640} 0xc000090810 0xc000090810 0 0}
&{{.noptrbss SHT_NOBITS SHF_WRITE+SHF_ALLOC 9180608 4986304 13176 0 0 32 0 13176} 0xc000090840 0xc000090840 0 0}
&{{.tbss SHT_NOBITS SHF_WRITE+SHF_ALLOC+SHF_TLS 0 0 8 0 0 8 8} 0xc000090870 0xc000090870 0 0}
&{{.zdebug_abbrev SHT_PROGBITS 0x0 9195520 4861952 274 0 0 8 0 274} 0xc0000908a0 0xc0000908a0 0 0}
&{{.zdebug_line SHT_PROGBITS 0x0 9195794 4862226 253610 0 0 8 0 253610} 0xc0000908d0 0xc0000908d0 0 0}
&{{.zdebug_frame SHT_PROGBITS 0x0 9449440 5115836 80024 0 0 8 0 80024} 0xc000090900 0xc000090900 0 0}
&{{.zdebug_pubnames SHT_PROGBITS 0x0 9529428 5195860 24975 0 0 8 0 24975} 0xc000090930 0xc000090930 0 0}
&{{.zdebug_pubtypes SHT_PROGBITS 0x0 9554403 5220835 38914 0 0 8 0 38914} 0xc000090960 0xc000090960 0 0}
&{{.debug_gdb_scripts SHT_PROGBITS 0x0 9593317 5259749 44 0 0 1 0 44} 0xc000090990 0xc000090990 0 0}
&{{.zdebug_info SHT_PROGBITS 0x0 9593361 5259793 497602 0 0 8 0 497602} 0xc0000909c0 0xc0000909c0 0 0}
&{{.zdebug_loc SHT_PROGBITS 0x0 10090963 5757395 279047 0 0 8 0 279047} 0xc0000909f0 0xc0000909f0 0 0}
&{{.zdebug_ranges SHT_PROGBITS 0x0 10370010 6036442 89953 0 0 8 0 89953} 0xc000090a20 0xc000090a20 0 0}
&{{.interp SHT_PROGBITS SHF_ALLOC 4198372 4068 28 0 0 1 0 28} 0xc000090a50 0xc000090a50 0 0}
&{{.note.go.buildid SHT_NOTE SHF_ALLOC 4198272 3968 100 0 0 4 0 100} 0xc000090a80 0xc000090a80 0 0}
&{{.symtab SHT_SYMTAB 0x0 0 6127616 199920 36 342 8 24 199920} 0xc000090ab0 0xc000090ab0 0 0}
&{{.strtab SHT_STRTAB 0x0 0 6327536 234833 0 0 1 0 234833} 0xc000090ae0 0xc000090ae0 0 0}
[bob@blinky 8-memory-management]$
```

There are also other Linux tools that we can use to investigate these ELF binaries. `readelf` will also print ELF files in a more human readable format. For example, we can take a look at an ELF file as follows:

```
bob@blinky:~/git/HighPerformanceWithGo/8-memory-management                         ×
File  Edit  View  Search  Terminal  Help
[bob@blinky 8-memory-management]$ readelf -l simpleServer

Elf file type is EXEC (Executable file)
Entry point 0x459630
There are 10 program headers, starting at offset 64

Program Headers:
  Type           Offset             VirtAddr           PhysAddr
                 FileSiz            MemSiz              Flags  Align
  PHDR           0x0000000000000040 0x0000000000400040 0x0000000000400040
                 0x0000000000000230 0x0000000000000230  R      0x1000
  INTERP         0x0000000000000fe4 0x0000000000400fe4 0x0000000000400fe4
                 0x000000000000001c 0x000000000000001c  R      0x1
      [Requesting program interpreter: /lib64/ld-linux-x86-64.so.2]
  NOTE           0x0000000000000f80 0x0000000000400f80 0x0000000000400f80
                 0x0000000000000064 0x0000000000000064  R      0x4
  LOAD           0x0000000000000000 0x0000000000400000 0x0000000000400000
                 0x00000000021d0b0 0x00000000021d0b0   R E    0x1000
  LOAD           0x00000000021e000 0x000000000061e000 0x000000000061e000
                 0x000000000024ecac 0x000000000024ecac  R      0x1000
  LOAD           0x000000000046d000 0x000000000086d000 0x000000000086d000
                 0x0000000000035700 0x0000000000057938  RW     0x1000
  DYNAMIC        0x000000000046d120 0x000000000086d120 0x000000000086d120
                 0x0000000000000130 0x0000000000000130  RW     0x8
  TLS            0x0000000000000000 0x0000000000000000 0x0000000000000000
                 0x0000000000000000 0x0000000000000008  R      0x8
  GNU_STACK      0x0000000000000000 0x0000000000000000 0x0000000000000000
                 0x0000000000000000 0x0000000000000000  RW     0x8
  LOOS+0x5041580 0x0000000000000000 0x0000000000000000 0x0000000000000000
                 0x0000000000000000 0x0000000000000000         0x8

Section to Segment mapping:
  Segment Sections...
   00
   01     .interp
   02     .note.go.buildid
   03     .text .plt .interp .note.go.buildid
   04     .rodata .rela .rela.plt .gnu.version .gnu.version_r .hash .dynstr .dynsym .typelink .itablink .gosymtab .gopclntab
   05     .got.plt .dynamic .got .noptrdata .data .bss .noptrbss
   06     .dynamic
   07     .tbss
   08
   09
[bob@blinky 8-memory-management]$
```

ELF files have a specific format. This format is as follows:

File Layout Portion	Description
File header	**Class field**: Defines 32 and 64 bit addresses as 52 or 64 bytes long, respectively. **Data**: Defines little or big endians. **Version**: Stores the ELF version (currently there is only one version, 01). **OS/ABI**: Defines the OS and the application binary interface. **Machine**: Tells you the machine type. **Type**: Indicates what type of file this is; common types are CORE, DYN (for shared objects), EXEC (for executable files), and REL (for relocatable files).

Program headers or segments	Contain instructions on how to create a process or memory image for execution at runtime. The kernel then uses these to map to a virtual address space using mmap.
Section headers or sections	`.text`: Executable code (instructions, static constants, literals) `.data`: Access controlled, initialized data `.rodata`: Read-only data `.bss`: Read/write uninitialized data

We can also compile a 32 bit version of this program to see the difference. As mentioned in Chapter 1, *Introduction to Performance in Go*, we can build Go binaries for different architectures. We can build a binary for an i386 Linux system using the following build parameters:

```
env GOOS=linux GOARCH=386 go build -o 386simpleServer simpleServer.go
```

Once this build has been completed, we can inspect the resulting ELF file and corroborate the fact that the resulting ELF is different from the one we processed before for my x86_64 computer. We'll use the –h flag just to view the headers for each file for brevity:

```
bob@blinky:~/git/HighPerformanceWithGo/8-memory-management

File  Edit  View  Search  Terminal  Help
[bob@blinky 8-memory-management]$ readelf -h 386simpleServer
ELF Header:
  Magic:   7f 45 4c 46 01 01 01 00 00 00 00 00 00 00 00 00
  Class:                             ELF32
  Data:                              2's complement, little endian
  Version:                           1 (current)
  OS/ABI:                            UNIX - System V
  ABI Version:                       0
  Type:                              EXEC (Executable file)
  Machine:                           Intel 80386
  Version:                           0x1
  Entry point address:               0x8095d90
  Start of program headers:          52 (bytes into file)
  Start of section headers:          276 (bytes into file)
  Flags:                             0x0
  Size of this header:               52 (bytes)
  Size of program headers:           32 (bytes)
  Number of program headers:         7
  Size of section headers:           40 (bytes)
  Number of section headers:         24
  Section header string table index: 3
[bob@blinky 8-memory-management]$
```

As you can see in the resulting output, this particular binary was generated for an i386 processor, as opposed to the x86_64 binary that was generated initially:

```
                bob@blinky:~/git/HighPerformanceWithGo/8-memory-management        ×

 File   Edit   View   Search   Terminal   Help
[bob@blinky 8-memory-management]$ readelf -h simpleServer
ELF Header:
  Magic:    7f 45 4c 46 02 01 01 00 00 00 00 00 00 00 00 00
  Class:                             ELF64
  Data:                              2's complement, little endian
  Version:                           1 (current)
  OS/ABI:                            UNIX - System V
  ABI Version:                       0
  Type:                              EXEC (Executable file)
  Machine:                           Advanced Micro Devices X86-64
  Version:                           0x1
  Entry point address:               0x459630
  Start of program headers:          64 (bytes into file)
  Start of section headers:          624 (bytes into file)
  Flags:                             0x0
  Size of this header:               64 (bytes)
  Size of program headers:           56 (bytes)
  Number of program headers:         10
  Size of section headers:           64 (bytes)
  Number of section headers:         37
  Section header string table index: 9
[bob@blinky 8-memory-management]$ █
```

Knowing the limitations of your system, your architecture, and your memory limits can help you to build Go programs that will run effectively on your hosts. In this section, we will deal with memory utilization.

Understanding memory utilization

Once we have our initial binary, we start building on the knowledge that we have of the ELF format to continue our understanding of memory utilization. The text, data, and bss fields are a foundation on which the heap and stack are laid. The heap begins at the end of the .bss and .data bits and grows continuously to form larger memory addresses.

The stack is an allocation of contiguous blocks of memory. This allocation happens automatically within the function call stack. When a function is called, its variables get memory allocated on the stack. After the function call is completed, the variable's memory is deallocated. The stack has a fixed size and can only be determined at compile time. Stack allocation is inexpensive from an allocation perspective because it only needs to push to the stack and pull from the stack for allocation.

The heap is a grouping of memory that is available to allocate and deallocate. Memory is allocated in random order, manually performed by the programmer. It is more expensive timewise and is slower to access because of its non-continuous blocks. It is, however, possible to resize elements in the heap. Heap allocation is expensive, as malloc searches for enough memory to hold the new data. As the garbage collector works later, it scans for objects in the heap that aren't referenced anymore, and deallocates them. These two processes are much more expensive than stack allocation/deallocation bits. Because of this, Go prefers allocation on the stack rather than the heap.

We can compile programs with a gcflag of –m in order to see how the Go compiler uses escape analysis (the process in which the compiler determines whether to use the stack or the heap for variables initialized at runtime).

We can create a very simple program as follows:

```
package main
import "fmt"
func main() {
    greetingString := "Hello Gophers!"
    fmt.Println(greetingString)
}
```

We can then compile our program with the escape analysis flag as follows:

```
bob@blinky:~/git/HighPerformanceWithGo/8-memory-management/escapeAnalysis                    ×

File  Edit  View  Search  Terminal  Help
[bob@blinky escapeAnalysis]$ go build -gcflags '-m' simpleEscapeAnalysis.go
# command-line-arguments
./simpleEscapeAnalysis.go:7:13: greetingString escapes to heap
./simpleEscapeAnalysis.go:7:13: main ... argument does not escape
[bob@blinky escapeAnalysis]$ 
```

In our resulting output, we can see that our simple `greetingString` is allocated to the heap. If we want additional verbosity with this flag, we can pass multiple m values. At the time of writing, passing up to 5 -m flags gives us different levels of verbosity. The following screenshot is of a build with 3 -m flags (for the sake of brevity):

```
bob@blinky:~/git/HighPerformanceWithGo/8-memory-management/escapeAnalysis                    ×

File  Edit  View  Search  Terminal  Help
[bob@blinky escapeAnalysis]$ go build -gcflags '-m -m -m' simpleEscapeAnalysis.g
o
# command-line-arguments
./simpleEscapeAnalysis.go:5:6: cannot inline main: function too complex: cost 89
 exceeds budget 80
./simpleEscapeAnalysis.go:6:2:[1] main esc: greetingString
./simpleEscapeAnalysis.go:6:2:[1] main esc: var greetingString string
./simpleEscapeAnalysis.go:6:17:[1] main esc: greetingString
./simpleEscapeAnalysis.go:6:20:[1] main esc: "Hello Gophers!"
./simpleEscapeAnalysis.go:6:17:[1] main esc: greetingString := "Hello Gophers!"
./simpleEscapeAnalysis.go:6:17:[1] main escassign: greetingString( a(true) g(1)
l(6) x(0) class(PAUTO) ld(1) tc(1) used)[NAME] = "Hello Gophers!"( l(6) tc(1))[L
ITERAL]
./simpleEscapeAnalysis.go:7:13:[1] main esc: fmt.Println
./simpleEscapeAnalysis.go:7:13:[1] main esc: greetingString
./simpleEscapeAnalysis.go:7:13:[1] main esc: greetingString
./simpleEscapeAnalysis.go:7:13:[1] main escassign: greetingString( l(7) esc(no)
ld(1) tc(1) implicit(true))[CONVIFACE] = greetingString( a(true) g(1) l(6) x(0)
class(PAUTO) ld(1) tc(1) used)[NAME]
./simpleEscapeAnalysis.go:7:13:[1] main esc: fmt.Println(greetingString)
./simpleEscapeAnalysis.go:7:13:[1] main escassign: ... argument( l(7) esc(no) ld
(1))[DDDARG] = greetingString( l(7) esc(no) ld(1) tc(1) implicit(true))[CONVIFAC
E]
./simpleEscapeAnalysis.go:7:13:[1] main escassign: .sink( x(0) class(PEXTERN) ld
(-1))[NAME] = *(... argument)( l(7) ld(1))[*]

escflood:0: dst .sink scope:<S>[-1]
escwalk: level:{0 0} depth:0  op=* *(... argument)( l(7) ld(1)) scope:main[1] ex
traloopdepth=-1
escwalk: level:{1 1} depth:1      op=DDDARG ... argument( l(7) esc(no) ld(1)) sco
pe:main[1] extraloopdepth=-1
escwalk: level:{0 0} depth:2          op=CONVIFACE greetingString( l(7) esc(n
o) ld(1) tc(1) implicit(true)) scope:main[1] extraloopdepth=-1
./simpleEscapeAnalysis.go:7:13: greetingString escapes to heap
./simpleEscapeAnalysis.go:7:13:        from ... argument (arg to ...) at ./simp
leEscapeAnalysis.go:7:13
./simpleEscapeAnalysis.go:7:13:        from *(... argument) (indirection) at ./
simpleEscapeAnalysis.go:7:13
./simpleEscapeAnalysis.go:7:13:        from ... argument (passed to call[argume
nt content escapes]) at ./simpleEscapeAnalysis.go:7:13
escwalk: level:{0 0} depth:3              op=NAME greetingString( a(true)
 g(1) l(6) x(0) class(PAUTO) ld(1) tc(1) used) scope:main[1] extraloopdepth=1
./simpleEscapeAnalysis.go:7:13: Reflooding main greetingString
./simpleEscapeAnalysis.go:7:13: main ... argument does not escape
[bob@blinky escapeAnalysis]$
```

Go variables that are statically assigned tend to live on the stack. Items that are pointers to memory or methods on interface types tend to be dynamic and therefore live on the heap generally.

If we want to see more available optimizations while performing our builds, we can see them using the following command: `go tool compile -help`.

Go runtime memory allocation

As we learned in `Chapter 3`, *Understanding Concurrency*, the Go runtime uses the `G` struct to represent stack parameters for a single goroutine. The `P` struct manages logical processors for execution. The malloc that is used as part of the Go runtime, defined at `https://golang.org/src/runtime/malloc.go`, does a lot of work. Go uses mmap to ask the underlying OS directly for memory. Small allocation sizes (memory allocations up to and including 32 kB) are handled separately from large memory allocations.

Memory allocation primer

Let's quickly discuss a couple of objects that are associated with Go's small object memory allocation.

 We can see the `mheap` and `mspan` structs in `https://golang.org/src/runtime/mheap.go`.

`mheap` is the main malloc heap. It keeps track of global data, as well as many other heap details. Some important ones are as follows:

Name	Description
lock	A mutex locking mechanism
free	An mTreap (a data structure that is a blend of a tree and a heap) of non-scavenged spans
scav	An mTreap of free and scavenged spans
sweepgen	An integer that keeps track of a span's swept status
sweepdone	Tracking whether all spans are swept
sweepers	The number of `sweepone` calls active

`mspan` is the main span malloc. It keeps track of all available spans. Spans are 8K or larger contiguous regions of memory. It also keeps many other span details. Some important ones to note are as follows:

Name	Description
next	The next span in the list; (nil) if one isn't present
previous	Previous span in the list; (nil) if there isn't one
list	A span list for debugging
startAddr	First byte of a span
npages	The number of pages in the span

Memory object allocation

There are three classifications of memory objects:

- Tiny: An object that is less than 16 bytes in size
- Small: An object that is greater than 16 bytes and less than or equal to 32 kB
- Large: An object that is larger than 32 kB in size

A tiny object in memory in Go performs the following process for memory allocation:

1. If `P`'s mcache has room, use that space.
2. Take the existing sub object in the mcache and round it to 8, 4, or 2 bytes.
3. Place the object in memory if it fits in the allocated space.

A small object in memory in Go follows a specific pattern for memory allocation:

1. The object's size gets rounded up and classified into one of the small size classes that are generated in `https://golang.org/src/runtime/mksizeclasses.go`. In the following output, we can see the `_NumSizeClasses` and the `class_to_size` variable allocations defined on my x86_64 machine. This value is then used to find a free bitmap within the mspan in P's mcache and will allocate accordingly if there's a free slot of memory available. The following screenshot illustrates this:

```
bob@blinky:~/git/go                                          ×
File  Edit  View  Search  Terminal  Help
[bob@blinky go]$ go run src/runtime/mksizeclasses.go --stdout=true | grep -iE '_
numSizeClasses |class_to_size'
        _NumSizeClasses = 67
var class_to_size = [_NumSizeClasses]uint16{0, 8, 16, 32, 48, 64, 80, 96, 112, 1
28, 144, 160, 176, 192, 208, 224, 240, 256, 288, 320, 352, 384, 416, 448, 480, 5
12, 576, 640, 704, 768, 896, 1024, 1152, 1280, 1408, 1536, 1792, 2048, 2304, 268
8, 3072, 3200, 3456, 4096, 4864, 5376, 6144, 6528, 6784, 6912, 8192, 9472, 9728,
 10240, 10880, 12288, 13568, 14336, 16384, 18432, 19072, 20480, 21760, 24576, 27
264, 28672, 32768}
[bob@blinky go]$ ▮
```

2. If there are no free spots in P's mspan, a new mspan is obtained from mcentral's mspan list that has enough space for the new memory object.
3. If that list is empty, a run of pages from the mheap is performed in order to find room for the mspan.
4. If that fails, is empty, or doesn't have a large enough page to allocate, a new group of pages is allocated from the OS. This is expensive, but is done in at least 1 MB chunks, which helps with the cost of having to talk to the OS.

Freeing objects from an mspan follow a similar process:

1. An mspan is returned to the mcache if it is being swept in response to an allocation.
2. If the mspan still has objects that are allocated to it, the mcentral free list receives this mspan for deallocation.
3. If the mspan is idle (it has no allocated objects), it gets returned to the mheap.
4. Once the mspan is idle for a given interval, these pages are returned to the underlying OS.

Large objects don't use the mcache or the mcentral; they just use the mheap directly.

We can use our previously created HTTP server in order to take a look at some memory stats. Using the runtime package, we can derive the amount of memory the program has retrieved from the OS, as well as the heap allocation for the Go program. Let's see how this happens step by step:

1. First, we initialize our package, perform our imports, and set up our first handler:

```
package main
import (
    "fmt"
    "io"
    "net/http"
    "runtime"
)

func main() {
    Handler := func(w http.ResponseWriter, req *http.Request) {
        io.WriteString(w, "Memory Management Test")
    }
```

2. We then write an anonymous function to capture our run statistics:

```
go func() {
    for {
        var r runtime.MemStats
        runtime.ReadMemStats(&r)
        fmt.Println("\nTime: ", time.Now())
        fmt.Println("Runtime MemStats Sys: ", r.Sys)
        fmt.Println("Runtime Heap Allocation: ", r.HeapAlloc)
        fmt.Println("Runtime Heap Idle: ", r.HeapIdle)
        fmt.Println("Runtime Head In Use: ", r.HeapInuse)
        fmt.Println("Runtime Heap HeapObjects: ", r.HeapObjects)
        fmt.Println("Runtime Heap Released: ", r.HeapReleased)
        time.Sleep(5 * time.Second)
    }
}()
http.HandleFunc("/", Handler)
http.ListenAndServe(":1234", nil)
}
```

3. After we execute this program, we can see the memory allocation for our service. The first printout in the following results shows the initial allocations of memory:

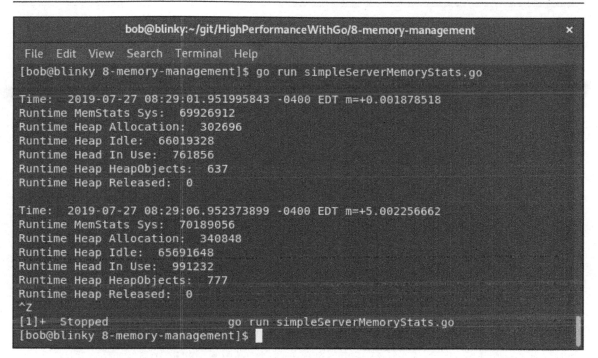

The second printout is after a request for `http://localhost:1234/` has been made. You can see that the system and heap allocations stay roughly the same, and that both the idle heap and the heap in use shift for utilization with the web request.

 Go's memory allocator was originally derived from TCMalloc, a thread caching malloc. More information about TCMalloc can be found at `http://goog-perftools.sourceforge.net/doc/tcmalloc.html`.

Go allocator, the Go memory allocator, uses thread-local cache and spans that are 8 K or larger contiguous regions of memory. These 8 K regions, also known as spans, are commonly used in one of three capacities:

- Idle: A span that can be reused for the heap/stack or returned to the OS
- In use: A span that is currently being used in the Go runtime
- Stack: A span that is used for the goroutine stack

If we create a program that doesn't have shared libraries, we should see a much smaller memory footprint for our program:

1. First, we initialize our package and import the required libraries:

```
package main
import (
    "fmt"
    "runtime"
    "time"
)
```

2. We then perform the same actions that we did for our previous simple http server, but we just use the `fmt` package to print a string. We then sleep so that we have the ability to see the memory utilization output:

```
func main() {
    go func() {
        for {
            var r runtime.MemStats
            runtime.ReadMemStats(&r)
            fmt.Println("\nTime: ", time.Now())
            fmt.Println("Runtime MemStats Sys: ", r.Sys)
            fmt.Println("Runtime Heap Allocation: ", r.HeapAlloc)
            fmt.Println("Runtime Heap Idle: ", r.HeapIdle)
            fmt.Println("Runtime Heap In Use: ", r.HeapInuse)
            fmt.Println("Runtime Heap HeapObjects: ", r.HeapObjects)
            fmt.Println("Runtime Heap Released: ", r.HeapReleased)
            time.Sleep(5 * time.Second)
        }
    }()
    fmt.Println("Hello Gophers")
    time.Sleep(11 * time.Second)
}
```

3. From the output from the execution of this program, we can see that the heap allocation for this executable is much smaller than our simple HTTP server:

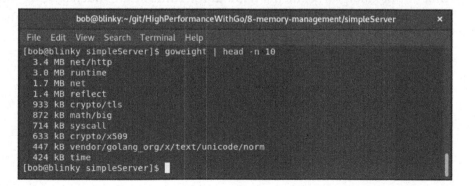

```
bob@blinky:~/git/HighPerformanceWithGo/8-memory-management/simpleProgramMemoryStats    ×

File  Edit  View  Search  Terminal  Help
[bob@blinky simpleProgramMemoryStats]$ go run simpleProgramMemoryStats.go
Hello Gophers

Time:  2020-02-09 20:43:23.219627431 -0500 EST m=+0.000179839
Runtime MemStats Sys:  69928960
Runtime Heap Allocation:  123576
Runtime Heap Idle:  66428928
Runtime Heap In Use:  385024
Runtime Heap HeapObjects:  193
Runtime Heap Released:  66428928

Time:  2020-02-09 20:43:28.219951858 -0500 EST m=+5.000504316
Runtime MemStats Sys:  70191104
Runtime Heap Allocation:  140752
Runtime Heap Idle:  66379776
Runtime Heap In Use:  401408
Runtime Heap HeapObjects:  223
Runtime Heap Released:  66379776

Time:  2020-02-09 20:43:33.220100237 -0500 EST m=+10.000742730
Runtime MemStats Sys:  70191104
Runtime Heap Allocation:  141072
Runtime Heap Idle:  66379776
Runtime Heap In Use:  401408
Runtime Heap HeapObjects:  234
Runtime Heap Released:  66379776
[bob@blinky simpleProgramMemoryStats]$
```

But why is this the case? We can use the goweight library [https://github.com/jondot/goweight] to see the size of the dependencies within our program. We just need to download this binary: `go get github.com/jondot/goweight`.

4. We can then determine what the large dependencies are in our Go program:

```
bob@blinky:~/git/HighPerformanceWithGo/8-memory-management/simpleServer    ×

File  Edit  View  Search  Terminal  Help
[bob@blinky simpleServer]$ goweight | head -n 10
  3.4 MB net/http
  3.0 MB runtime
  1.7 MB net
  1.4 MB reflect
  933 kB crypto/tls
  872 kB math/big
  714 kB syscall
  633 kB crypto/x509
  447 kB vendor/golang_org/x/text/unicode/norm
  424 kB time
[bob@blinky simpleServer]$
```

We can see that the `net/http` library takes up a lot of space, as do the runtime and the net library.

In contrast, let's look at our simple program with memory stats:

```
bob@blinky:~/git/HighPerformanceWithGo/8-memory-management/simpleProgramMemoryStats    ×

File   Edit   View   Search   Terminal   Help
[bob@blinky simpleProgramMemoryStats]$ goweight simpleProgramMemoryStats.go
 3.0 MB runtime
 1.4 MB reflect
 714 kB syscall
 424 kB time
 390 kB fmt
 319 kB os
 247 kB strconv
 225 kB unicode
 204 kB math
 180 kB internal/poll
 132 kB io
 120 kB sync
  32 kB internal/cpu
  26 kB unicode/utf8
  24 kB math/bits
  18 kB sync/atomic
  15 kB internal/bytealg
  13 kB internal/testlog
  11 kB runtime/internal/sys
  10 kB runtime/internal/atomic
 6.4 kB internal/syscall/unix
 4.1 kB errors
 3.6 kB internal/race
[bob@blinky simpleProgramMemoryStats]$
```

We can see that our next largest segments without the runtime are much smaller than the
`net/http` and `net` libraries. It's always important to know exactly where our resources are
being utilized in order to make more efficient binaries.

If we take a look at the OS level calls with strace, we can next see the difference between the interaction with our simple web server and our simple program. An example of our simple web server is as follows:

```
bob@blinky:~/git/HighPerformanceWithGo/8-memory-management/simpleServerMemoryStats    ×

 File  Edit  View  Search  Terminal  Help
[bob@blinky simpleServerMemoryStats]$ go build simpleServerMemoryStats.go
[bob@blinky simpleServerMemoryStats]$ strace ./simpleServerMemoryStats
execve("./simpleServerMemoryStats", ["./simpleServerMemoryStats"], 0x7fffabc6347
0 /* 69 vars */) = 0
brk(NULL)                               = 0x1c84000
arch_prctl(0x3001 /* ARCH_??? */, 0x7ffc239d98b0) = -1 EINVAL (Invalid argument)
access("/etc/ld.so.preload", R_OK)      = -1 ENOENT (No such file or directory)
openat(AT_FDCWD, "/etc/ld.so.cache", O_RDONLY|O_CLOEXEC) = 3
fstat(3, {st_mode=S_IFREG|0644, st_size=143179, ...}) = 0
mmap(NULL, 143179, PROT_READ, MAP_PRIVATE, 3, 0) = 0x7f5e18308000
close(3)                                = 0
openat(AT_FDCWD, "/lib64/libpthread.so.0", O_RDONLY|O_CLOEXEC) = 3
read(3, "\177ELF\2\1\1\3\0\0\0\0\0\0\0\0\3\0>\0\1\0\0\0\340q\0\0\0\0\0\0"..., 83
2) = 832
fstat(3, {st_mode=S_IFREG|0755, st_size=258624, ...}) = 0
mmap(NULL, 8192, PROT_READ|PROT_WRITE, MAP_PRIVATE|MAP_ANONYMOUS, -1, 0) = 0x7f5
e18306000
lseek(3, 808, SEEK_SET)                 = 808
read(3, "\4\0\0\0\20\0\0\0\5\0\0\0GNU\0\2\0\0\300\4\0\0\0\3\0\0\0\0\0\0\0", 32)
= 32
mmap(NULL, 136384, PROT_READ, MAP_PRIVATE|MAP_DENYWRITE, 3, 0) = 0x7f5e182e4000
mmap(0x7f5e182ea000, 65536, PROT_READ|PROT_EXEC, MAP_PRIVATE|MAP_FIXED|MAP_DENYW
RITE, 3, 0x6000) = 0x7f5e182ea000
mmap(0x7f5e182fa000, 24576, PROT_READ, MAP_PRIVATE|MAP_FIXED|MAP_DENYWRITE, 3, 0
x16000) = 0x7f5e182fa000
mmap(0x7f5e18300000, 8192, PROT_READ|PROT_WRITE, MAP_PRIVATE|MAP_FIXED|MAP_DENYW
RITE, 3, 0x1b000) = 0x7f5e18300000
mmap(0x7f5e18302000, 13504, PROT_READ|PROT_WRITE, MAP_PRIVATE|MAP_FIXED|MAP_ANON
YMOUS, -1, 0) = 0x7f5e18302000
close(3)                                = 0
openat(AT_FDCWD, "/lib64/libc.so.6", O_RDONLY|O_CLOEXEC) = 3
read(3, "\177ELF\2\1\1\3\0\0\0\0\0\0\0\0\3\0>\0\1\0\0\0 E\2\0\0\0\0\0"..., 832)
= 832
lseek(3, 792, SEEK_SET)                 = 792
read(3, "\4\0\0\0\24\0\0\0\3\0\0\0GNU\0\273\200t>\36\363\345\222B\324P\35\374\25
7\331h"..., 68) = 68
fstat(3, {st_mode=S_IFREG|0755, st_size=2786576, ...}) = 0
lseek(3, 792, SEEK_SET)                 = 792
read(3, "\4\0\0\0\24\0\0\0\3\0\0\0GNU\0\273\200t>\36\363\345\222B\324P\35\374\25
7\331h"..., 68) = 68
lseek(3, 864, SEEK_SET)                 = 864
read(3, "\4\0\0\0\20\0\0\0\5\0\0\0GNU\0\2\0\0\300\4\0\0\0\3\0\0\0\0\0\0\0", 32)
= 32
mmap(NULL, 1857568, PROT_READ, MAP_PRIVATE|MAP_DENYWRITE, 3, 0) = 0x7f5e1811e000
mprotect(0x7f5e18140000, 1679360, PROT_NONE) = 0
mmap(0x7f5e18140000, 1363968, PROT_READ|PROT_EXEC, MAP_PRIVATE|MAP_FIXED|MAP_DEN
YWRITE, 3, 0x22000) = 0x7f5e18140000
mmap(0x7f5e1828d000, 311296, PROT_READ, MAP_PRIVATE|MAP_FIXED|MAP_DENYWRITE, 3,
```

An example of our simple program can be seen here:

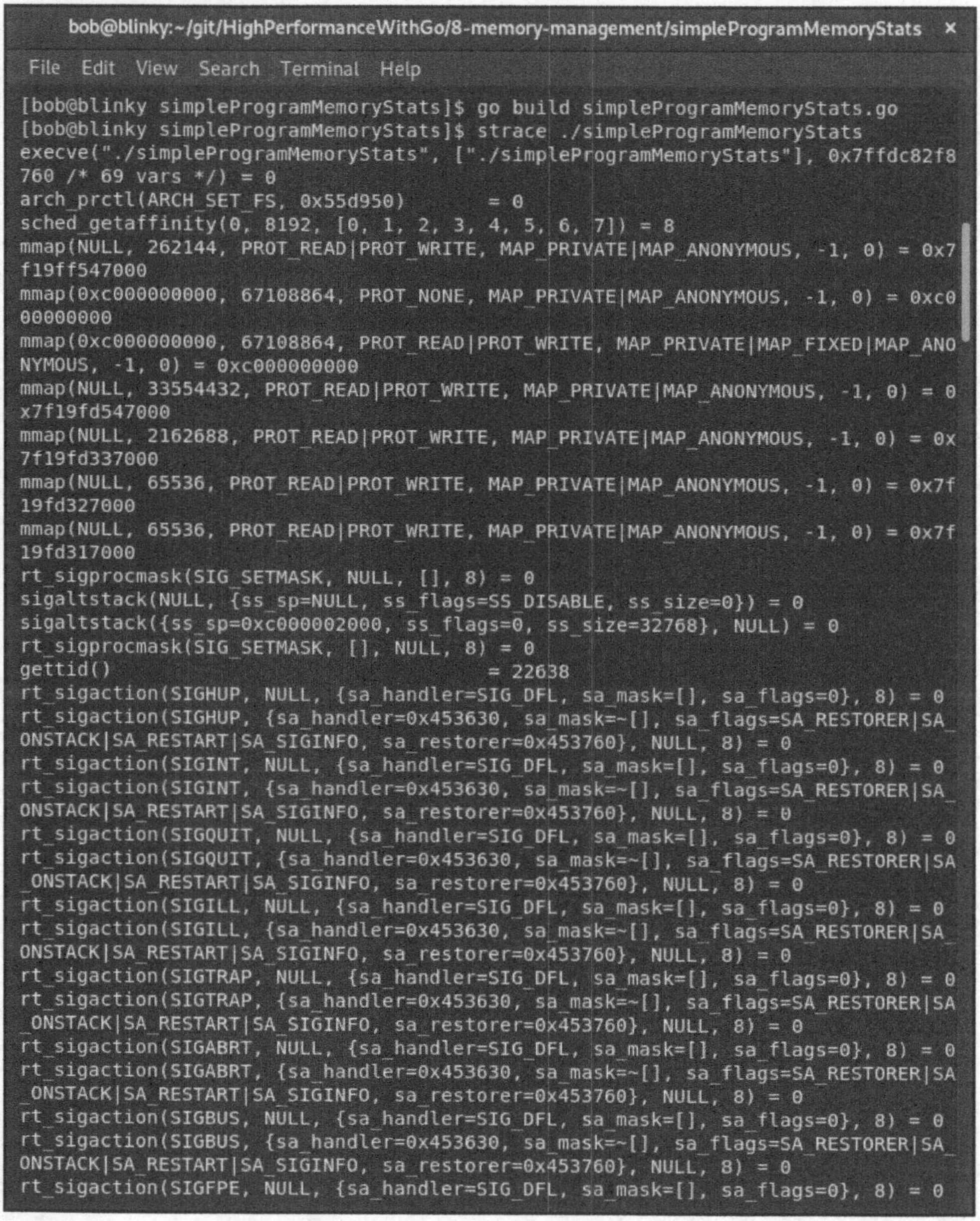

```
bob@blinky:~/git/HighPerformanceWithGo/8-memory-management/simpleProgramMemoryStats   ×

File   Edit   View   Search   Terminal   Help

[bob@blinky simpleProgramMemoryStats]$ go build simpleProgramMemoryStats.go
[bob@blinky simpleProgramMemoryStats]$ strace ./simpleProgramMemoryStats
execve("./simpleProgramMemoryStats", ["./simpleProgramMemoryStats"], 0x7ffdc82f8
760 /* 69 vars */) = 0
arch_prctl(ARCH_SET_FS, 0x55d950)        = 0
sched_getaffinity(0, 8192, [0, 1, 2, 3, 4, 5, 6, 7]) = 8
mmap(NULL, 262144, PROT_READ|PROT_WRITE, MAP_PRIVATE|MAP_ANONYMOUS, -1, 0) = 0x7
f19ff547000
mmap(0xc000000000, 67108864, PROT_NONE, MAP_PRIVATE|MAP_ANONYMOUS, -1, 0) = 0xc0
00000000
mmap(0xc000000000, 67108864, PROT_READ|PROT_WRITE, MAP_PRIVATE|MAP_FIXED|MAP_ANO
NYMOUS, -1, 0) = 0xc000000000
mmap(NULL, 33554432, PROT_READ|PROT_WRITE, MAP_PRIVATE|MAP_ANONYMOUS, -1, 0) = 0
x7f19fd547000
mmap(NULL, 2162688, PROT_READ|PROT_WRITE, MAP_PRIVATE|MAP_ANONYMOUS, -1, 0) = 0x
7f19fd337000
mmap(NULL, 65536, PROT_READ|PROT_WRITE, MAP_PRIVATE|MAP_ANONYMOUS, -1, 0) = 0x7f
19fd327000
mmap(NULL, 65536, PROT_READ|PROT_WRITE, MAP_PRIVATE|MAP_ANONYMOUS, -1, 0) = 0x7f
19fd317000
rt_sigprocmask(SIG_SETMASK, NULL, [], 8) = 0
sigaltstack(NULL, {ss_sp=NULL, ss_flags=SS_DISABLE, ss_size=0}) = 0
sigaltstack({ss_sp=0xc000002000, ss_flags=0, ss_size=32768}, NULL) = 0
rt_sigprocmask(SIG_SETMASK, [], NULL, 8) = 0
gettid()                                 = 22638
rt_sigaction(SIGHUP, NULL, {sa_handler=SIG_DFL, sa_mask=[], sa_flags=0}, 8) = 0
rt_sigaction(SIGHUP, {sa_handler=0x453630, sa_mask=~[], sa_flags=SA_RESTORER|SA_
ONSTACK|SA_RESTART|SA_SIGINFO, sa_restorer=0x453760}, NULL, 8) = 0
rt_sigaction(SIGINT, NULL, {sa_handler=SIG_DFL, sa_mask=[], sa_flags=0}, 8) = 0
rt_sigaction(SIGINT, {sa_handler=0x453630, sa_mask=~[], sa_flags=SA_RESTORER|SA_
ONSTACK|SA_RESTART|SA_SIGINFO, sa_restorer=0x453760}, NULL, 8) = 0
rt_sigaction(SIGQUIT, NULL, {sa_handler=SIG_DFL, sa_mask=[], sa_flags=0}, 8) = 0
rt_sigaction(SIGQUIT, {sa_handler=0x453630, sa_mask=~[], sa_flags=SA_RESTORER|SA
_ONSTACK|SA_RESTART|SA_SIGINFO, sa_restorer=0x453760}, NULL, 8) = 0
rt_sigaction(SIGILL, NULL, {sa_handler=SIG_DFL, sa_mask=[], sa_flags=0}, 8) = 0
rt_sigaction(SIGILL, {sa_handler=0x453630, sa_mask=~[], sa_flags=SA_RESTORER|SA_
ONSTACK|SA_RESTART|SA_SIGINFO, sa_restorer=0x453760}, NULL, 8) = 0
rt_sigaction(SIGTRAP, NULL, {sa_handler=SIG_DFL, sa_mask=[], sa_flags=0}, 8) = 0
rt_sigaction(SIGTRAP, {sa_handler=0x453630, sa_mask=~[], sa_flags=SA_RESTORER|SA
_ONSTACK|SA_RESTART|SA_SIGINFO, sa_restorer=0x453760}, NULL, 8) = 0
rt_sigaction(SIGABRT, NULL, {sa_handler=SIG_DFL, sa_mask=[], sa_flags=0}, 8) = 0
rt_sigaction(SIGABRT, {sa_handler=0x453630, sa_mask=~[], sa_flags=SA_RESTORER|SA
_ONSTACK|SA_RESTART|SA_SIGINFO, sa_restorer=0x453760}, NULL, 8) = 0
rt_sigaction(SIGBUS, NULL, {sa_handler=SIG_DFL, sa_mask=[], sa_flags=0}, 8) = 0
rt_sigaction(SIGBUS, {sa_handler=0x453630, sa_mask=~[], sa_flags=SA_RESTORER|SA_
ONSTACK|SA_RESTART|SA_SIGINFO, sa_restorer=0x453760}, NULL, 8) = 0
rt_sigaction(SIGFPE, NULL, {sa_handler=SIG_DFL, sa_mask=[], sa_flags=0}, 8) = 0
```

From the output, we can notice a couple of things:

- The output from our `simpleWebServer` is much longer than our `simpleProgram` (this has been truncated in the screenshots, but if it is generated we can see that the response length is longer).
- The `simpleWebServer` loads a lot more C libraries (we can see `ld.so.preload`, `libpthread.so.0`, and `libc.so.6` in our strace capture in the screenshot).
- There are quite a lot more memory allocations in our `simpleWebServer` than our `simpleProgram` output.

We can take a look at where these are pulled in. The `net/http` library doesn't have any C references, but its parent library net does. In all of the cgo packages in the net library, we have documentation that tells us how we can skip using underlying CGO resolvers for packages: https://golang.org/pkg/net/#pkg-overview.

This documentation shows us how we can use the Go and cgo resolvers:

```
export GODEBUG=netdns=go    # force pure Go resolver
export GODEBUG=netdns=cgo   # force cgo resolver
```

Let's use this to enable just the Go resolver in our example web server by executing the following command:

```
export CGO_ENABLED=0
go build -tags netgo
```

In the following screenshot, we can see the process that is executing for our `simpleServer` without the C resolver:

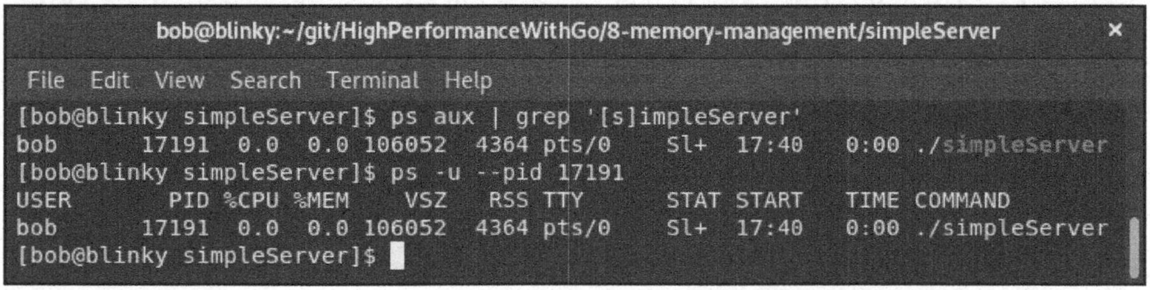

We can see that our VSZ and RSS are low. Compare that to using the C resolver by typing the following command:

```
export CGO_ENABLED=1
go build -tags cgo
```

We can see the output of our `simpleServer` using the following C resolver:

Our VSZ is significantly lower in our server that wasn't compiled with the cgo resolver. Next, we will discuss limited memory situations and how to account for and build them.

Briefing on limited memory situations

If you are running Go on an embedded device or a device with very constrained memory, it's sometimes smart to understand some of the underlying processes within the runtime to make informed decisions regarding your processes. The Go garbage collector *prioritizes low latency and simplicity*. It uses a non-generational concurrent tri-color mark and sweep garbage collector. By default, it manages memory allocation automatically.

Go has a function in the debug standard library that will force a garbage collection and return memory to the OS. The Go garbage collector returns unused memory to the OS after 5 minutes. If you are running on a low memory device, this function, `FreeOSMemory()`, can be found here: `https://golang.org/pkg/runtime/debug/#FreeOSMemory`.

We can also use the `GC()` function, which can be found here: `https://golang.org/pkg/runtime/#GC`.

The `GC()` function may also block the entire program. Use both of these functions at your own risk, because they can lead to unintended consequences.

Summary

In this chapter, we've learned about how Go allocates the heap and stack. We've also learned how to effectively monitor VSZ and RSS memory, and how we can optimize our code to make better use of available memory. Being able to do this allows us to effectively scale with the resources we have, serving more concurrent requests with the same amount of hardware.

In the next chapter, we will be discussing GPU processing in Go.

GPU Parallelization in Go 9

GPU accelerated programming is becoming more and more important in today's high-performance computing stacks. It is commonly used in fields such as **Artificial Intelligence (AI)** and **Machine Learning (ML)**. GPUs are commonly used for these tasks because they tend to be excellent for parallel computation.

In this chapter, we will learn about Cgo, GPU accelerated programming, **CUDA** (short for **Compute Unified Device Architecture**), make commands, C style linking for Go programs, and executing a GPU enabled process within a Docker container. Learning all of these individual things will help us to use a GPU to power a Go backed CUDA program. Doing this will help us to determine how we can use the GPU effectively to help solve computational problems using Go:

- Cgo – writing C in Go
- GPU-accelerated computing – utilizing the hardware
- CUDA on GCP
- CUDA – powering the program

Cgo – writing C in Go

Cgo is a library that is built into the standard library of Go that allows users to invoke calls to underlying C programs in their Go code. Cgo is often used as a delegator for things that are currently coded in C but don't have equivalent Go code written.

Cgo should be used sparingly and only when there isn't an equivalent Go library available for a system. Cgo adds a few limitations to your Go programs:

- Needless complexity
- Difficulty troubleshooting
- Added complexity of building and compiling C code
- Much of Go's tooling is not available for use in Cgo programs
- Cross-compiling doesn't work as expected or at all
- The complexity of C code
- Native Go calls are much faster than Cgo calls
- Slower build times

If you can (or must) live with all of these stipulations, Cgo may be a necessary resource for the project that you're working on.

There are a few instances where it is appropriate to use Cgo. A couple of primary examples are as follows:

- When you must use a proprietary **Software Development Kit (SDK)** or proprietary library.
- When you have a legacy piece of software in C that would be difficult to port to Go because of business logic validation.
- You've exhausted the Go runtime to its limit and you need further optimization. It is very rare that we get to this particular case.

More excellent cgo documentation can be found at the following URLs:

- `https://golang.org/cmd/cgo/`
- `https://blog.golang.org/c-go-cgo`

In the next section, we are going to take a look at a simple cgo example in order to familiarize ourselves with how Cgo works, along with some of its highlights and shortcomings.

A simple Cgo example

Let's take a look at a relatively straightforward Cgo example. In this example, we will write a simple function to print "Hello Gophers" from a C binding and then we will call that C code from our Go program. In this function, we return a constant character string. We then call the `hello_gophers` C function within our Go program. We also use the `C.GoString` function to convert the C string type and the Go string type:

```
package main

/*

 #include <stdio.h>
 const char* hello_gophers() {
     return "Hello Gophers!";
 }
*/

import "C"
import "fmt"
func main() {
    fmt.Println(C.GoString(C.hello_gophers()))
}
```

Once this program has been executed, we can see a simple `Hello Gophers!` output:

```
bob@blinky:~/git/HighPerformanceWithGo/9-gpu-parallelization-in-go/cgo                    ×
[bob@blinky cgo]$ go run cgo.go
Hello Gophers!
[bob@blinky cgo]$ 
```

This example, while simple, shows us how we can bind C functions in our Go programs. To further emphasize the difference in execution time, we can look at a benchmark of our Cgo function and our Go function:

```
package benchmark

/*
 #include <stdio.h>
 const char* hello_gophers() {
     return "Hello Gophers!";
 }
*/

import "C"
```

```
import "fmt"

func CgoPrint(n int) {
    for i := 0; i < n; i++ {
        fmt.Sprintf(C.GoString(C.hello_gophers()))
    }
}

func GoPrint(n int) {
    for i := 0; i < n; i++ {
        fmt.Sprintf("Hello Gophers!")
    }
}
```

We can then use these functions for benchmarking our bound C function in comparison to just a normal `GoPrint` function:

```
package benchmark

import "testing"

func BenchmarkCPrint(b *testing.B) {
    CgoPrint(b.N)
}

func BenchmarkGoPrint(b *testing.B) {
    GoPrint(b.N)
}
```

After we execute this, we can see the following output:

```
bob@blinky:~/git/HighPerformanceWithGo/9-gpu-parallelization-in-...   ×

File  Edit  View  Search  Terminal  Help
[bob@blinky cgo]$ go test -bench=. -v
goos: linux
goarch: amd64
BenchmarkCPrint-8          6202881              178 ns/o
p
BenchmarkGoPrint-8        14439451             83.2 ns
/op
PASS
ok      /home/bob/git/HighPerformanceWithGo/9-gpu-para
llelization-in-go/cgo   2.595s
[bob@blinky cgo]$ 
```

Note that the bound Cgo function takes about an order of magnitude longer than the native Go functionality. This is okay in some cases. This benchmark is just further verifying the fact that we should use Cgo bindings only when it makes sense. It's important to remember that there are specific times where we can justify using Cgo, such as when we have to perform actions that aren't available natively as Go functionality.

In the next section, we are going to learn about GPU-accelerated programming and NVIDIA's CUDA platform.

GPU-accelerated computing – utilizing the hardware

In today's modern computers, we have a couple of pieces of hardware that do most of the work for the system. The CPU performs most instructional operations from other parts of the computer and delivers the results of those operations. The memory is a fast, short-term location for data storage and manipulation. Hard disks are used for longer-term data storage and manipulation, and networking devices are used to send these bits of data between computing devices across a network. A device that is often also used in a modern computing system is a discrete GPU. Whether it is to display the latest computer games with high-fidelity graphics, decoding 4K video, or performing financial number-crunching, GPUs are becoming a more popular option for high-speed computing.

GPUs are designed for performing specific tasks in an efficient manner. Use of GPUs as **General-Purpose Graphics Processing Units (GPGPUs)** is becoming more commonplace as high-throughput computing is seeing wider adoption.

There are many different APIs available for GPU programming to use GPUs to their fullest extent, including the following:

- OpenCL: https://www.khronos.org/opencl/
- OpenMP: https://www.openmp.org/
- NVIDIA's CUDA platform: https://developer.nvidia.com/cuda-zone

NVIDIA's CUDA library is mature, performant, and widely accepted. We are going to use the CUDA library in our examples in this chapter. Let's talk more about the CUDA platform.

NVIDIA's CUDA platform is an API written by the NVIDIA team that is used to increase parallelism and improve speed with a CUDA-enabled graphics card. Using a GPGPU for performing parallel algorithms on data structures can seriously improve compute time. Many of the current ML and AI toolsets use CUDA under the hood, including, but not limited to, the following:

- TensorFlow: `https://www.tensorflow.org/install/gpu`
- Numba: `https://devblogs.nvidia.com/gpu-accelerated-graph-analytics-python-numba/`
- PyTorch: `https://pytorch.org/`

CUDA provides an API for accessing these processing idioms in C++. It uses the concept of kernels, which are functions called from the C++ code that get executed on the GPU device. Kernels are the parts of the code that get executed in parallel. CUDA uses C++ syntax rules in order to process instructions.

There are many places you can use GPUs in the cloud to perform compute jobs, such as the following:

- Google Cloud GPUs: `https://cloud.google.com/gpu/`
- AWS EC2 instances with GPU: `https://aws.amazon.com/nvidia/`
- Paperspace: `https://www.paperspace.com/`
- FloydHub: `https://www.floydhub.com/`

You can also run CUDA programs on your local workstation. The requirements for doing so are as follows:

- A GPU that is CUDA capable (I used a NVIDIA GTX670 in my example)
- An **Operating System (OS)** that has a GCC compiler and toolchain (I used Fedora 29 in my example)

In the next section, we'll run through how to get our workstation set up for CUDA processing:

1. First, we'll have to install the proper kernel development tools and kernel headers for our host. We can do this on our example Fedora host by executing the following:

```
sudo dnf install kernel-devel-$(uname -r) kernel-headers-$(uname -r)
```

2. We also need to install `gcc` and the appropriate build tools. We can do so with the following:

```
sudo dnf groupinstall "Development Tools"
```

3. After we have the prerequisites installed, we can retrieve the local `.run` file installer that NVIDIA gives us for CUDA. At the time of writing, the `cuda_10.2.89_440.33.01_linux.run` package was the latest available. You can find the latest CUDA toolkit package for download from https://developer.nvidia.com/cuda-downloads:

```
wget
http://developer.download.nvidia.com/compute/cuda/10.2/Prod/local_i
nstallers/cuda_10.2.89_440.33.01_linux.run
```

4. We can then install this package with the following code:

```
sudo ./cuda_10.2.89_440.33.01_linux.run
```

This will give us an installation prompt, as seen in the following screenshot:

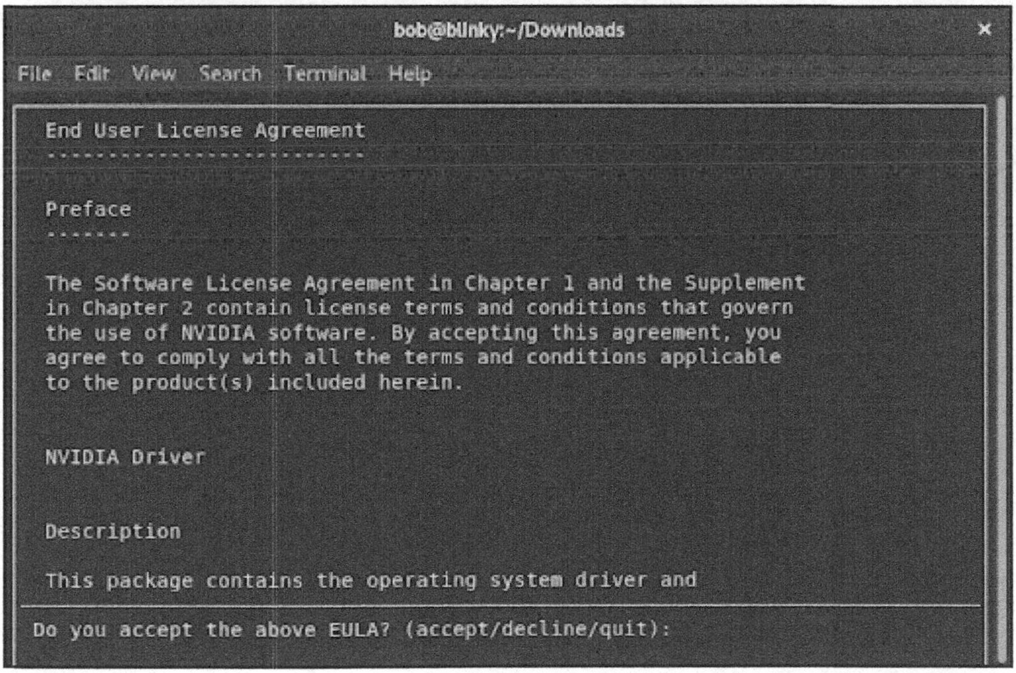

5. After we accept the EULA, we can choose the necessary dependencies to install and select `Install`:

```
                    bob@blinky:~/Downloads                              ×

File  Edit  View  Search  Terminal  Help

  CUDA Installer
  - [X] Driver
      [X] 440.33.01
  + [X] CUDA Toolkit 10.2
    [X] CUDA Samples 10.2
    [X] CUDA Demo Suite 10.2
    [X] CUDA Documentation 10.2
    Options
    Install

  Up/Down: Move | Left/Right: Expand | 'Enter': Select | 'A': Advanced options
```

After you accept the installation prompt, the CUDA installer should successfully complete the installation. If you have any errors during your installation, looking in the following locations may help you to sort out your installation:

- `/var/log/cuda-installer.log`
- `/var/log/nvidia-installer.log`

In the next section, we are going to discuss how to use the host machine for CUDA processes.

CUDA – utilizing host processes

After you've successfully installed CUDA, you'll need to set some environment variables in order to add the installed bits to your execution path. This functionality works as expected if you don't have access to Docker on your host or if you'd rather use your bare machine to perform GPU-intensive operations. If you'd like to use a more reproducible build, you can use the Docker configuration defined in the following *Docker for GPU-enabled programming* section.

We'll need to update our `PATH` to include the CUDA binary paths that we just installed. We can do this by executing the following: `export PATH=$PATH:/usr/local/cuda-10.2/bin:/usr/local/cuda-10.2/NsightCompute-2019.1.`

We also need to update our `LD_LIBRARY_PATH` variable, which is an environment variable that your OS looks for when linking dynamic and shared libraries. We can add the CUDA libraries by executing `export LD_LIBRARY_PATH=:/usr/local/cuda-10.2/lib64`.

This will add the CUDA libraries to your library path. We will add these to our path programmatically with a GNU Makefile for our examples in the closing sections of this chapter. In the next section, we'll discuss how to utilize CUDA with Docker.

Docker for GPU-enabled programming

If you'd like to use Docker for your GPU-enabled programming in this chapter, you can perform the following steps, but to use this, you must have a compatible NVIDIA CUDA GPU in your computer. You can find a full list of enabled cards at `https://developer.nvidia.com/cuda-gpus`.

 We might not use Docker in this way in a production environment for GPU-accelerated computing, because you'd most likely want to be as close to the hardware as possible for GPU-accelerated programming, but I've chosen to use this methodology in this chapter in order to have a reproducible build for the consumer of this book to use. Most of the time a reproducible build is an acceptable trade off for the slight performance penalty of using containerized methodologies.

If you're unsure of what your NVIDIA-enabled GPU supports, you can use the `cuda-z` utility to find more information about your graphics card. The executable for this program can be found at `http://cuda-z.sourceforge.net/`.

After you download the version for your particular OS, you should be able to execute the file like so:

```
./CUDA-Z-0.10.251-64bit.run
```

You'll see an output that gives you all sorts of information about the card you're currently using:

Once you're certain your card supports the GPU processing required, we can use Docker to hook into your GPU for processing. To do so, we will go through the following steps:

1. Enable the NVIDIA container toolkit for your computer. With my Fedora test system, I had to make a small tweak to this by changing my distribution to `centos7`—the installed RPMs still worked as expected:

```
distribution=$(. /etc/os-release;echo $ID$VERSION_ID)
curl -s -L
https://nvidia.github.io/nvidia-docker/$distribution/nvidia-docker.
repo | sudo tee /etc/yum.repos.d/nvidia-docker.repo
```

The full instructions for installing this on other OSes can be found at
`https://github.com/NVIDIA/nvidia-docker#quickstart`.

2. Install the `nvidia-container-toolkit`:

```
sudo yum install -y nvidia-container-toolkit
```

3. Restart Docker in order to pick up these new changes:

```
sudo systemctl restart docker
```

4. Disable SELINUX so that your computer has the ability to use your GPU for these requests:

```
setenforce 0 #as root
```

5. Execute a test `docker run` to ensure that you are able to perform GPU actions within Docker and inspect the information about your particular NVIDIA card:

```
docker run --gpus all tensorflow/tensorflow:latest-gpu nvidia-smi
```

In the next section, we'll go through how to set up a CUDA GPU enabled machine in Google Cloud Platform.

CUDA on GCP

If you don't have the necessary hardware or you'd like to run your workloads for your GPU-enabled code in the cloud, you may decide that you'd rather use CUDA on a shared hosting environment. In the following example, we'll show you how to get set up using GPUs on GCP.

There are many other hosted GPU providers (you can see all of them listed in the *GPU-accelerated computing – utilizing the hardware* section of this chapter)—we are going to use GCP's GPU instances as an example here.

You can learn more about GCP's GPU offerings at `https://cloud.google.com/gpu`.

Creating a VM with a GPU

We need to create a Google Compute Engine instance in order to be able to utilize GPUs on GCP.

 You may need to increase your GPU quota. To do so, you can follow the steps at the following URL:
https://cloud.google.com/compute/quotas#requesting_additional_quota

At the time of writing, the NVIDIA P4 GPU is the least expensive on the platform, and has ample power to demonstrate our work. You can verify your quota by checking the NVIDIA P4 GPUs metric on the IAM Admin quotas page:

To do this, we can visit the **VM instances** page on the Google Cloud console. A screenshot of this page follows. Click on the **Create** button in the center of the screen:

VM instances

Compute Engine
VM instances

Compute Engine lets you use virtual machines that run on Google's infrastructure. Create micro-VMs or larger instances running Debian, Windows, or other standard images. Create your first VM instance, import it using a migration service, or try the quickstart to build a sample app.

[Create]   or   [Import]   or   [Take the quickstart]

Compute Engine

- VM instances
- Instance groups
- Instance templates
- Sole-tenant nodes
- Machine images
- Disks
- Snapshots
- Images
- TPUs
- Committed use discounts
- Metadata
- Health checks
- Zones
- Network endpoint groups
- Operations
- Security scans
- OS patch management
- Settings
- Marketplace

Google Cloud Platform — high-performance-in-go-tracing

We next create an Ubuntu 18.04 VM with a GPU attached. Our VM instance configuration for this example is shown in the following screenshot:

We are using Ubuntu 18.04 here as an example, rather than Fedora 29, to show how to set CUDA up for multiple architectures.

Our OS and other configuration parameters are shown in the following screenshot:

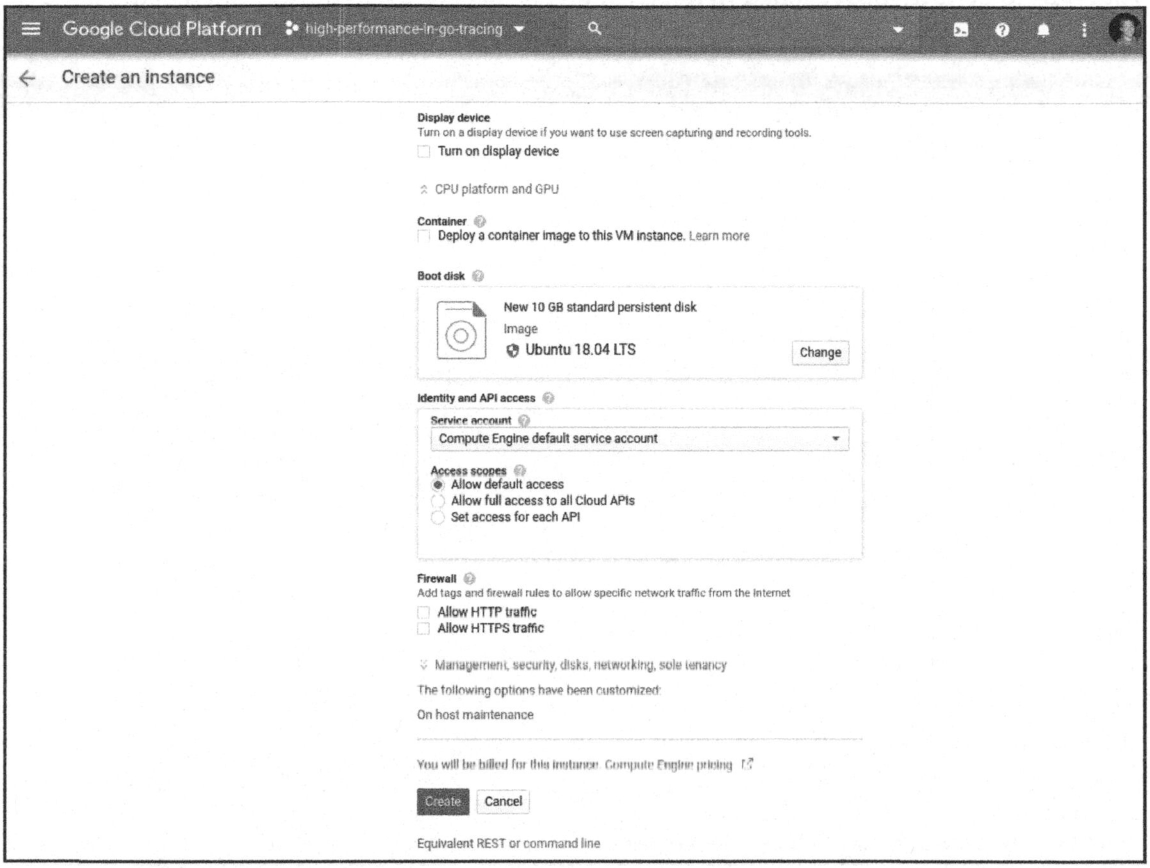

After we click the **Create** button, we are taken back to the **VM instances** page. Wait for your VM to be fully provisioned (it'll have a green checkmark to the left of its name):

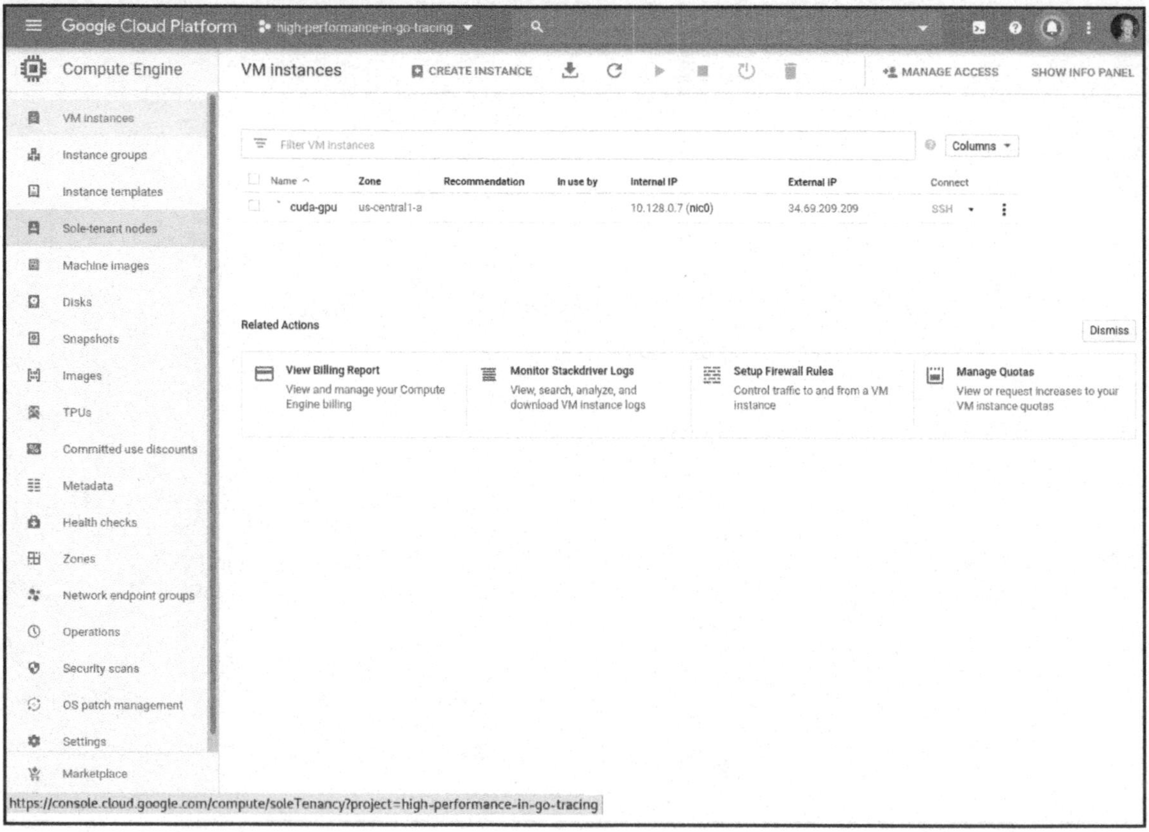

Next, we can SSH to the instance, as seen in the following screenshot:

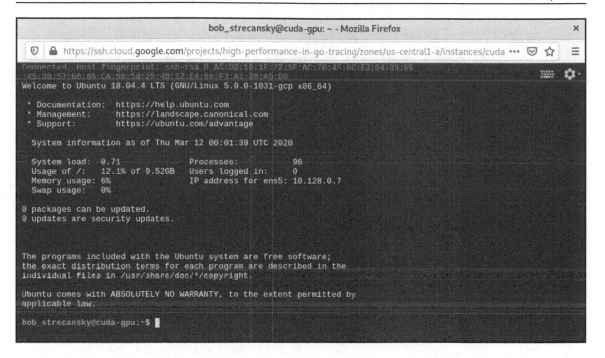

In the next subsections, we will install all the necessary dependencies for running our GPU enabled CGo program. I've also included a script that performs all these actions at the end of the explanation for your convenience.

Install the CUDA driver

Follow the instructions from `https://cloud.google.com/compute/docs/gpus/install-drivers-gpu` to get the NVIDIA CUDA drivers installed:

1. Retrieve the CUDA repository:

```
curl -O
http://developer.download.nvidia.com/compute/cuda/repos/ubuntu1804/
x86_64/cuda-repo-ubuntu1804_10.0.130-1_amd64.deb
```

2. Install the `.deb` package:

```
sudo dpkg -i cuda-repo-ubuntu1804_10.0.130-1_amd64.deb
```

3. Add the NVIDIA GPG key to the apt sources keyring:

```
sudo apt-key adv --fetch-keys
http://developer.download.nvidia.com/compute/cuda/repos/ubuntu1804/
x86_64/7fa2af80.pub
```

4. Install the NVIDIA CUDA drivers:

```
sudo apt-get update && sudo apt-get install cuda
```

5. We now have a CUDA-enabled GPU on our GCP VM. We can validate this with the `nvidia-smi` command:

```
nvidia-smi
```

6. We will see the following output in the screenshot:

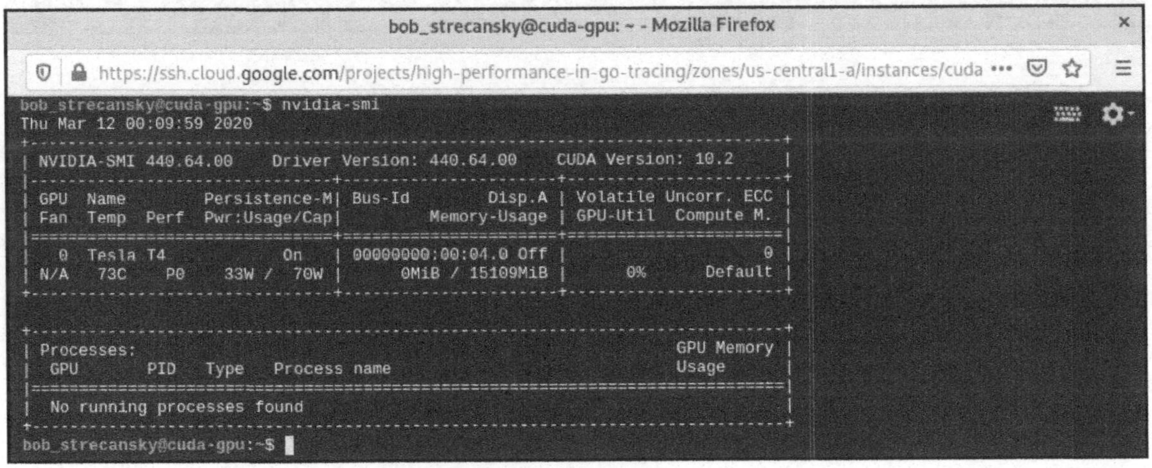

Install Docker CE on GCP

We next need to install Docker CE on our CUDA enabled GCE VM. To install Docker CE on our VM, we can follow the instructions on this page:

```
https://docs.docker.com/install/linux/docker-ce/ubuntu/
```

At the time of writing this book, the following steps were necessary:

1. Validate there aren't any other docker versions on the host:

   ```
   sudo apt-get remove docker docker-engine docker.io containerd runc
   ```

2. Make sure our repositories are up to date:

   ```
   sudo apt-get update
   ```

3. Install the necessary dependencies to install docker CE:

   ```
   sudo apt-get install apt-transport-https ca-certificates curl
   gnupg-agent software-properties-common
   ```

4. Add the docker CE repository:

   ```
   curl -fsSL https://download.docker.com/linux/ubuntu/gpg | sudo apt-
   key add
   sudo add-apt-repository "deb [arch=amd64]
   https://download.docker.com/linux/ubuntu $(lsb_release -cs) stable"
   ```

5. Run an update to ensure the docker CE repository is up to date:

   ```
   sudo apt-get update
   ```

6. Install the necessary docker dependencies:

   ```
   sudo apt-get install docker-ce docker-ce-cli containerd.io
   ```

We now have a working instance of Docker CE on our host.

Installing NVIDIA Docker on GCP

To install the NVIDIA docker driver on our VM, we can follow the instructions on this page:

```
https://github.com/NVIDIA/nvidia-docker#ubuntu-16041804-debian-
jessiestretchbuster
```

1. Set a distribution variable:

   ```
   distribution=$(. /etc/os-release;echo $ID$VERSION_ID)
   ```

2. Add the `nvidia-docker` repo gpg key and apt repository:

```
curl -s -L https://nvidia.github.io/nvidia-docker/gpgkey | sudo
apt-key add -
curl -s -L
https://nvidia.github.io/nvidia-docker/$distribution/nvidia-docker.
list | sudo tee /etc/apt/sources.list.d/nvidia-docker.list
```

3. Install the nvidia-container-toolkit:

```
sudo apt-get update && sudo apt-get install -y nvidia-container-
toolkit
```

4. Restart your VM for this driver to take effect.

Scripting it all together

The following bash script performs all of the previous actions together. First, we install the CUDA driver:

```
#!/bin/bash

# Install the CUDA driver
curl -O
http://developer.download.nvidia.com/compute/cuda/repos/ubuntu1804/x86_64/c
uda-repo-ubuntu1804_10.0.130-1_amd64.deb
dpkg -i cuda-repo-ubuntu1804_10.0.130-1_amd64.deb
apt-key adv --fetch-keys
http://developer.download.nvidia.com/compute/cuda/repos/ubuntu1804/x86_64/7
fa2af80.pub
apt-get -y update && sudo apt-get -y install cuda
```

We then install Docker CE:

```
# Install Docker CE
apt-get remove docker docker-engine docker.io containerd runc
apt-get update
apt-get -y install apt-transport-https ca-certificates curl gnupg-agent
software-properties-common
curl -fsSL https://download.docker.com/linux/ubuntu/gpg | sudo apt-key add
-
add-apt-repository "deb [arch=amd64]
https://download.docker.com/linux/ubuntu $(lsb_release -cs) stable"
apt-get -y update
apt-get -y install docker-ce docker-ce-cli containerd.io
```

Finally we install the `nvidia-docker` driver:

```
# Install nvidia-docker
distribution=$(. /etc/os-release;echo $ID$VERSION_ID)
curl -s -L https://nvidia.github.io/nvidia-docker/gpgkey | sudo apt-key add
-
curl -s -L
https://nvidia.github.io/nvidia-docker/$distribution/nvidia-docker.list |
sudo tee /etc/apt/sources.list.d/nvidia-docker.list
apt-get -y update && sudo apt-get -y install nvidia-container-toolkit
usermod -aG docker $USER
systemctl restart docker
```

This is included in the repo at `https://git/HighPerformanceWithGo/9-gpu-parallelization-in-go/gcp_scripts` and can be executed by running:

```
sudo bash nvidia-cuda-gcp-setup.sh
```

within the directory. In the next section, we'll go through an example CUDA program that is executed using Cgo.

CUDA – powering the program

After we have all of our CUDA dependencies installed and running, we can start out with a simple CUDA C++ program:

1. First, we'll include all of our necessary header files and define the number of elements we'd like to process. `1 << 20` is 1,048,576, which is more than enough elements to show an adequate GPU test. You can shift this if you'd like to see the difference in processing time:

```
#include <cstdlib>
#include <iostream>

const int ELEMENTS = 1 << 20;
```

Our `multiply` function is wrapped in a `__global__` specifier. This allows `nvcc`, the CUDA-specific C++ compiler, to run a particular function on the GPU. This multiply function is relatively straightforward: it takes the `a` and `b` arrays, multiplies them together using some CUDA magic, and returns the value in the `c` array:

```
__global__ void multiply(int j, float * a, float * b, float * c) {

    int index = threadIdx.x * blockDim.x + threadIdx.x;
    int stride = blockDim.x * gridDim.x;

    for (int i = index; i < j; i += stride)
        c[i] = a[i] * b[i];
}
```

This CUDA magic is referencing the parallel-processing functionality of the GPU. The variables are defined as follows:

- `gridDim.x`: The number of thread blocks available on the processor
- `blockDim.x`: The number of threads in each block
- `blockIdx.x`: The index of the current block within the grid
- `threadId.x`: The index of the current thread within the block

We then need to add an `extern "C"` call to have a C-style linkage for this particular function, so we can effectively call this function from our Go code. This `cuda_multiply` function creates three arrays:

- `a` and `b`, which store random numbers between 1 and 10
- `c`, which stores the result of the multiplication of `a` and `b`

```
extern "C" {

    int cuda_multiply(void) {
        float * a, * b, * c;
        cudaMallocManaged( & a, ELEMENTS * sizeof(float));
        cudaMallocManaged( & b, ELEMENTS * sizeof(float));
        cudaMallocManaged( & c, ELEMENTS * sizeof(float));
```

2. We then create our arrays of random floats:

```
for (int i = 0; i < ELEMENTS; i++) {
  a[i] = rand() % 10;
  b[i] = rand() % 10;
}
```

We then perform our multiply function (which we defined at the beginning of our file) based on a block size. We calculate the number of blocks we'd like to use based on the number:

```
int blockSize = 256;
int numBlocks = (ELEMENTS + blockSize - 1) / blockSize;
multiply << < numBlocks, blockSize >>> (ELEMENTS, a, b, c);
```

After our multiplication is completed, we will wait for the GPU to finish before accessing our information on the host: `cudaDeviceSynchronize();`.

3. We can then print the values of the multiplication that we performed to the screen in order to let the end user see the computations we are performing. This is commented out in the code, as printing to `stdout` doesn't show a very good performance story for this particular code. You can uncomment it if you'd like to see the computation that is occurring:

```
//for (int k = 0; k < ELEMENTS; k++) {
    //std::cout << k << ":" << a[k] << "*" << b[k] << "=" << c[k] <<
"\n";
    //}
```

4. We then free the GPU memory that we allocated for the multiply function with `cudaMallocManaged()` by calling `cudaFree` on each of our array pointers, followed by returning 0 to finish up our program:

```
        cudaFree(a);
        cudaFree(b);
        cudaFree(c);
        return 0;
    }
  }
```

5. We will then add our header file, `cuda_multiply.h`:

```
    int cuda_multiply(void);
```

Our Go program in this chapter is just a wrapper around the `cuda_multiply.cu` function that we've created with a little syntactical sugar.

6. We instantiate `main` and import the necessary packages:

```
package main

import (
    "fmt"
    "time"
)
```

7. We then add the necessary `CFLAGS` and `LDFLAGS` that we need in order to reference the libraries that we have created with our nvcc make, as well as the system libraries. It's important to note here that these comments, referred to as *preambles* in cgo code, are used as the header while compiling the C parts of our package. We can include any C code that is necessary here in order to make the Go portion of our code more palatable. If you're planning on using any of the following styles of flags, they must be preempted with a `#cgo` directive to tweak the behavior of the underlying compiler:

   - CFLAGS
   - CPPFLAGS
   - CXXFLAGS
   - FFLAGS
   - LDFLAGS

8. We then import the pseudo-package `C`, which allows us to execute the C that we wrote (recall our `extern C` call in our `cuda_multiply.cu` file). We also add a timing wrapper around this function in order to see how long it takes to execute this function:

```
//#cgo CFLAGS: -I.
//#cgo LDFLAGS: -L. -lmultiply
//#cgo LDFLAGS: -lcudart
//#include <cuda_multiply.h>

import "C"
func main() {
    fmt.Printf("Invoking cuda library...\n")
    start := time.Now()
    C.cuda_multiply()
    elapsed := time.Since(start)
    fmt.Println("\nCuda Execution took", elapsed)
}
```

Chapter 9

9. A Makefile is provided for the Docker container that we are going to build next. Our Makefile defines a method to build our nvcc library, run our Go code, and clean up our nvcc library:

```
//target:
    nvcc -o libmultiply.so --shared -Xcompiler -fPIC
cuda_multiply.cu
//go:
    go run cuda_multiply.go

//clean:
    rm *.so
```

Our Dockerfile ties it all together for our demonstration to be very easily reproducible:

```
FROM tensorflow/tensorflow:latest-gpu
ENV LD_LIBRARY_PATH=/usr/local/cuda-10.1/lib64
RUN ln -s /usr/local/cuda-10.1/lib64/libcudart.so
/usr/lib/libcudart.so
RUN apt-get install -y golang
COPY . /tmp
WORKDIR /tmp
RUN make
RUN mv libmultiply.so /usr/lib/libmultiply.so
ENTRYPOINT ["/usr/bin/go", "run", "cuda_multiply.go"]
```

10. Next, we will build and run our Docker container. The following is the output from a cached build to truncate the build steps for brevity:

```
$ sudo docker build -t cuda-go .
Sending build context to Docker daemon  8.704kB
Step 1/9 : FROM tensorflow/tensorflow:latest-gpu
 ---> 3c0df9ad26cc
Step 2/9 : ENV LD_LIBRARY_PATH=/usr/local/cuda-10.1/lib64
 ---> Using cache
 ---> 65aba605af5a
Step 3/9 : RUN ln -s /usr/local/cuda-10.1/lib64/libcudart.so
/usr/lib/libcudart.so
 ---> Using cache
 ---> a0885eb3c1a8
Step 4/9 : RUN apt-get install -y golang
 ---> Using cache
 ---> bd85bd4a8c5e
Step 5/9 : COPY . /tmp
 ---> 402d800b4708
Step 6/9 : WORKDIR /tmp
 ---> Running in ee3664a4669f
```

[231]

```
Removing intermediate container ee3664a4669f
 ---> 96ba0678c758
Step 7/9 : RUN make
 ---> Running in 05df1a58cfd9
nvcc -o libmultiply.so --shared -Xcompiler -fPIC cuda_multiply.cu
Removing intermediate container 05df1a58cfd9
 ---> 0095c3bd2f58
Step 8/9 : RUN mv libmultiply.so /usr/lib/libmultiply.so
 ---> Running in 493ab6397c29
Removing intermediate container 493ab6397c29
 ---> 000fcf47898c
Step 9/9 : ENTRYPOINT ["/usr/bin/go", "run", "cuda_multiply.go"]
 ---> Running in 554b8bf32a1e
Removing intermediate container 554b8bf32a1e
 ---> d62266019675
Successfully built d62266019675
Successfully tagged cuda-go:latest
```

We can then execute our Docker container with the following command (optionally with sudo depending on how your docker daemon is configured):

```
sudo docker run --gpus all -it --rm cuda-go
```

The follwing is the output of the preceding command:

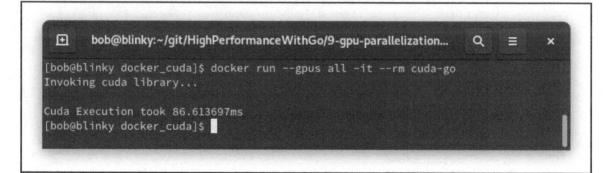

Pretty impressive for such a large multiplication calculation! With high computational workloads, GPU programming can often be a good solution for very quick calculations. An equivalent C++ program using just the CPU takes roughly 340 ms to run on the same machine.

Summary

In this chapter, we learned about cgo, GPU-accelerated programming, CUDA, Make commands, C-style linking for Go programs, and executing a GPU-enabled process within a Docker container. Learning about all of these individual elements helped us to develop a performant GPU-driven application that can make some very large mathematical calculations. These steps could be repeated to do a lot of very large-scale computations in a performant manner. We also learned how to set up a GPU enabled VM in GCP so that we can use cloud resources to perform our GPU computations.

In the next chapter, we'll discuss runtime evaluations in Go.

10
Compile Time Evaluations in Go

The Go authors have written the language in a way that minimizes dependencies and each file declares its own dependencies. Regular syntax and module support also helps a developer improve compile times, as well as interface satisfaction. In this chapter, we will see how runtime evaluations help make Go compilation quicker, alongside using containers for building Go code and utilizing the Go build cache.

In this chapter, we will cover the following topics:

- The Go runtime
- `GCTrace`
- `GOGC`
- `GOMAXPROCS`
- `GOTRACEBACK`
- The Go build cache
- Vendoring
- Caching
- Debugging
- `KeepAlive`
- `NumCPU`
- `ReadMemStats`

These are all valuable topics for understanding how the Go runtime works and how you can use it to write performant code.

Exploring the Go runtime

Within the Go source code, we can see the runtime source by looking at `https://golang.org/src/runtime/`. The runtime package contains operations that interact with the Go runtime. This package is used to control things such as goroutines, garbage collection, reflection, and scheduling, which are all functions that are essential to the operation of the language. Within the runtime package, we have many environment variables that help us change the runtime behavior of Go executables. Let's review some of the most important environment variables we can talk about with respect to the Go runtime.

GODEBUG

GODEBUG is the controller of the variables and is used for debugging within the Go runtime. This variable contains a list of `name=val` key-value pairs, separated by commas. These named variables are used to tune the output of the debugging information the binary will return. One of the nice things about this variable is that the runtime allows you to apply this directly to a precompiled binary, rather than invoking it at build time. This is nice because it allows you to debug a binary that has already been built (and potentially already causing harm in a production environment). The variables you can pass to GODEBUG are as follows:

GODEBUG variables	Enable value	Description
allocfreetrace	1	Used in order to profile every allocation. A stack trace is printed for each object's allocation and is freed. Each stack trace contains the memory block, size, type, goroutine ID, and stack trace of the individual element.
clobberfree	1	The GC clobbers the content of an object with bad content when it frees the object.
cgocheck	0 – Disabled 1 (default) – Cheap checks 2 – Expensive checks	Checks for packages that use cgo for incorrectly passed go pointers to non-Go code. Set 0 for disabled, 1 for cheap checks that may miss some errors (default), or 2 for expensive checks that will slow your program down.
efence	1	The allocator will ensure each object is allocated on a unique page and that memory addresses aren't recycled.
gccheckmark	1	Verifies the GC's current mark phase by doing a second mark pass. The world is stopped during this second mark pass. If the second pass finds an object that wasn't found by the concurrent mark, the GC will panic.

gcpacertrace	1	Prints information about the concurrent pacer's internal state with respect to the garbage collector.
gcshrinkstackoff	1	Moving goroutines cannot move onto smaller stacks. A Goroutine's stack only grows in this mode.
gcstoptheworld	1 – Disables GC 2 – Disables GC and concurrent sweeping	1 disables concurrent garbage collection. This turns each GC event into a stop the world situation. 2 disables GC and disables concurrent sweeping after the completion of garbage collection.
gctrace	1	See the GCTrace header on the subsequent page.
madvdontneed	1	Returns memory to the kernel with MADV_DONTNEED instead of MADV_FREE on Linux. Using this flag makes for less efficient memory utilization, but also makes RSS memory values drop more quickly.
mcmprofilerate	0 – Turn of profiling 1 – Include every allocated block X – Updates the value of MemProfileRate	Controls memory allocation fractions that are reported and recorded within the memory profile. Changing X controls the fraction of memory allocations that are recorded.
invalidptr	0 – Disables this check 1 – Crashes if an invalid pointer is found	The garbage collector and stack copier will crash if a value for an invalid pointer is found where a pointer is stored.
sbrk	1	Swaps in a trivial allocator from the OS that doesn't reclaim memory, instead of using the default memory allocator and garbage collector.
scavenge	1	The heap scavenger debugging mode is enabled.
scheddetail	1 (in conjunction with schedtrace=X)	The scheduler returns information that pertains to the scheduler, processor, thread, and goroutine processes every X milliseconds.
schedtrace	X	A single line is emitted to STDERR every X milliseconds with a scheduler state summary.
tracebackancestors	N	Tracebacks of where goroutines are crated with their associated stacks are extended, reporting N ancestor goroutines. No ancestry information is returned if N = 0.

Other packages also have variables that are able to be passed to GODEBUG. These are usually very well-known packages that may need runtime performance tweaks, such as crypto/tls and net/http. Packages should contain documentation if they have GODEBUG flags that are available at runtime.

GCTRACE

GCTRACE is utilized during runtime to view a single line that's been printed to stderr showing the total memory collected and the length of the pause during each collection. At the time of writing, this line is organized as follows:

```
gc# @#s #%: #+#+# ms clock, #+#/#/#+# ms cpu, #->#-># MB, # MB goal, #P
```

We can instrument a simple HTTP server to provide an example of how this works. First, we write a simple HTTP server with a simple response of Hello Gophers to the root of localhost:8080:

```
package main
import (
    "fmt"
    "net/http"
)

func hello(w http.ResponseWriter, r *http.Request) {
    fmt.Fprintf(w, "Hello Gophers")
}

func main() {
    http.HandleFunc("/", hello)
    err := http.ListenAndServe(":8080", nil)
    if err != nil {
        fmt.Println(err)
    }
}
```

Next, we can build and run this simple web server, and then we can use Apache bench (https://httpd.apache.org/docs/2.4/programs/ab.html) to simulate some load to the host:

```
Q          bob@localhost:~/git/HighPerformanceWithGo/10-runtime-evalu...    ⊞    ☰    ✕

[bob@blinky runtime]$ ab -n 1000 -c 1000 http://localhost:8080/
This is ApacheBench, Version 2.3 <$Revision: 1843412 $>
Copyright 1996 Adam Twiss, Zeus Technology Ltd, http://www.zeustech.net/
Licensed to The Apache Software Foundation, http://www.apache.org/

Benchmarking localhost (be patient)
Completed 100 requests
Completed 200 requests
Completed 300 requests
Completed 400 requests
Completed 500 requests
Completed 600 requests
Completed 700 requests
Completed 800 requests
Completed 900 requests
Completed 1000 requests
Finished 1000 requests

Server Software:
Server Hostname:        localhost
Server Port:            8080

Document Path:          /
Document Length:        13 bytes

Concurrency Level:      1000
Time taken for tests:   0.154 seconds
Complete requests:      1000
Failed requests:        0
Total transferred:      130000 bytes
HTML transferred:       13000 bytes
Requests per second:    6494.77 [#/sec] (mean)
Time per request:       153.970 [ms] (mean)
Time per request:       0.154 [ms] (mean, across all concurrent requests)
Transfer rate:          824.53 [Kbytes/sec] received

Connection Times (ms)
              min  mean[+/-sd] median   max
Connect:        0    41  15.1     40      78
Processing:    21    31  10.9     26      79
Waiting:        1    29  12.2     25      60
Total:         51    73  11.2     71     104

Percentage of the requests served within a certain time (ms)
  50%     71
  66%     77
  75%     80
  80%     82
  90%     88
  95%     96
  98%    101
  99%    102
 100%    104 (longest request)
[bob@blinky runtime]$ █
```

After we see this output from Apache bench, showing that our test has completed, we will see some garbage collection statistics in our Terminal where we initially instantiated our simple HTTP daemon:

```
Q      bob@localhost:~/git/HighPerformanceWithGo/10-runtime-evalu...    ⊞    ≡    ✕

[bob@blinky runtime]$ go build gctraceExample.go
[bob@blinky runtime]$ GODEBUG=gctrace=1 ./gctraceExample
gc 1 @6.131s 0%: 0.016+2.1+0.023 ms clock, 0.067+2.8/1.9/0+0.093 ms cpu, 4->4->3
 MB, 5 MB goal, 4 P
gc 2 @6.165s 0%: 0.31+3.0+0.005 ms clock, 1.2+4.4/2.5/0+0.023 ms cpu, 6->6->2 MB
, 7 MB goal, 4 P
gc 3 @6.189s 0%: 0.014+1.8+0.027 ms clock, 0.058+2.0/1.7/0.96+0.11 ms cpu, 4->4-
>3 MB, 5 MB goal, 4 P
```

Let's break down the garbage collection output of this example:

Output	Description
gc 1	The garbage collection number. This number is incremented at each garbage collection.
@6.131s	This garbage collection occurred 6.131 s after the program was started.
0%	The percentage of time spent in GC since the program was started.
0.016+2.1+0.023 ms clock	The wallclock/CPU times that occur for the phases of the GC. This can be expressed as $Tgc = Tseq + Tmark + Tsweep$. **Tseq**: User Go routines time stop (stop the world sweep termination). **Tmark**: The heap making time (concurrent mark and scan time). **Tsweep**: Heap sweeping time (sweep the world mark termination).
4->4->3 MB	GC start, GC end, and live heap sizes.
5 MB goal	The goal heap size.
4 P	4 processors being used.

If we wait a couple of moments, our Terminal should produce an output, as follows:

```
scvg1: 57 MB released
scvg1: inuse: 1, idle: 61, sys: 63, released: 57, consumed: 5 (MB)
```

This is an output that occurs using `gctrace > 0`. It produces a summary whenever the Go runtime releases memory back to the system, also known as **scavenging**. At the time of writing, this output follows the following format:

Output	Description
scvg1: 57 MB released	The scavenge cycle number. This number is incremented at each scavenge. This data point also lets us know the size of the memory block that is released back to the OS.
inuse: 1	The size in MB of memory used in our program (this can also indicate partially used spans).
idle: 61	The size in MB of spans pending scavenging.
sys: 3	The size in MB of memory that's been mapped from the system.
released: 57	The size in MB of memory released to the system.
consumed: 5	The size in MB of memory allocated from the system.

Both the garbage collection and scavenging output examples are important—they can tell us the current state of memory utilization in our system in a simple to read manner.

GOGC

The `GOGC` variable allows us to tune the intensity of the Go garbage collection system. The garbage collector (instantiated at `https://golang.org/src/runtime/mgc.go`) reads the `GOGC` variable and determines the value of the garbage collector. A value of `off` sets the garbage collector off. This is often useful for debugging but not sustainable in the long term as the program needs to free memory that is collected within the executable's heap. Setting this value to less than the default value of 100 will cause the garbage collector to execute more frequently. Setting this value larger than the default value of 100 will cause the garbage collector to execute less frequently. Very often for multi-core large machines, garbage collection happens too frequently and we can improve performance if we have garbage collection happen less frequently. We can use a compilation of the standard library to see how changing garbage collection will influence compile times. In the following code sample, we can see examples of the build of the standard library and their respective timings:

```
#!/bin/bash

export GOGC=off
printf "\nBuild with GOGC=off:"
time go build -a std
printf "\nBuild with GOGC=50:"
export GOGC=50
time go build -a std
```

```
for i in 0 500 1000 1500 2000
do
    printf "\nBuild with GOGC = $i:"
    export GOGC=$i
    time go build -a std
done
```

Our output shows us the respective timings of the Go standard library compile times:

We can see that there is a vast difference in compile times by tuning the garbage collection. This will vary greatly, depending on your architecture, system specs, and Go version. It is important to recognize this is a knob we can turn for our Go programs. This knob is often turned for build times or highly monitored, latency-sensitive binaries that need to squeeze out more performance during their execution time.

GOMAXPROCS

GOMAXPROCS is a variable that can be tuned to allow us to control the number of threads that our operating system will allocate to our goroutines within our Go binary. By default, GOMAXPROCS is equal to the number of cores available to the application. This is dynamically configurable via the runtime package. It is important to note that as of Go 1.10, GOMAXPROCS will have no upper bound limit.

If we have a function that is CPU-intensive and parallelized (such as goroutine sorting strings), we will see some serious improvements if we adjust the number of GOMAXPROCS we have. In the following code example, we are going to test building the standard library with a different number set for GOMAXPROCS:

```bash
#!/bin/bash
for i in 1 2 3 4
do
    export GOMAXPROCS=$i
    printf "\nBuild with GOMAXPROCS=$i:"
    time go build -a std
done
```

In our results, we can see what happens when we manipulate the total number of GOMAXPROCS:

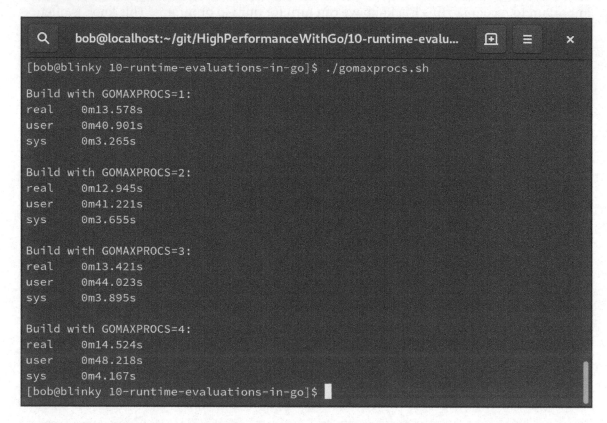

Realistically, we should never set GOMAXPROCS manually. There are rare occasions where you might want to limit CPU utilization for a particular binary based on the resources you have available to you on a system, or you may really need to optimize based on the resources you have on hand. For most cases, however, the default GOMAXPROCS value is sane.

GOTRACEBACK

GOTRACEBACK allows you to control the generated output from a Go program with unexpected runtime conditions or unrecovered panic states. Setting a GOTRACEBACK variable will allow you to see more or less granular information about the goroutines that are instantiated for your specific error or panic. An example of panic from a channel/goroutine interrupt is as follows:

```
package main
import (
    "time"
)

func main() {
    c := make(chan bool, 1)
    go panicRoutine(c)
    for i := 0; i < 2; i++ {
        <-c
    }
}

func panicRoutine(c chan bool) {
    time.Sleep(100 * time.Millisecond)
    panic("Goroutine Panic")
    c <- true
}
```

If we tweak the GOTRACEBACK variable in our output, we will see different varying levels of stack trace. Setting GOTRACEBACK=none or GOTRACEBACK=0 gives us a minimal amount of information about this panic:

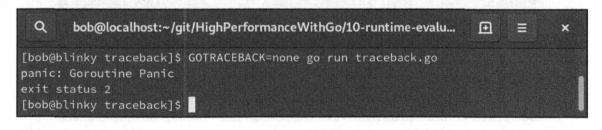

Setting GOTRACEBACK=single (the default option in the Go runtime) will emit a single stack trace for the current goroutine for our particular request, as follows:

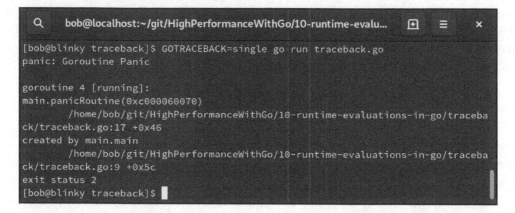

Setting GOTRACEBACK=all or GOTRACEBACK=1 will send us back the stack traces for all of the goroutines that were created by the user:

```
[bob@blinky traceback]$ GOTRACEBACK=all go run traceback.go
panic: Goroutine Panic

goroutine 4 [running]:
main.panicRoutine(0xc000060070)
        /home/bob/git/HighPerformanceWithGo/10-runtime-evaluations-in-go/traceba
ck/traceback.go:17 +0x46
created by main.main
        /home/bob/git/HighPerformanceWithGo/10-runtime-evaluations-in-go/traceba
ck/traceback.go:9 +0x5c

goroutine 1 [chan receive]:
main.main()
        /home/bob/git/HighPerformanceWithGo/10-runtime-evaluations-in-go/traceba
ck/traceback.go:11 +0x7c
exit status 2
[bob@blinky traceback]$
```

Setting GOTRACEBACK=system or GOTRACEBACK=2 will add all of the runtime stack frames for functions and goroutines that are created by the runtime.

Finally, we can set GOTRACEBACK=crash. This functions similarly to the system but allows the operating system to trigger a core dump.

Most of the time, the default of `GOTRACEBACK=single` gives us enough information about the current context in order to make an informed decision about why our program ended in a way that we did not expect.

Go build cache

In this chapter, we've discussed a couple of ways to optimize the runtime for Go builds. We also have the ability to improve Go build times with a couple of simple tweaks. Go's team has been optimizing for runtime, not for build time. Go has the ability to cache build time dependencies, which helps to reuse common artifacts from previous builds. These artifacts are kept in `$GOPATH/pkg/`. We can keep these intermediate results by using the `-i` flag while calling go build in order to reutilize those artifacts. If we want to debug what is happening during our build, we can run our build with a `-x` flag in order to produce a more verbose output from the Go build system.

Vendoring dependencies

Vendoring is also a popular choice for improving build consistency and quality. Within the project structure, the authors of the language were receptive to the feedback of keeping support for vendoring dependencies. Keeping your dependencies within your repository makes it very large, but it can help with keeping third party dependencies available locally during build time. When we are using Go version 1.11 or greater, we can use Go modules flagging to allow vendored builds. We can use `go mod vendor` to capture all of the dependencies in the `vendor/` directory, followed by using `go build -mod vendor` at build time.

Caching and vendoring improvements

In order to see the improvements we can make with built and cached assets, let's build a project with a third-party dependency. Prometheus [https://prometheus.io/] is a popular time-series database (also written in Go) that is commonly used for metrics gathering and collection. We may want to start up a Prometheus metrics server in any of our applications in order to learn more about our current running binary, from a systems perspective. To do this, we can import the Prometheus library as follows:

```
package main
import (
    "net/http"
```

```
        "github.com/prometheus/client_golang/prometheus/promhttp"
)

func main() {
    http.Handle("/promMetrics", promhttp.Handler())
    http.ListenAndServe(":1234", nil)
}
```

After we instantiate our `prometheus` server in a basic binary, we can build our binary and execute it. To perform a force rebuild of packages that are already up to date, we can use the `-a` flag with `go build`. If you're curious as to what's taking forever in our super long build time, you can also add the `-x` flag – it'll give you a very verbose output as to what's happening during the build process.

By default, newer versions of Golang will define a GOCACHE. You can see where it's located using `go env GOCACHE`. Using a combination of GOCACHE and mod vendor, we can see that our build time has significantly improved. Our first build in the list is a cold build, forcing packages to be rebuilt so they're up to date. Our second build, which has some items stored from the mod vendor stanza, is much quicker. Our third build, which should have most build elements cached, is very quick in comparison. The following screenshot illustrates this:

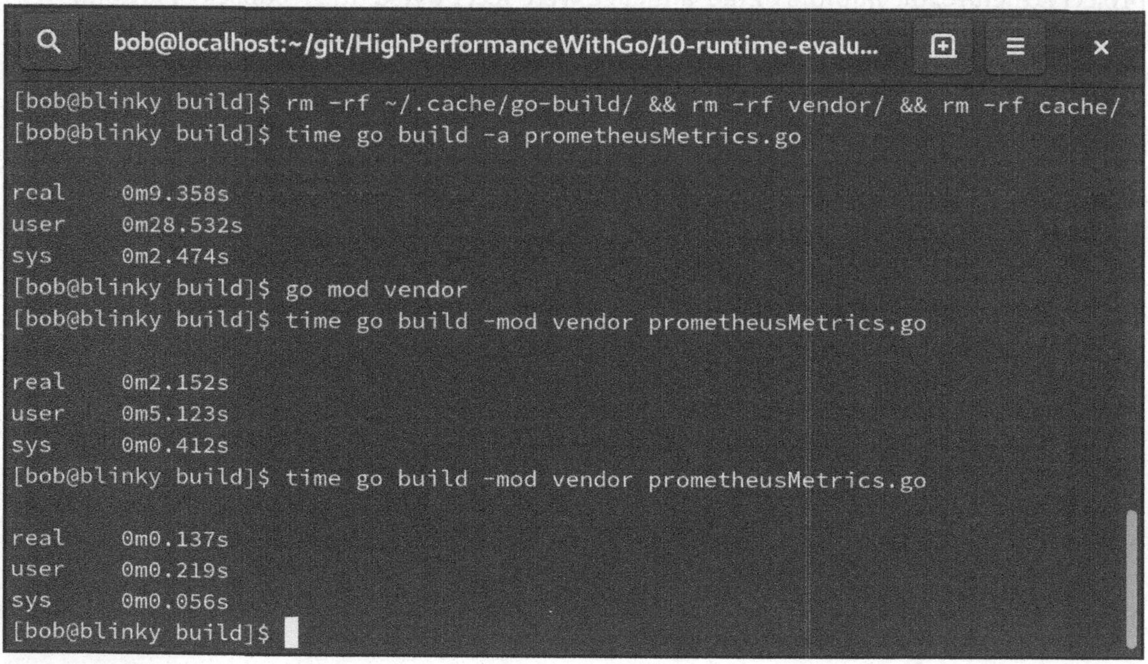

Debug

The debug package within the runtime gives us many functions and types that are available for debugging. We have the ability to do the following:

- Force a garbage collection using `FreeOSMemory()`.
- Print the stack trace that was generated at runtime. Stack to stderr using `PrintStack()`.
- Read our garbage collection stats using `ReadGCStats()`.
- Set our garbage collection percentage using `SetGCPercent()`.
- Set our max stack size for a single goroutine using `SetMaxStack()`.
- Set our maximum number of OS threads using `SetMaxThreads()`.
- Control the runtime behavior while faulting on an unexpected address using `SetPanicOndefault()`.
- Set the amount of traceback using `SetTraceback()`.
- Return the stack trace of a goroutine using `Stack()`.
- Write a heap dump using `WriteHeapDump()`.

PProf/race/trace

We will cover the details of profiling and tracing Go programs in `Chapter 12`, *Profiling Go Code*, and `Chapter 13`, *Tracing Go Code*, respectively. It is prudent to know that the runtime library is a key driver in these utilities. Being able to use pprof/race/trace can help you debug your code in a meaningful way and be able to find nascent errors In the next section, we will learn about runtime functions and how they are prudent to the Go runtime library.

Understanding functions

The Go runtime library also has functions that you can inject into your program's runtime to emit runtime data. Let's run through a couple of prime examples. A full list of all of the available runtime functions can be found at `https://golang.org/pkg/runtime/#pkg-index`. Many of the functions that are available in this package are also included in the `runtime/pprof` package, which we will investigate in more detail in `Chapter 12`, *Profiling Go Code*.

KeepAlive

The `runtime.KeepAlive()` function expects `interface{}` and ensures that the object passed to it isn't freed and that its finalizer (as defined by `runtime.SetFinalizer`) is not run. This keeps the argument passed to `KeepAlive` reachable. The compiler sets up `OpKeepAlive`, as defined in the **static single assignment (SSA)** package (`https://golang.org/src/cmd/compile/internal/gc/ssa.go#L2947`) – this allows the compiler to know the state of the interface as a variable and allows the keep alive context to be kept.

As a rule of thumb, we should not call `KeepAlive` in normal implementations. It's used to ensure that the garbage collector doesn't reclaim memory from a *no longer* referenced value within a function.

NumCPU

The `NumCPU` function returns the usable number of logical CPUs of the current process. When the binary is invoked, the runtime validates the number of CPUs that are available at startup. A simple example of this can be found in the following code snippet:

```
package main

import (
    "fmt"
    "runtime"
)

func main() {
    fmt.Println("Number of CPUs Available: ", runtime.NumCPU())
}
```

Now, we can see the number of CPUs currently available to the process. In my case, this value ended up being 4:

With this, we can see that my computer has 4 CPUs available for use.

ReadMemStats

The ReadMemStats() function reads memory allocator statistics and populates them into a variable, say, m. The MemStats struct has a lot of really valuable information about in-flight memory utilization. Let's take a deep look into what values it can produce for us. An HTTP handler function that allows us to see the memory utilization of the binary may be helpful as we make more requests in our system and wish to see where our memory allocation is utilized:

1. First, we can instantiate the program and the function:

```
package main
import (
    "fmt"
    "net/http"
    "runtime"
)
func memStats(w http.ResponseWriter, r *http.Request) {
    var memStats runtime.MemStats
    runtime.ReadMemStats(&memStats)
```

2. Next, we can print all of the values of the individual memory statistics that the runtime provides us with. Let's start with Alloc, Mallocs, and Frees:

```
fmt.Fprintln(w, "Alloc:", memStats.Alloc)
fmt.Fprintln(w, "Total Alloc:", memStats.TotalAlloc)
fmt.Fprintln(w, "Sys:", memStats.Sys)
fmt.Fprintln(w, "Lookups:", memStats.Lookups)
fmt.Fprintln(w, "Mallocs:", memStats.Mallocs)
fmt.Fprintln(w, "Frees:", memStats.Frees)
```

3. Now, let's look at heap information:

```
fmt.Fprintln(w, "Heap Alloc:", memStats.HeapAlloc)
fmt.Fprintln(w, "Heap Sys:", memStats.HeapSys)
fmt.Fprintln(w, "Heap Idle:", memStats.HeapIdle)
fmt.Fprintln(w, "Heap In Use:", memStats.HeapInuse)
fmt.Fprintln(w, "Heap Released:", memStats.HeapReleased)
fmt.Fprintln(w, "Heap Objects:", memStats.HeapObjects)
```

4. Next, we look at stack/span/cache/bucket allocations:

```
fmt.Fprintln(w, "Stack In Use:", memStats.StackInuse)
fmt.Fprintln(w, "Stack Sys:", memStats.StackSys)
fmt.Fprintln(w, "MSpanInuse:", memStats.MSpanInuse)
fmt.Fprintln(w, "MSpan Sys:", memStats.MSpanSys)
fmt.Fprintln(w, "MCache In Use:", memStats.MCacheInuse)
fmt.Fprintln(w, "MCache Sys:", memStats.MCacheSys)
fmt.Fprintln(w, "Buck Hash Sys:", memStats.BuckHashSys)
```

5. Then, we look at garbage collection information:

```
fmt.Fprintln(w, "EnableGC:", memStats.EnableGC)
fmt.Fprintln(w, "GCSys:", memStats.GCSys)
fmt.Fprintln(w, "Other Sys:", memStats.OtherSys)
fmt.Fprintln(w, "Next GC:", memStats.NextGC)
fmt.Fprintln(w, "Last GC:", memStats.LastGC)
fmt.Fprintln(w, "Num GC:", memStats.NumGC)
fmt.Fprintln(w, "Num Forced GC:", memStats.NumForcedGC)
```

6. Now, let's look at garbage collection interruption information:

```
fmt.Fprintln(w, "Pause Total NS:", memStats.PauseTotalNs)
fmt.Fprintln(w, "Pause Ns:", memStats.PauseNs)
fmt.Fprintln(w, "Pause End:", memStats.PauseEnd)
fmt.Fprintln(w, "GCCPUFraction:", memStats.GCCPUFraction)
fmt.Fprintln(w, "BySize Size:", memStats.BySize)
```

7. Next, we instantiate a simple HTTP server:

```
func main() {
    http.HandleFunc("/", memStats)
    http.ListenAndServe(":1234", nil)
}
```

Here, we can use our Apache bench tool to generate a bit of load on our memory allocator:

```
ab -n 1000 -c 1000 http://localhost:1234/
```

Finally, we can see some active HTTP server information, along with a response, by making a request to `localhost:1234`:

```
Q        bob@localhost:~/git/HighPerformanceWithGo/10-runtime-evalu...    ⊞    ≡    ✕

[bob@blinky memstats]$ curl localhost:1234
Alloc: 248392
Total Alloc: 248392
Sys: 69928960
Lookups: 0
Mallocs: 648
Frees: 12
Heap Alloc: 248392
Heap Sys: 66781184
Heap Idle: 65953792
Heap In Use: 827392
Heap Released: 0
Heap Objects: 636
Stack In Use: 327680
Stack Sys: 327680
MSpanInuse: 12096
MSpan Sys: 16384
MCache In Use: 6944
MCache Sys: 16384
Buck Hash Sys: 2620
EnableGC: true
GCSys: 2240512
Other Sys: 544196
Next GC: 4473924
Last GC: 0
Num GC: 0
Num Forced GC: 0
Pause Total NS: 0
Pause Ns: [0 0 0 0 0 0 0 0 0 0 0 0 0 0 0 0 0 0 0 0 0 0 0 0 0 0 0 0 0 0 0 0
 0 0 0 0 0 0 0 0 0 0 0 0 0 0 0 0 0 0 0 0 0 0 0 0 0 0 0 0 0 0 0 0
 0 0 0 0 0 0 0 0 0 0 0 0 0 0 0 0 0 0 0 0 0 0 0 0 0 0 0 0 0 0 0 0
 0 0 0 0 0 0 0 0 0 0 0 0 0 0 0 0 0 0 0 0 0 0 0 0 0 0 0 0 0 0 0 0
 0 0 0 0 0 0 0 0 0 0 0 0 0 0 0 0 0 0 0 0 0 0 0 0 0 0 0 0 0 0 0 0
 0 0 0 0 0 0 0 0 0 0 0 0 0 0 0 0 0 0 0 0 0 0 0 0 0 0 0 0 0 0 0 0
 0 0 0 0 0 0 0 0 0 0 0 0 0 0 0 0 0]
Pause End: [0 0 0 0 0 0 0 0 0 0 0 0 0 0 0 0 0 0 0 0 0 0 0 0 0 0 0 0 0 0
 0 0 0 0 0 0 0 0 0 0 0 0 0 0 0 0 0 0 0 0 0 0 0 0 0 0 0 0 0 0 0 0
 0 0 0 0 0 0 0 0 0 0 0 0 0 0 0 0 0 0 0 0 0 0 0 0 0 0 0 0 0 0 0 0
 0 0 0 0 0 0 0 0 0 0 0 0 0 0 0 0 0 0 0 0 0 0 0 0 0 0 0 0 0 0 0 0
 0 0 0 0 0 0 0 0 0 0 0 0 0 0 0 0 0 0 0 0 0 0 0 0 0 0 0 0 0 0 0 0
 0 0 0 0 0 0 0 0 0 0 0 0 0 0 0 0 0 0 0 0 0 0 0 0 0 0 0 0 0 0 0 0
 0 0 0 0 0 0 0 0 0 0 0 0 0 0 0 0 0]
GCCPUFraction: 0
BySize Size: [[0 0 0] {8 11 0} {16 263 0} {32 58 0} {48 88 0} {64 32 0} {80 13 0
} {96 15 0} {112 2 0} {128 8 0} {144 2 0} {160 15 0} {176 4 0} {192 0 0} {208 17
 0} {224 2 0} {240 0 0} {256 9 0} {288 7 0} {320 2 0} {352 10 0} {384 21 0} {416
 5 0} {448 0 0} {480 1 0} {512 4 0} {576 3 0} {640 3 0} {704 2 0} {768 0 0} {896
 8 0} {1024 3 0} {1152 3 0} {1280 1 0} {1408 1 0} {1536 0 0} {1792 5 0} {2048 1
0} {2304 2 0} {2688 2 0} {3072 0 0} {3200 0 0} {3456 0 0} {4096 4 0} {4864 0 0}
{5376 1 0} {6144 1 0} {6528 0 0} {6784 0 0} {6912 0 0} {8192 1 0} {9472 4 0} {97
28 0 0} {10240 0 0} {10880 0 0} {12288 0 0} {13568 0 0} {14336 0 0} {16384 0 0}
{18432 0 0} {19072 0 0}]
[bob@blinky memstats]$
```

The definitions for all of the MemStats values can be found in the documentation at
https://golang.org/pkg/runtime/#MemStats.

Summary

In this chapter, we learned about the GODEBUG, GCTRACE, GOGC, GOMAXPROCS, and GOTRACEBACK runtime optimizations. We also learned about the GOBUILDCACHE and Go vendoring dependencies. Lastly, we learned about debugging and calling runtime functions from code. Using these techniques while troubleshooting your Go code will help you spot your problems and bottlenecks more easily.

In the next chapter, we will discuss the proper way to deploy Go code effectively.

3
Section 3: Deploying, Monitoring, and Iterating on Go Programs with Performance in Mind

In this section, you will understand all of the different idiomatic ways to program performant Go code. Hence, in this section, we will work to establish writing performant Go code in real-world scenarios.

This section contains the following chapters:

- Chapter 11, *Building and Deploying Go Code*
- Chapter 12, *Profiling Go Code*
- Chapter 13, *Tracing Go Code*
- Chapter 14, *Clusters and Job Queues*
- Chapter 15, *Comparing Code Quality Across Versions*

Building and Deploying Go Code

11

Once we have come up with a method to write performant Go code, we need to ship it, validate it, and continue iterating it. The first step of this process is to deploy the new Go code. Go's code is compiled into binaries, which allows for the modular deployment of new Go code as we iterate through code development. We can push this out to one or multiple places in order to test against different environments. Doing this will allow us to optimize our code to fully utilize the throughput that will be available to us in our system.

In this chapter, we will learn all about the Go build process. We'll look at how the Go compiler builds binaries, and we'll use this knowledge to build right-sized, optimized binaries for the platform at hand. We will cover the following topics:

- Building Go binaries
- Using `go clean` to remove object files
- Using `go get` to download and install dependencies
- Using `go mod` for dependency management
- Using `go list` to list packages and modules
- Using `go run` to execute programs
- Using `go install` to install packages

These topics will help us build efficient Go binaries from our source code.

Building Go binaries

In Chapter 10, *Compile Time Evaluations in Go*, we discussed some Go build optimizations that can potentially help optimize our build strategy. Go's build system has quite a few options that can help the system operator add additional parameterization to their build strategy.

The Go tool has many different methodologies for building our source code. Let's investigate top-level understandings of each, and then we will discuss each package in more depth. Knowing the key differences between these commands may help you to understand how they interplay with one another and choose the right tool for the job. Let's have a look at them:

- `go build`: Builds a binary for your project, compiling packages and dependencies
- `go clean`: Removes object and cached files from package source directories
- `go get`: Downloads and installs packages and their dependencies
- `go mod`: Go's (relatively new) built-in dependency module system
- `go list`: Lists named packages and modules and can display important build information about files, imports, and dependencies
- `go run`: Runs and compiles a named Go program
- `go install`: Builds the binary for your project, moves the binary to `$GOPATH/bin`, and caches all non-main packages

In this chapter, we are going to investigate these different pieces of the Go build system. As we learn more about how these programs interoperate with one another, we will be able to see how to use them to our advantage to build slim, feature-filled binaries that will work as we expect them to on the supported architectures and operating systems.

In the next section, we shall see through `go build`.

Go build – building your Go code

The invocation stanza for go build is as follows:

```
go build [-o output] [build flags] [packages]
```

Defining an output with –o compiles a binary using a specifically named file. This is helpful when you have a particular naming convention that you want to keep for your file, or if you want to name binaries based on different build parameters (platform/OS/git SHA and others).

Packages can be defined as a list of go source files or they can be omitted. If a list of go source files is specified, the build program will use the list of files that were passed as a group that specifies a single package. If no packages are defined, the build program will validate that the packages within the directory can be built, but it will discard the results of the build.

Build flags

Go's build flags are all shared by the build, clean, install, list, run, and test commands. A table stating the build flags and their usage descriptions is as follows:

Build flag	Description
-a	Forces packages to be rebuilt. This can be especially handy if you'd like to make sure that all of your dependencies are up to date.
-n	Prints the commands that the compiler utilizes but doesn't run the commands (akin to a dry run in other languages). This is useful to see how a package gets compiled.
-p n	Parallelizes your build commands. By default, this value is set to the number of CPUs that are available to the build system.
-race	Enables race detection. Only certain architectures have the ability to detect race detections: • linux/amd64 • freebsd/amd64 • darwin/amd64 • windows/amd64
-msan	Detects uninitialized memory reads in C. This is only supported on Linux with amd64 or arm64 architectures, and it is necessary to use a clang/LLVM compiler for the host. This can be called with CC=clang go build -msan example.go.
-v	As the program is compiled, the names of the packages that are built are listed to stdout. This can help verify which packages are used for the build.

`-work`	Prints the value of the temporary work directory Go uses in order to build the binary. This is usually stored in `/tmp/` by default.
`-x`	Shows all of the commands that were used during the build process. This can be helpful to determine how a package is built. See the *Build information* section for more information.
`-asmflags '[pattern=]arg list'`	A list of arguments to pass when `go tool asm` is invoked.
`-buildmode=type`	This tells the build command which type of object file we'd like to build. There are currently a couple of type options for `buildmode`: • `archive`: Builds non-main packages into `.a` files. • `c-archive`: Builds the main package and all of its imports into a C archive file. • `c-shared`: Builds the main package and its imports into a C shared library. • `default`: A list of main packages is created. • `shared`: Combines all non-main packages into a single shared library. • `exe`: Builds main packages and their imports into executables. • `pie`: Builds main packages and their imports into **position-independent executables (PIE)**. • `plugin`: Builds main packages and their imports into a Go plugin.
`-compiler name`	Determines which compiler to use. Common uses are `gccgo` and `gc`.
`-gccgoflags`	`gccgo` compiler and linker invocation flags.
`-gcflags`	`gc` compiler and linker invocation flags. See the *Compiler and linker* section for more details.
`-installsuffix suffix`	Adds a suffix to the name of the package installation directory. This is used in order to keep the output separate from default builds.
`-ldflags '[pattern=]arg list'`	Go tool link invocation arguments. See the *Compiler and linker* section for more details.
`-linkshared`	After a `-buildmode=shared` invocation occurs, this flag links against the newly created shared libraries.
`-mod`	Determines which module download mode to use. At the time of writing, there are two options: `- readonly` or `vendor`.
`-pkgdir dir`	Utilize the `dir` defined to install and load all packages.
`-tags tag,list`	A list of build tags that are to be satisfied during the build. This list is passed as a comma-separated list.
`-trimpath`	The resulting built executable will use a different naming scheme for filesystem paths during an executable build. These are as follows: • Go (for the standard library) • path @version (for go modules) • plain import path (while using `GOPATH`)

`-toolexec 'cmd args'`	Invokes toolchain programs, such as debuggers or other interactive programs. This is used for programs such as vet and asm.

With all of this information, you'll be able to build correct linker flags impactfully.

Build information

To garner some understanding of the build process, let's take a look at some build examples so we can gain some insight into how the build tooling works together.

Let's say we want to build a simple HTTP server that has a Prometheus exporter. We can create an exporter like so:

```
package main
import (
    "fmt"
    "net/http"
    "github.com/prometheus/client_golang/prometheus/promhttp"
)

func main() {
    http.Handle("/", promhttp.Handler())
    port := ":2112"
    fmt.Println("Prometheus Handler listening on port ", port)
    http.ListenAndServe(port, nil)
}
```

After we have our package ready, we can build our package with the following:

```
go build -p 4 -race -x prometheusExporterExample.go
```

As we build this binary, we will see a couple of things coming back to stdout (since we passed the -x flag to see the commands that were used during the process). Let's take a look:

1. We are going to truncate the output so that the results are easier to read. If you test this out yourself, you'll see a much larger build output:

   ```
   WORK=/tmp/go-build924967855
   ```

This sets a temporary working directory for the build. As we mentioned previously, this usually lives in the /tmp/ directory unless otherwise specified:

```
mkdir -p $WORK/b001/
```

2. A sub-working directory is also created by the compiler:

```
cat >$WORK/b001/importcfg.link << 'EOF' # internal
```

3. A linking configuration is created and added. This adds all sorts of different arguments to the linking configuration:

```
packagefile command-line-arguments=/home/bob/.cache/go-
build/aa/aa63d73351c57a147871fde4964d74c9a39330b467c6d73640815775e6
673084-d
```

4. The package for command-line arguments is referenced from the cache:

```
packagefile fmt=/home/bob/.cache/go-
build/74/749e110dc104578def1859fbd4ca5c5546f4032f02ffd5ea4d14c730fb
d65b81-d
```

fmt is the printing package we use to display fmt.Println("Prometheus Handler listening on port ", port). This is referenced like so:

```
packagefile
github.com/prometheus/client_golang/prometheus/promhttp=/home/bob/.
cache/go-
build/e9/e98940b17504e2f647dccc7832793448aa4e8a64047385341c94c1c443
1d59cf-d
```

5. The compiler also adds the package for the Prometheus HTTP client library. After this, there are many other references that are added to the build. This has been truncated for brevity.

The end of the file is signified with EOF.

6. An executable directory is created:

```
mkdir -p $WORK/b001/exe/
```

7. The compiler then builds the binary using the importcfg that was created earlier:

```
/usr/lib/golang/pkg/tool/linux_amd64/link -o $WORK/b001/exe/a.out -
importcfg $WORK/b001/importcfg.link -installsuffix race -
buildmode=exe -
```

```
buildid=bGYa4XecCYqWj3VjKraU/eHfXIjk2XJ_C2azyW4yU/8YHxpy5Xa69CGQ4FC
9Kb/bGYa4XecCYqWj3VjKraU -race -extld=gcc /home/bob/.cache/go-
build/aa/aa63d73351c57a147871fde4964d74c9a39330b467c6d73640815775e6
673084-
```

8. A buildid is then added:

```
/usr/lib/golang/pkg/tool/linux_amd64/buildid -w
$WORK/b001/exe/a.out # internal
```

9. Next, the binary is renamed to the filename we had for our exporter example (since we did not specify a different binary name with -o):

cp $WORK/b001/exe/a.out prometheusExporterExample

10. Finally, the work directory is removed:

rm -r $WORK/b001/

The output of the work from this program is a Go binary. In the next section, we'll talk about compiler and linker flags.

Compiler and linker flags

While building a Go binary, the -gcflags flag lets you pass optional compiler arguments, while the -ldflags flag lets you pass optional linker arguments. A full list of compiler and linker flags can be found by invoking the following commands:

```
go tool compile -help
go tool link -help
```

Let's look at an example of utilizing compiler and linker flags. We can build a simple program that returns the value of an uninitialized string variable. The following program seems innocuous enough:

```
package main
import "fmt"

var linkerFlag string
func main() {
    fmt.Println(linkerFlag)
}
```

If we build this with some of the common compiler and linker flags, we will see some helpful output:

```
bob@blinky:~/git/HighPerformanceWithGo/11-deploying-go-code/compilerLinker          ×

File  Edit  View  Search  Terminal  Help
[bob@blinky compilerLinker]$ go build -gcflags="-m -m -N -l" -ldflags "-X main.l
inkerFlag=Hi_Gophers -s -w" compilerLinkerFlags.go
# command-line-arguments
./compilerLinkerFlags.go:8:13: linkerFlag escapes to heap
./compilerLinkerFlags.go:8:13:   from ... argument (arg to ...) at ./compilerLink
erFlags.go:8:13
./compilerLinkerFlags.go:8:13:   from *(... argument) (indirection) at ./compiler
LinkerFlags.go:8:13
./compilerLinkerFlags.go:8:13:   from ... argument (passed to call[argument conte
nt escapes]) at ./compilerLinkerFlags.go:8:13
./compilerLinkerFlags.go:8:13: main ... argument does not escape
[bob@blinky compilerLinker]$
```

The compiler flags that we passed here achieve the following:

- `"-m -m"`: Prints information about the compiler's optimization decisions. This is the output that we can see in the preceding screenshot after the build command.
- `"-N"`: Disables optimizations within the Go binary.
- `"-l"`: Disables inlining.

The linker flags that we passed do the following:

- `"-X main.linkerFlag=Hi_Gophers"`: Sets a value for the `linkerFlag` variable in `main`. Being able to add a variable during build time is important as many developers want to add some sort of build parameter to their code during compilation time. We can pass a build date using `` `date -u +.%Y%m%d%.H%M%S` `` or a git commit version using `git rev-list -1 HEAD`. These values can be helpful later for referencing the state of the build.
- `"-s"`: Disables the symbol table, a data structure that stores each identifier in the source code alongside declaration information. This is often not needed for production binaries.
- `"-w"`: Disables DWARF generation. The dwarf table often doesn't need to be saved since the Go binary includes basic type information, PC-to-line data, and a symbol table.

If we build the binary using a standard method followed by using some of the compiler and linker flags we have available, we will be able to see a difference in binary size:

- Non-optimized build:

```
$ go build -ldflags "-X main.linkerFlag=Hi_Gophers" -o nonOptimized
```

- Optimized build:

```
$ go build -gcflags="-N -l" -ldflags "-X main.linkerFlag=Hi_Gophers
-s -w" -o Optimized
```

As we can see, the `Optimized` binary is 28.78% smaller than the `nonOptimized` binary:

```
bob@blinky:~/git/HighPerformanceWithGo/11-deploying-go-code/compilerLinker          ×

 File  Edit  View  Search  Terminal  Help
[bob@blinky compilerLinker]$ go build -ldflags "-X main.linkerFlag=Hi_Gophers" -
o nonOptimized
[bob@blinky compilerLinker]$ go build -gcflags="-N -l" -ldflags "-X main.linkerF
lag=Hi_Gophers -s -w" -o Optimized
[bob@blinky compilerLinker]$ ls -al
total 3204
drwxrwxr-x. 2 bob bob    4096 Sep  8 09:21 .
drwxr-xr-x. 5 bob bob    4096 Sep  8 08:50 ..
-rw-rw-r--. 1 bob bob      92 Sep  8 08:52 compilerLinkerFlags.go
-rwxrwxr-x. 1 bob bob 1906785 Sep  8 09:22 nonOptimized
-rwxrwxr-x. 1 bob bob 1357856 Sep  8 09:22 Optimized
[bob@blinky compilerLinker]$
```

Both of these binaries will perform the same function for the end user, so consider removing some of the build optimizations using compiler and linker flags in order to reduce the end resulting binary size. This can be beneficial during the storage and deployment of said binaries.

Build constraints

If you'd like to add a build constraint to your Go build, you can add a comment line at the beginning of the file that's only preceded by blank lines and other comments. The form of this comment is `// +build darwin,amd64,!cgo, android,386,cgo`.

This corresponds to a boolean output of `darwin AND amd64 AND (NOT cgo)) OR (android AND 386 AND cgo`.

This needs to proceed with the package declaration with a newline between the build constraint and the package initialization. This takes the following form:

```
// +build [OPTIONS]

package main
```

The complete list of build constraints can be found at `https://golang.org/pkg/go/build/` `#hdr-Build_Constraints`. This list includes the following build constraints:

- `GOOS`
- `GOARCH`
- Compiler type (`gc` or `gccgo`)
- `cgo`
- All the 1.x Go versions (no build tags for beta or minor releases)
- Additional words that are listed in `ctxt.BuildTags`

If you have a file in your library that you'd like to exclude from your build, you can also add a comment in the following form:

```
// +build ignore
```

Inversely, you can restrict file builds to specific `GOOS`, `GOARCH`, and `cgo` bits using a comment in the following form:

```
// +build windows, 386, cgo
```

This will only build a file when you're using `cgo` and building on a 386 processor in a Windows operating system. This is a powerful construct in the Go language because you have the ability to build packages based on the necessary build parameters.

Filename conventions

If a file matches the `GOOS` and `GOARCH` patterns after stripping any extensions and the `_test` suffix (for test cases), the file will be built for that particular `GOOS` or `GOARCH` pattern. Patterns like so are often referenced as follows:

- `*_GOOS`
- `*_GOARCH`
- `*_GOOS_GOARCH`

For example, if you have a file that's named `example_linux_arm.go`, it will only be built as part of the Linux arm builds.

In the next section, we will explore the `go clean` command.

Go clean – cleaning your build directory

The Go command builds binaries in a temporary directory. The go clean command was created in order to remove extraneous object files that are created by other tools or when go build is manually invoked. Go clean has a usage stanza of `go clean [clean flags] [build flags] [packages]`.

The following flags are available for the clean command:

- The `-cache` flag removes the entire go build cache. This can be helpful if you're trying to compare a fresh build across multiple systems or if you'd like to see the amount of time a fresh build takes.
- The `-i` flag removes the archive or binary that go install creates.
- The `-n` flag is a noop; printing the result removes commands but doesn't execute them.
- The `r` flag applies logic recursively to all the dependencies of the import path's packages.
- The `-x` flag prints and executes the remove commands that were generated.
- The `-cache` flag removes the whole go build cache.
- The `-testcache` flag removes the test results in the build cache.
- The `-modcache` flag removes the module download cache.

If we want to attempt a clean build with no existing dependencies, we can use a command to remove items from many of the important caches in the go build system. Let's take a look:

1. We will build our `prometheusExporterExample` in order to validate the size of the build cache changing. We can find our build cache location using the go environment `GOCACHE` variable:

```
[bob@blinky promExporter]$ go env | grep GOCACHE
GOCACHE="/home/bob/.cache/go-build"
[bob@blinky promExporter]$
```

2. For our validation, we'll use a couple of commands in a row. First, we'll remove our entire cache directory with `rm -rf ~/.cache/go-build/`.

3. Next, we can build our Go binary by running the `go build prometheusExporterExample.go` command.

4. Then, we can validate that the cache has grown significantly in size by checking its size with `du -sh ~/.cache/go-build/`.

5. Now, we can clean the caches using the go clean program, that is, `go clean -cache -modcache -i -r 2&>/dev/null`.

It's important to note that some of the cache information is stored in main libraries, so that can't be removed by a normal user. We can get around this if needed by running the clean command as a superuser, but this isn't often recommended.

Then, we can validate that the cache has shrunk in size. If we look into the cache directory after the clean, we'll see that we only have three items left in the cache directory:

- A `README` file explaining the directory.
- A `log.txt` file that tells us about cache information.
- A `trim.txt` file, which tells us the time of the last completed cache trim. In the following screenshot, we can see a cleaned build cache:

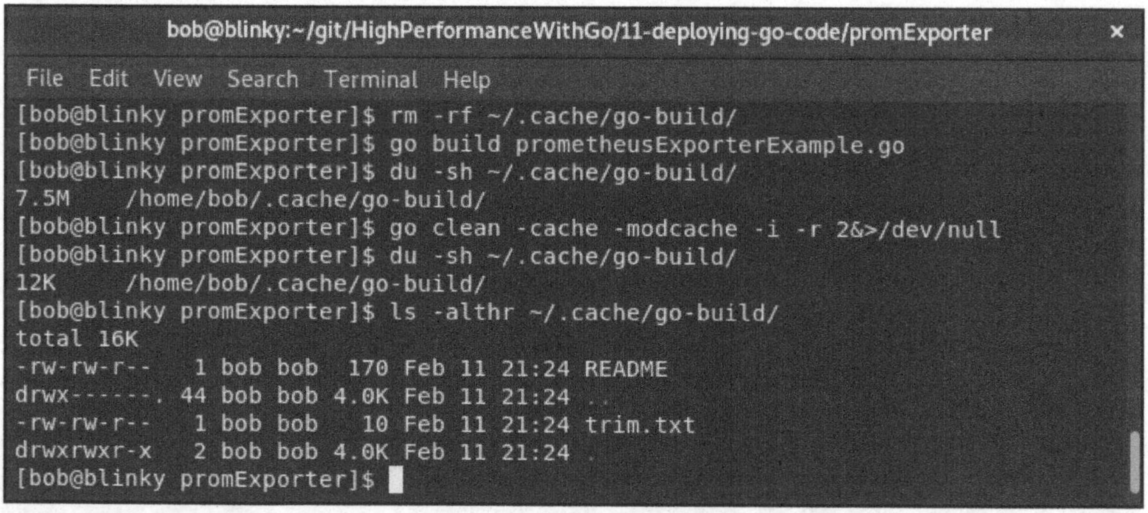

```
bob@blinky:~/git/HighPerformanceWithGo/11-deploying-go-code/promExporter          ×

File   Edit   View   Search   Terminal   Help
[bob@blinky promExporter]$ rm -rf ~/.cache/go-build/
[bob@blinky promExporter]$ go build prometheusExporterExample.go
[bob@blinky promExporter]$ du -sh ~/.cache/go-build/
7.5M     /home/bob/.cache/go-build/
[bob@blinky promExporter]$ go clean -cache -modcache -i -r 2&>/dev/null
[bob@blinky promExporter]$ du -sh ~/.cache/go-build/
12K      /home/bob/.cache/go-build/
[bob@blinky promExporter]$ ls -althr ~/.cache/go-build/
total 16K
-rw-rw-r--    1 bob bob  170 Feb 11 21:24 README
drwx------. 44 bob bob 4.0K Feb 11 21:24 ..
-rw-rw-r--    1 bob bob   10 Feb 11 21:24 trim.txt
drwxrwxr-x   2 bob bob 4.0K Feb 11 21:24 .
[bob@blinky promExporter]$ 
```

Validating that you're caching the correct things as part of the build will speed up the build process and make for a less toilsome development experience.

In the next section, we'll look at the `go get` and `go mod` commands.

Retrieving package dependencies with go get and go mod

As you construct Go programs, you'll likely run into places where you'd like to add dependencies. `go get` downloads and installs packages and their dependencies. The invocation stanza for `go get` is `go get [-d] [-f] [-t] [-u] [-v] [-fix] [-insecure] [build flags] [packages]`.

Go 1.11 added preliminary support for Go modules. We learned how to utilize Go modules in `Chapter 6`, *Composing Readable Go Code*, under the *Go modules* section.

A Go mod vendor is often included as part of the Go build system since we can use vendored dependencies in our Go programs. There are positives and negatives to vendoring dependencies in your code base. Having all of the required dependencies available locally during build time can make the build faster. If the upstream repository that you're using for your build dependencies changes or is removed, you'll have a build failure. This is because your program won't be able to satisfy its upstream dependencies.

The negatives to having vendored dependencies include the fact that vendoring dependencies puts the onus of keeping the packages up to date on the programmer – updates from the upstream such as security updates, performance improvements, and stability enhancements could be lost if a dependency is vendored and not updated.

Many enterprises take the vendored approach as they feel the safety of storing all of the required dependencies outweighs the need to update the vendored directory with newer packages from upstream as they become available.

After we initialize our go module, we vendor our dependencies and build them using our vendored modules:

```
bob@blinky:~/git/HighPerformanceWithGo/11-deploying-go-code/promExporter    ✕

File  Edit  View  Search  Terminal  Help
[bob@blinky promExporter]$ go mod init github.com/bobstrecansky/HighPerformanceW
ithGo/11-deploying-go-code/promExporter
go: creating new go.mod: module github.com/bobstrecansky/HighPerformanceWithGo/1
1-deploying-go-code/promExporter
[bob@blinky promExporter]$ go mod vendor
go: finding github.com/prometheus/client_golang/prometheus/promhttp latest
go: finding github.com/prometheus/client_golang/prometheus latest
[bob@blinky promExporter]$ go build -mod vendor
[bob@blinky promExporter]$ ls -atlhr vendor/
total 20K
drwxrwxr-x. 3 bob bob 4.0K Sep  8 10:43 ..
drwxrwxr-x. 6 bob bob 4.0K Sep  8 10:43 github.com
drwxrwxr-x. 3 bob bob 4.0K Sep  8 10:43 golang.org
-rw-rw-r--. 1 bob bob  924 Sep  8 10:43 modules.txt
drwxrwxr-x. 4 bob bob 4.0K Sep  8 10:43 .
[bob@blinky promExporter]$ ▐
```

As shown in the preceding output, we have vendored dependencies (from `https://github.com/` and `https://golang.org/`) that are needed to satisfy our build constraints in our project. We can use `go mod tidy` in our builds to validate that `go.mod` contains all of the necessary elements for the repository.

`go mod tidy` adds missing modules and removes unused modules in order to validate our source code with the directory's `go.mod` matches.

In the following section, we will learn about the `go list` command.

Go list

`go list` performs the action of listing named packages and modules, as well as displaying important build information about files, imports, and dependencies. The invocation stanza for go list is `usage: go list [-f format] [-json] [-m] [list flags] [build flags] [packages]`.

Having access to the data structures that are the main pieces of the build process is powerful. We can use `go list` to find out a lot about the programs that we are building. For example, take the following simple program, which prints a message and computes a square root for the end user:

```
package main


import (
    "fmt"
    "math"
)


func main() {
    fmt.Println("Hello Gophers")
    fmt.Println(math.Sqrt(64))
}
```

If we want to find out about all the dependencies that we have for our particular project, we can invoke the `go list -f '{{.Deps}}'` command.

The result will be a slice of all of the dependencies that our repository contains:

```
bob@blinky:~/git/HighPerformanceWithGo/11-deploying-go-code/goList                    ×

File   Edit   View   Search   Terminal   Help
[bob@blinky goList]$ go list -f '{{.Deps}}'
[errors fmt internal/bytealg internal/cpu internal/poll internal/race internal/s
yscall/unix internal/testlog io math math/bits os reflect runtime runtime/intern
al/atomic runtime/internal/sys strconv sync sync/atomic syscall time unicode uni
code/utf8 unsafe]
[bob@blinky goList]$ ▮
```

The go list data structure can be found here: https://golang.org/cmd/go/#hdr-List_ packages_or_modules. It has many different parameters. One of the other popular outputs from the go list program is the JSON formatted output. In the following screenshot, you can see the output from executing go list -json for our listExample.go:

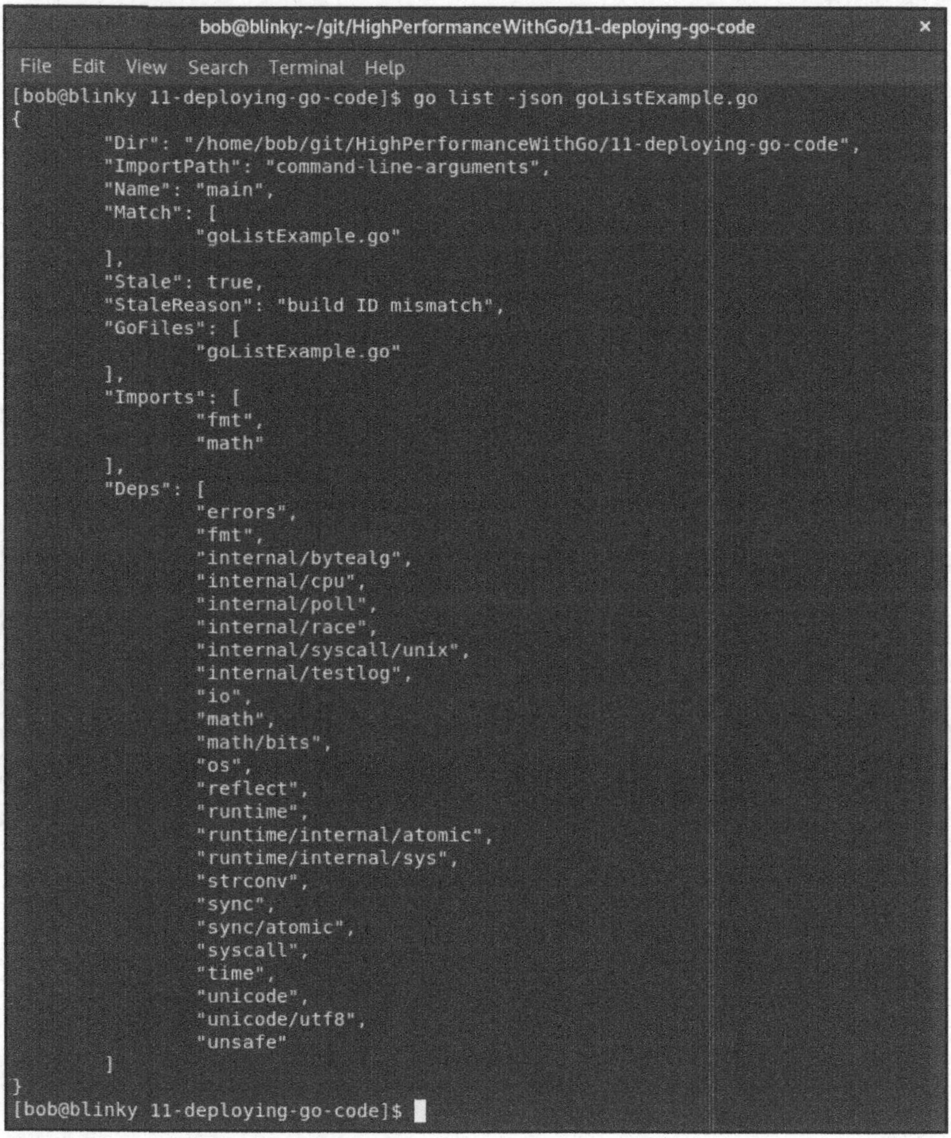

```
bob@blinky:~/git/HighPerformanceWithGo/11-deploying-go-code                          ×

File  Edit  View  Search  Terminal  Help
[bob@blinky 11-deploying-go-code]$ go list -json goListExample.go
{
        "Dir": "/home/bob/git/HighPerformanceWithGo/11-deploying-go-code",
        "ImportPath": "command-line-arguments",
        "Name": "main",
        "Match": [
                "goListExample.go"
        ],
        "Stale": true,
        "StaleReason": "build ID mismatch",
        "GoFiles": [
                "goListExample.go"
        ],
        "Imports": [
                "fmt",
                "math"
        ],
        "Deps": [
                "errors",
                "fmt",
                "internal/bytealg",
                "internal/cpu",
                "internal/poll",
                "internal/race",
                "internal/syscall/unix",
                "internal/testlog",
                "io",
                "math",
                "math/bits",
                "os",
                "reflect",
                "runtime",
                "runtime/internal/atomic",
                "runtime/internal/sys",
                "strconv",
                "sync",
                "sync/atomic",
                "syscall",
                "time",
                "unicode",
                "unicode/utf8",
                "unsafe"
        ]
}
[bob@blinky 11-deploying-go-code]$ 
```

`go list -m -u all` will also show you the dependencies that you have. The resulting output will also have a second version listed in brackets, if they have available upgrades. This can be helpful if we want to closely monitor our dependencies and their upgrades using the `go mod` package.

If we use our Prometheus exporter example, we can see whether or not our packages have dependencies that need upgrading:

```
bob@blinky:~/git/HighPerformanceWithGo/11-deploying-go-code/promExporter      ×

File   Edit   View   Search   Terminal   Help
[bob@blinky promExporter]$ go list -m -u all
go: finding github.com/prometheus/client_model latest
go: finding github.com/modern-go/concurrent latest
go: finding github.com/kr/logfmt latest
go: finding golang.org/x/sync latest
go: finding golang.org/x/crypto latest
go: finding golang.org/x/sys latest
go: finding golang.org/x/net latest
go: finding github.com/mwitkow/go-conntrack latest
go: finding gopkg.in/check.v1 latest
github.com/bobstrecansky/HighPerformanceWithGo/11-deploying-go-code/promExporter
github.com/beorn7/perks v1.0.1
github.com/davecgh/go-spew v1.1.1
github.com/go-kit/kit v0.8.0 [v0.9.0]
github.com/go-logfmt/logfmt v0.4.0
github.com/golang/protobuf v1.3.2
github.com/google/go-cmp v0.3.0 [v0.3.1]
github.com/google/gofuzz v1.0.0
github.com/json-iterator/go v1.1.7
github.com/julienschmidt/httprouter v1.2.0
github.com/konsorten/go-windows-terminal-sequences v1.0.1 [v1.0.2]
github.com/kr/logfmt v0.0.0-20140226030751-b84e30acd515
github.com/matttproud/golang_protobuf_extensions v1.0.1
github.com/modern-go/concurrent v0.0.0-20180306012644-bacd9c7ef1dd
github.com/modern-go/reflect2 v1.0.1
github.com/mwitkow/go-conntrack v0.0.0-20161129095857-cc309e4a2223 [v0.0.0-20190
716064945-2f068394615f]
github.com/pkg/errors v0.8.0 [v0.8.1]
github.com/pmezard/go-difflib v1.0.0
github.com/prometheus/client_golang v1.1.0
github.com/prometheus/client_model v0.0.0-20190129233127-fd36f4220a90 [v0.0.0-20
190812154241-14fe0d1b01d4]
github.com/prometheus/common v0.6.0
github.com/prometheus/procfs v0.0.3 [v0.0.4]
github.com/sirupsen/logrus v1.2.0 [v1.4.2]
github.com/stretchr/objx v0.1.1 [v0.2.0]
github.com/stretchr/testify v1.3.0 [v1.4.0]
golang.org/x/crypto v0.0.0-20190308221718-c2843e01d9a2 [v0.0.0-20190907121410-71
b5226ff739]
```

In this example, we can see that there are a couple of packages that have available upgrades. If we invoke go get for one of these dependencies, we'll be able to upgrade them effectively. We can upgrade the errors package listed in the preceding screenshot from v0.8.0 to v0.8.1 using `go get github.com/pkg/errors@v0.8.1`.

After we complete this upgrade, we can validate that the dependency has been upgraded by running `go list -m -u github.com/pkg/errors`.

We can see this output in the following screenshot:

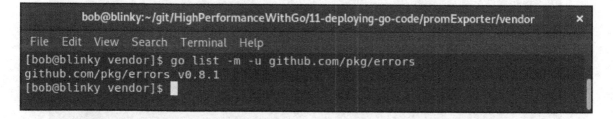

In our preceding output, we can see that the errors package that's being referenced is now v0.8.1, rather than v0.8.0, which was shown in our previous output.

Next, let's take a look at what `go run` is.

Go run – executing your packages

`go run` runs and compiles a named Go program. The invocation stanza for `go run` is `go run [build flags] [-exec xprog] package [arguments...]`.

Go run allows a developer to quickly compile and run a go binary in one operation. During this process, `go run` builds the executable file, runs it, and then deletes the executable file. This is particularly helpful in a development environment. As you rapidly iterate on your Go program, `go run` can be used as a shortcut to validate that the code you are changing will result in a build artifact that you deem acceptable for use. As we learned earlier in this chapter, the build flags for many of these tools are consistent.

`goRun.go` is one of the simplest possible go programs. It has no arguments, just an empty `main()` function invocation. We are using this as an example to show this process with no additional dependencies or overhead:

```
package main
func main() {}
```

We can see the work output associated with a `go run` invocation by executing the `go run -x goRun.go` command.

When we perform this action, we will be able to see the build parameters that are being called as part of the `go run` program:

```
                   bob@blinky:~/git/HighPerformanceWithGo/11-deploying-go-code/goRun          x

  File   Edit   View   Search   Terminal   Help
[bob@blinky goRun]$ go run -x goRun.go
WORK=/tmp/go-build272352258
mkdir -p $WORK/b001/
cat >$WORK/b001/importcfg << 'EOF' # internal
# import config
packagefile runtime=/home/bob/.cache/go-build/f6/f66035ee3750d60d972d10c946891dc
141c0adfe111de4899fd622ec4d98b338-d
EOF
cd /home/bob/git/HighPerformanceWithGo/11-deploying-go-code/goRun
/usr/lib/golang/pkg/tool/linux_amd64/compile -o $WORK/b001/_pkg_.a -trimpath $WO
RK/b001 -p main -complete -buildid uZdSfAgZi5LdEKfj-C4u/uZdSfAgZi5LdEKfj-C4u -dw
arf=false -goversion go1.11.12 -D /home/bob/git/HighPerformanceWithGo/11-deploy
ing-go-code/goRun -importcfg $WORK/b001/importcfg -pack -c=4 ./goRun.go
/usr/lib/golang/pkg/tool/linux_amd64/buildid -w $WORK/b001/_pkg_.a # internal
cp $WORK/b001/_pkg_.a /home/bob/.cache/go-build/68/G80a546071fcd162fcbcad055ef9d
6a9a8bec28df0b3a48e71f1cca671369261-d # internal
cat >$WORK/b001/importcfg.link << 'EOF' # internal
packagefile command-line-arguments=$WORK/b001/_pkg_.a
packagefile runtime=/home/bob/.cache/go-build/f6/f66035ee3750d60d972d10c946891dc
141c0adfe111de4899fd622ec4d98b338-d
packagefile internal/bytealg=/home/bob/.cache/go-build/0f/0f35ff3a238cc5b0289b0d
23bc7d9e9d17acf675c2de62e30ff5d094c3f4e3e0-d
packagefile internal/cpu=/home/bob/.cache/go-build/5f/5fc2feddcb16d176b21694d05f
2d1555df1fba231b5f38dc84e701cc143a2c30-d
packagefile runtime/internal/atomic=/home/bob/.cache/go-build/e6/e600cfc9bd5d973
f25ef4b202401c37c72d7c91228fe947c90902a9ba62260f5-d
packagefile runtime/internal/sys=/home/bob/.cache/go-build/cf/cfb0b97860bd94f74d
50db7e359b3f96ba2abd58b7445ff7c9148949d801a687-d
EOF
mkdir -p $WORK/b001/exe/
cd .
/usr/lib/golang/pkg/tool/linux_amd64/link -o $WORK/b001/exe/goRun -importcfg $WO
RK/b001/importcfg.link -s -w -buildmode=exe -buildid=YmcLafQ0fff_UalwniOY/uZdSfA
gZi5LdEKfj-C4u/14u_Rxgk-or1YP--UMZa/YmcLafQ0fff_UalwniOY -extld=gcc $WORK/b001/_
pkg_.a
$WORK/b001/exe/goRun
[bob@blinky goRun]$
```

This should seem eerily familiar as the output closely resembles the output we saw in our go build example. Then, we can see our package being invoked.

If we were to perform this same action with our Prometheus HTTP server, we would see that our Prometheus HTTP server is started and run as the result of executing the `go run` program. After we kill our process during this go run invocation, we'll notice that we don't have any binaries stored in our local directory. The `go run` invocation doesn't save these outputs by default.

The Go command in the next section (`go install`) is the last one for this chapter. Let's see what it is all about.

Go install – installing your binaries

`go install` compiles and installs a named Go program. The invocation stanza for go run is `go install [-i] [build flags] [packages]`

These are imported to `$GOPATH/pkg`. Cached items will be used on the next compilation if they haven't been modified. The resulting output from go install is an executable file that is the same as the one that gets compiled with a go build command, installed on the `$GOBIN` path on the system. For example, if we wanted to install our Prometheus HTTP server on our host, we could invoke a go install command, that is, `GOBIN=~/prod-binaries/ go install -i prometheusExporterExample.go`.

Setting our `GOBIN` variable tells the compiler where to install the compiled binary after compilation is complete. The go install program allows us to install the binary to our `GOBIN` location. The `-i` flag installs the dependencies of the named packages. We can see this in the following screenshot:

```
bob@blinky:~/git/HighPerformanceWithGo/11-deploying-go-code/promExporter      x

File  Edit  View  Search  Terminal  Help
[bob@blinky promExporter]$ mkdir ~/prod-binaries/
[bob@blinky promExporter]$ GOBIN=~/prod-binaries/ go install -i prometheusExport
erExample.go
[bob@blinky promExporter]$ ls -al ~/prod-binaries/
total 10196
drwxrwxr-x.  2 bob bob     4096 Sep  8 12:43 .
drwx--x--x. 30 bob bob     4096 Sep  8 12:43 ..
-rwxrwxr-x.  1 bob bob 10428886 Sep  8 12:43 prometheusExporterExample
[bob@blinky promExporter]$ 
```

After this is completed, we can see that we have a `prometheusExporterExample` binary available in the `GOBIN` location that we defined in our example.

In the upcoming and the last section of this chapter, we shall see how to build Go binaries with Docker.

Building Go binaries with Docker

Depending on your target architecture, you may wish to build your Go binaries with Docker to maintain a reproducible build, limit your build size, and minimize the attack vectors for your service. Using multistage Docker builds can help us to accomplish this task.

 To perform these actions, you must have a recent version of Docker installed. The multistage builds feature that we are going to use requires Docker version 17.05 or higher in both the daemon and the client. You can find the most recent version of Docker for your OS, as well as instructions on how to install it, at `https://docs.docker.com/install/`.

Consider the following simple package that logs a debug message to the screen:

```
package main
import "go.uber.org/zap"
func main() {
  zapLogger: = zap.NewExample()
  defer zapLogger.Sync()
  zapLogger.Debug("Hi Gophers - from our Zap Logger")
}
```

If we want to build this and execute it within a Docker container while minimizing dependencies, we can use a multistage Docker build. To do so, we can perform the following steps:

1. Initialize the current directory as the root of a module by executing the following:

    go mod init github.com/bobstrecansky/HighPerformanceWithGo/11-deploying-go-code/multiStageDockerBuild

2. Add the `vendor` repositories by executing the following:

    go mod vendor

We now have all of the required vendor packages (in our case, the Zap logger) available in our repository. This can be seen in the following screenshot:

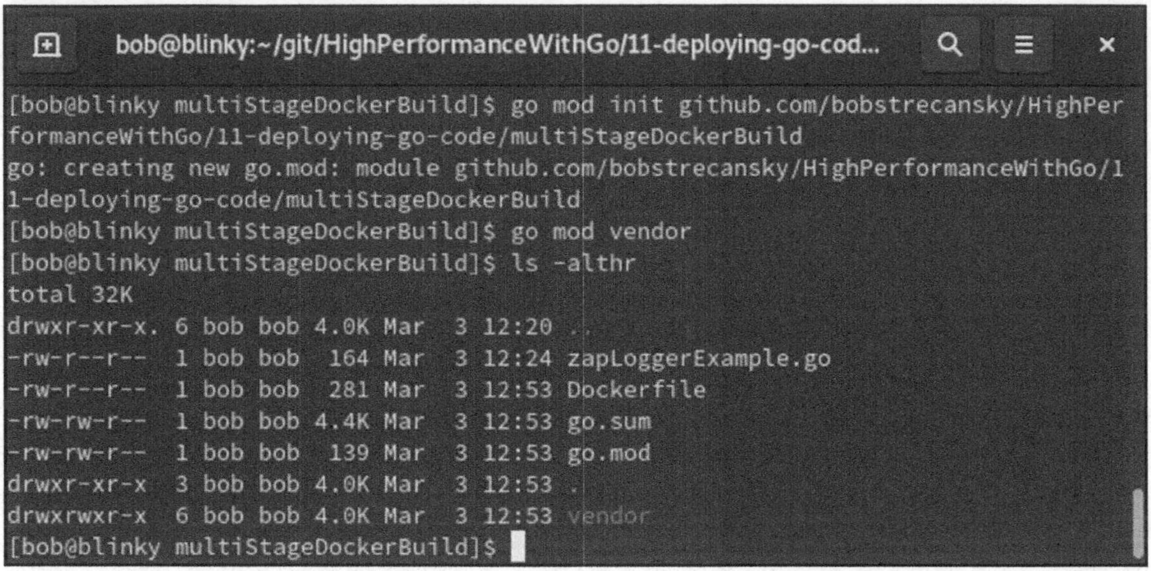

3. Build our `zapLoggerExample` Docker container. We can build our container using the following Dockerfile:

```
# Builder - stage 1 of 2
FROM golang:alpine as builder
COPY . /src
WORKDIR /src
RUN CGO_ENABLED=0 GOOS=linux go build -mod=vendor -o
zapLoggerExample
# Executor - stage 2 of 2
FROM alpine:latest
WORKDIR /src/
COPY --from=builder /src/zapLoggerExample .
CMD ["./zapLoggerExample"]
```

Please note that we use the `golang:alpine` image for building the Go binary, as it's one of the simplest Docker images that contains the necessary elements to successfully build our Go binary. We use the `alpine:latest` image for executing the Go binary, as it's one of the simplest Docker images that contains the necessary elements to successfully run our Go binary.

In this Dockerfile example, we are using a multistage Docker build to build and execute our binary. In stage 1 of 2 (the builder stage), we use a golang alpine image as a base. We copy all of our files from our current directory into the `/src/` directory on the Docker container, we make `/src/` our working directory, and we build our Go binary. Disabling cgo, building for our Linux architecture, and adding the vendor directory we created in *step 1* can all help minimize build size and time.

In stage 2 of 2 (the executor stage), we use a basic alpine Docker image, make `/src/` our working directory, and copy the binary we built in the first stage to this Docker container. We then execute our logger as the final command within this Docker build.

4. After we have our necessary dependencies together, we can build our Docker container. We do this by performing the following command:

    ```
    docker build -t zaploggerexample .
    ```

5. Once we have our Docker container built, we can execute it by performing the following command:

    ```
    docker run -it --rm zaploggerexample
    ```

In the following screenshot, you can see our build and execution steps being completed:

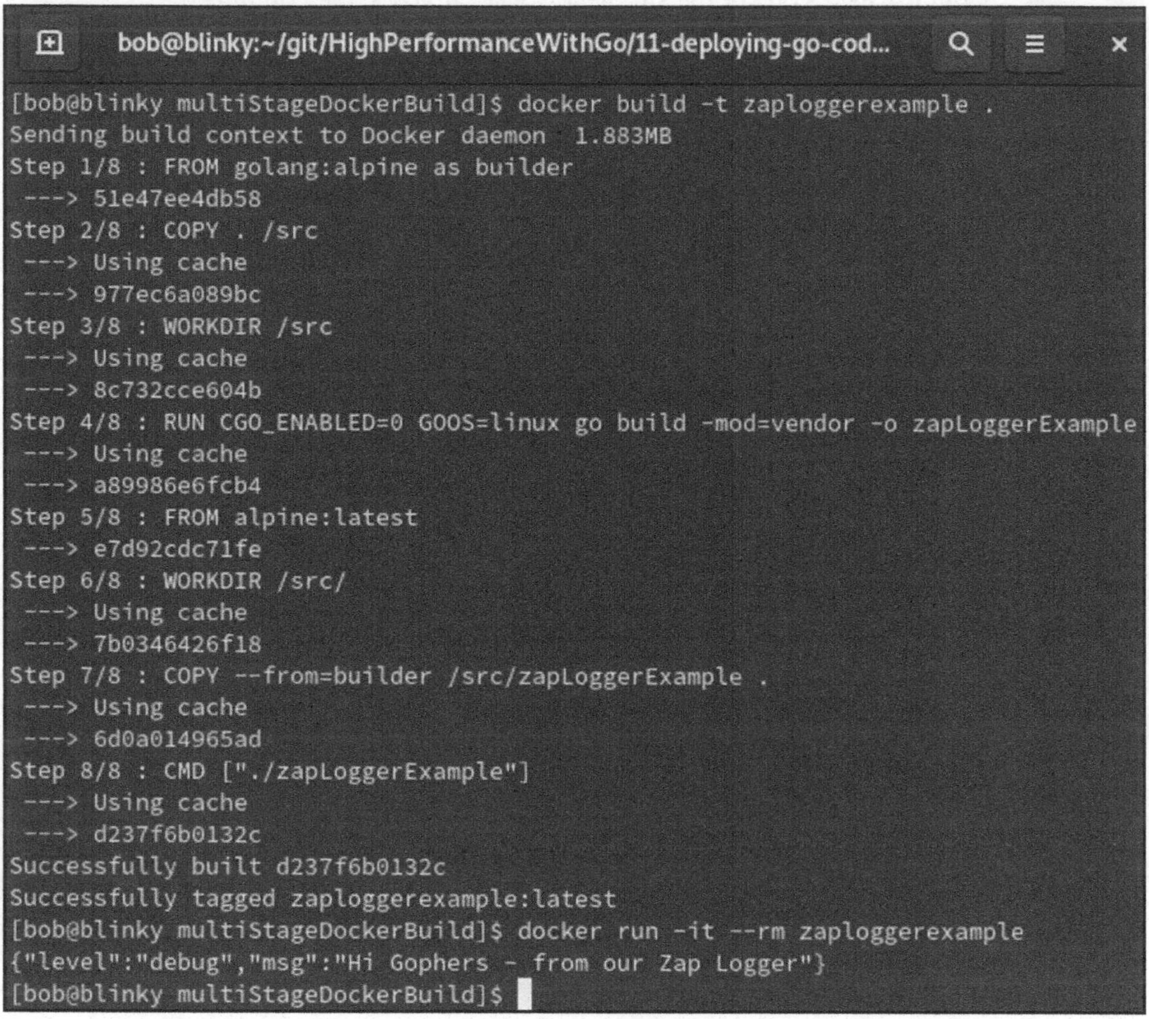

```
 ⊞        bob@blinky:~/git/HighPerformanceWithGo/11-deploying-go-cod...      Q   ☰   ✕

[bob@blinky multiStageDockerBuild]$ docker build -t zaploggerexample .
Sending build context to Docker daemon  1.883MB
Step 1/8 : FROM golang:alpine as builder
 ---> 51e47ee4db58
Step 2/8 : COPY . /src
 ---> Using cache
 ---> 977ec6a089bc
Step 3/8 : WORKDIR /src
 ---> Using cache
 ---> 8c732cce604b
Step 4/8 : RUN CGO_ENABLED=0 GOOS=linux go build -mod=vendor -o zapLoggerExample
 ---> Using cache
 ---> a89986e6fcb4
Step 5/8 : FROM alpine:latest
 ---> e7d92cdc71fe
Step 6/8 : WORKDIR /src/
 ---> Using cache
 ---> 7b0346426f18
Step 7/8 : COPY --from=builder /src/zapLoggerExample .
 ---> Using cache
 ---> 6d0a014965ad
Step 8/8 : CMD ["./zapLoggerExample"]
 ---> Using cache
 ---> d237f6b0132c
Successfully built d237f6b0132c
Successfully tagged zaploggerexample:latest
[bob@blinky multiStageDockerBuild]$ docker run -it --rm zaploggerexample
{"level":"debug","msg":"Hi Gophers - from our Zap Logger"}
[bob@blinky multiStageDockerBuild]$ █
```

Building our Go programs in multistage Docker containers can be helpful in creating reproducible builds, limiting binary size, and minimizing the attack vectors for our services by using only the bits and pieces we need.

Summary

In this chapter, we looked at how to build Go binaries. We learned how to do this effectively and permanently. We also learned how to understand and manage dependencies, test go code with `go run`, and install go binaries to a specific location using go install. Understanding how these binaries work will help you iterate more effectively on your code.

In the next chapter, we'll be looking at how to profile Go code to find functional bottlenecks.

12
Profiling Go Code

Profiling is a practice that can be used to measure the resources utilized in a computer system. Profiling is often done to understand the CPU or memory utilization within a program in order to optimize for execution time, size, or reliability. Alongside profiling, in this chapter, we are going to learn the following:

- How to profile requests in Go with `pprof`
- How to compare multiple profiles
- How to read the resulting profiles and flame graphs

Performing profiling will help you to deduce where you can make improvements within your function and how much time individual pieces take within your function call with respect to the overall system.

Understanding profiling

Profiling Go code is one of the best ways to determine where the bottlenecks are within your code base. We have physical limitations to our computer systems (CPU clock speed, memory size/speed, I/O read/write speeds, and network throughput, to give a few examples), but we can often optimize our programs to more efficiently utilize our physical hardware. After a profile of a computer program is taken with a profiler, a report is created. This report, often called a profile, can tell you information about the program that you ran. There are many reasons why you might want to understand the CPU and memory utilization of your program. A couple of examples are listed as follows:

CPU profiling reasons:

- Check performance improvements in new releases of software
- Validate how much CPU is being utilized for each task
- Limit CPU utilization in order to save money
- Understanding where latency comes from

Memory profiling reasons:

- Incorrect usage of global variables
- Goroutines that don't complete
- Incorrect reflection usage
- Large string allocation

We will next talk about exploring instrumentation methodologies.

Exploring instrumentation methodologies

The `pprof` tool has many different methodologies for incorporating profiling into your code. The Go language creators wanted to make sure that it was simple and effective in implementing the profiling necessary to write performant programs. We can implement profiling in many stages of Go software development—namely, engineering, the creation of new functions, testing, and production.

It is important to remember that profiling does add a small performance penalty, as more metrics are being collected on a continuous basis in your running binaries. Many companies (Google included) feel that this trade-off is acceptable. Adding an additional 5% overhead for CPU and memory profiling is worth the cost in order to consistently write performant code.

Implementing profiling with go test

You can create both CPU and memory profiles using the `go test` command. This can be useful if you'd like to compare the outputs from multiple test runs. These outputs will often be stored in long-term storage for comparison over a longer date range. To execute CPU and memory profiles for a test, execute the `go test -cpuprofile /tmp/cpu.prof -memprofile /tmp/mem.prof -bench` command.

This will create two output files, `cpu.prof` and `mem.prof`, which will both be stored in the `/tmp/` folder. These resulting profiles can be analyzed using the techniques in the *Analyzing profiles* section later in this chapter.

Manually instrumenting profiling in code

If there is a particular place in your code that you'd like to profile specifically, you can implement profiling directly around that code. This can be especially useful if you only want to profile a smaller segment of your code, if you want the pprof output to be smaller and more concise, or if you don't want to add additional overhead to known expensive parts of your code by implementing profiling around them. There are separate methodologies for performing CPU and memory profiling around different segments of a code base.

Profiling CPU utilization for a specific chunk of code would look as follows:

```
function foo() {
pprof.StartCPUProfile()
defer pprof.StopCPUProfile()
...
code
...
}
```

Profiling memory utilization for a specific chunk of code would look as follows:

```
function bar() {
runtime.GC()
defer pprof.WriteHeapProfile()
...
code
...
}
```

Hopefully, we won't have to implement individual segments of code if we design effectively, iterate with impact, and implement our profiling using the idioms from the next section, but it is nice to know that this is always a potential option for profiling code and retrieving meaningful output.

Profiling running service code

The most commonly utilized method for implementing profiling in Go code is enabling the profiler in your HTTP handler function. This can be useful for debugging live production systems. Being able to profile your production system in real time lets you make decisions based on real, live production data, rather than your local development environment.

Sometimes, errors only occur when the order of magnitude of data for a particular system reaches a specific scale. A method or function that can handle 1,000 data points effectively might not be able to handle 1,000,000 data points effectively on the underlying hardware that the function or method is running on. This is especially important while running on hardware that changes. Whether you are running on Kubernetes with noisy neighbors, a new piece of physical hardware with unknown specs, or with a new version of a piece of code or third-party library, understanding the performance impact of changes is paramount in creating reliability and resilience.

Being able to receive the data from a production system, where your end users and the order of magnitude of their data may be larger than what you use locally, can help you to make performance improvements impacting the end user that you might not have ever spotted when iterating locally.

If we'd like to implement the `pprof` library in our HTTP handler, we can use the `net/http/pprof` library. This can be done by importing `_ "net/http/pprof"` into your main package.

Your HTTP handler will then have HTTP handlers registered for your profiling. Make sure that you aren't performing this action on a publicly exposed HTTP server; having the breakdown of your program's profile would expose some serious security vulnerabilities. The index of the `pprof` package displays paths that become available to you when you utilize this package. The following is a screenshot of the index of the `pprof` tool:

We can take a look at the exposed HTTP `pprof` paths and their descriptions. The paths and related descriptions can be found in the following table:

Name	HTTP path	Description
allocs	/debug/pprof/allocs	Memory allocation information.
block	/debug/pprof/block	Information on where the goroutines block waits. This typically happens on synchronization primitives.
cmdline	/debug/pprof/cmdline	Values of the invocation of the command line of our binary.
goroutine	/debug/pprof/goroutine	Stack traces of goroutines that are currently running.
heap	/debug/pprof/heap	Memory allocations sampling (for monitoring memory usage and leaks).
mutex	/debug/pprof/mutex	Contended mutex stack traces.
profile	/debug/pprof/profile	The CPU profile.
symbol	/debug/pprof/symbol	Request program counters.
threadcreate	/debug/pprof/threadcreate	OS thread creation stack traces.
trace	/debug/pprof/trace	Current program trace. This will be discussed in depth in Chapter 13, *Tracing Go Code*.

In the next section, we will discuss CPU profiling.

Briefing on CPU profiling

Let's perform some example profiling on a simple Go program in order to understand how the profiler works. We will create a sample program with a couple of sleep parameters in order to see the timings for different function calls:

1. First, we instantiate our package and add all of our imports:

```
import (
    "fmt"
    "io"
    "net/http"
    _ "net/http/pprof"
    "time"
)
```

2. Next, in our `main` function, we have an HTTP handler that has two sleep functions that are called as part of the handler:

```
func main() {
    Handler := func(w http.ResponseWriter, req *http.Request) {
        sleep(5)
        sleep(10)
        io.WriteString(w, "Memory Management Test")
    }
    http.HandleFunc("/", Handler)
    http.ListenAndServe(":1234", nil)
}
```

Our `sleep` function just sleeps for a particular millisecond duration and prints the resulting output:

```
func sleep(sleepTime int) {
    time.Sleep(time.Duration(sleepTime) * time.Millisecond)
    fmt.Println("Slept for ", sleepTime, " Milliseconds")
}
```

3. When we run our program, we see the output `go run httpProfiling.go`. To generate a profile from this particular code, we need to call `curl -s "localhost:1234/debug/pprof/profile?seconds=10" > out.dump`. This will run a profile for 10 seconds and return the results to a file named `out.dump`. By default, the `pprof` tool will run for 30 seconds and return the binary to `STDOUT`. We want to make sure that we limit the time of this test to something that is reasonable for the test duration, and we need to redirect the output in order to be able to capture something meaningful to look at in our profiling tools.

4. Next, we generate a test load for our function. We can use Apache Bench to accomplish this task, generating 5,000 requests with a concurrency of 10; we set this up using `ab -n 5000 -c 10 http://localhost:1234/`.

5. Once we get the output from this test, we can take a look at our `out.dump` file, `go tool pprof out.dump`. This will take you into the profiler. This is a slight variant of the C++ profiler `pprof`. This tool has quite a bit of functionality.

6. We can use the `topN` command to look at the top *N* samples that are contained in the profile we generated, as shown in the following screenshot:

```
                bob@blinky:~/git/HighPerformanceWithGo/12-profiling-go-code    ×

 File  Edit  View  Search  Terminal  Help
 [bob@blinky 12-profiling-go-code]$ go tool pprof out.dump
 File: httpProfiling
 Type: cpu
 Time: Sep 18, 2019 at 5:07pm (EDT)
 Duration: 10s, Total samples = 190ms ( 1.90%)
 Entering interactive mode (type "help" for commands, "o" for options)
 (pprof) top10
 Showing nodes accounting for 160ms, 84.21% of 190ms total
 Showing top 10 nodes out of 80
       flat  flat%   sum%        cum   cum%
       50ms 26.32% 26.32%       60ms 31.58%  syscall.Syscall
       30ms 15.79% 42.11%       30ms 15.79%  runtime.futex
       10ms  5.26% 47.37%       10ms  5.26%  runtime.casgstatus
       10ms  5.26% 52.63%       10ms  5.26%  runtime.epollctl
       10ms  5.26% 57.89%       10ms  5.26%  runtime.gcTrigger.test
       10ms  5.26% 63.16%       10ms  5.26%  runtime.gentraceback
       10ms  5.26% 68.42%       10ms  5.26%  runtime.mallocgc
       10ms  5.26% 73.68%       10ms  5.26%  runtime.mapiterinit
       10ms  5.26% 78.95%       10ms  5.26%  runtime.rawstring
       10ms  5.26% 84.21%       10ms  5.26%  runtime.reentersyscall
 (pprof)
 (pprof)
```

While the profiler is being executed, Go stops the program roughly 100 times per second. During this time, it records the program counters on the goroutine's stack. We can also use the cumulative flag (-cum) in order to sort by the cumulative values that we have in our current profile sampling:

```
                bob@blinky:~/git/HighPerformanceWithGo/12-profiling-go-code    ×

 File  Edit  View  Search  Terminal  Help
 (pprof) top10 -cum
 Showing nodes accounting for 50ms, 26.32% of 190ms total
 Showing top 10 nodes out of 80
       flat  flat%   sum%        cum   cum%
          0     0%     0%       90ms 47.37%  net/http.(*conn).serve
       50ms 26.32% 26.32%       60ms 31.58%  syscall.Syscall
          0     0% 26.32%       50ms 26.32%  internal/poll.(*FD).Write
          0     0% 26.32%       50ms 26.32%  syscall.Write
          0     0% 26.32%       50ms 26.32%  syscall.write
          0     0% 26.32%       40ms 21.05%  bufio.(*Writer).Flush
          0     0% 26.32%       40ms 21.05%  net.(*conn).Write
          0     0% 26.32%       40ms 21.05%  net.(*netFD).Write
          0     0% 26.32%       40ms 21.05%  net/http.(*response).finishRequest
          0     0% 26.32%       40ms 21.05%  net/http.checkConnErrorWriter.Write
 (pprof)
```

7. We also have the ability to display a visual representation of the trace in graph form. After we make sure that the `graphviz` package is installed (it should be included in your package manager, or it can be downloaded from `http://www.graphviz.org/` by simply typing the `web` command)

This will give us a visual representation of the profile that we generated from within our program:

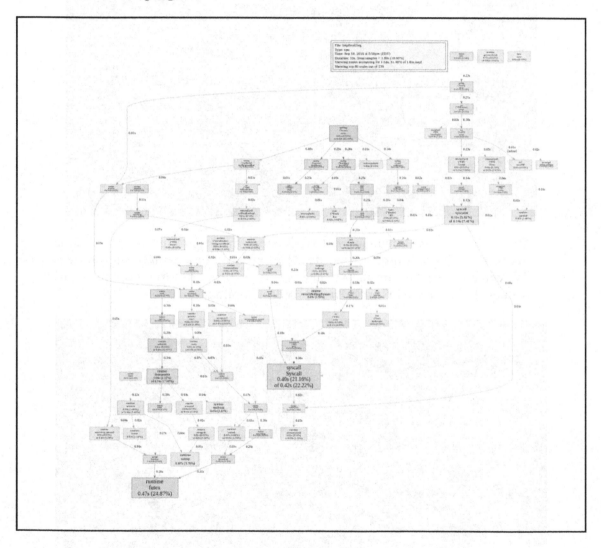

The red boxes in the profile are the code paths that are the most impactful to the request flow. We can take a look at these boxes, and, as we'd expect, we can see that a good portion of our sample program takes time in sleeping and writing responses back to the client. We can take a look at the specific functions in this same web format by passing the name of the function that we want to see a web graph for. For example, if we want to see a detailed view of our `sleep` function, we can just type the `(pprof) web sleep` command.

8. We'll then get an SVG with the image focused on the sleep call:

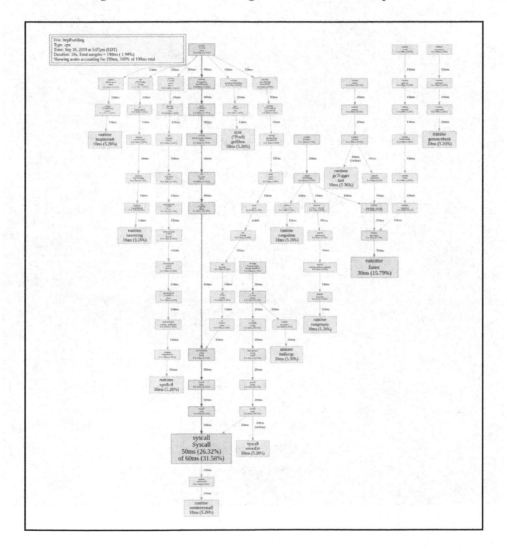

9. After we get this breakdown, we may want to take a look into what the sleep function is actually performing. We can use the `list` command in `pprof` in order to get the output that profiles the invocation of the `sleep` command and its subsequent calls. The following screenshot shows this; the code is shortened for the sake of brevity:

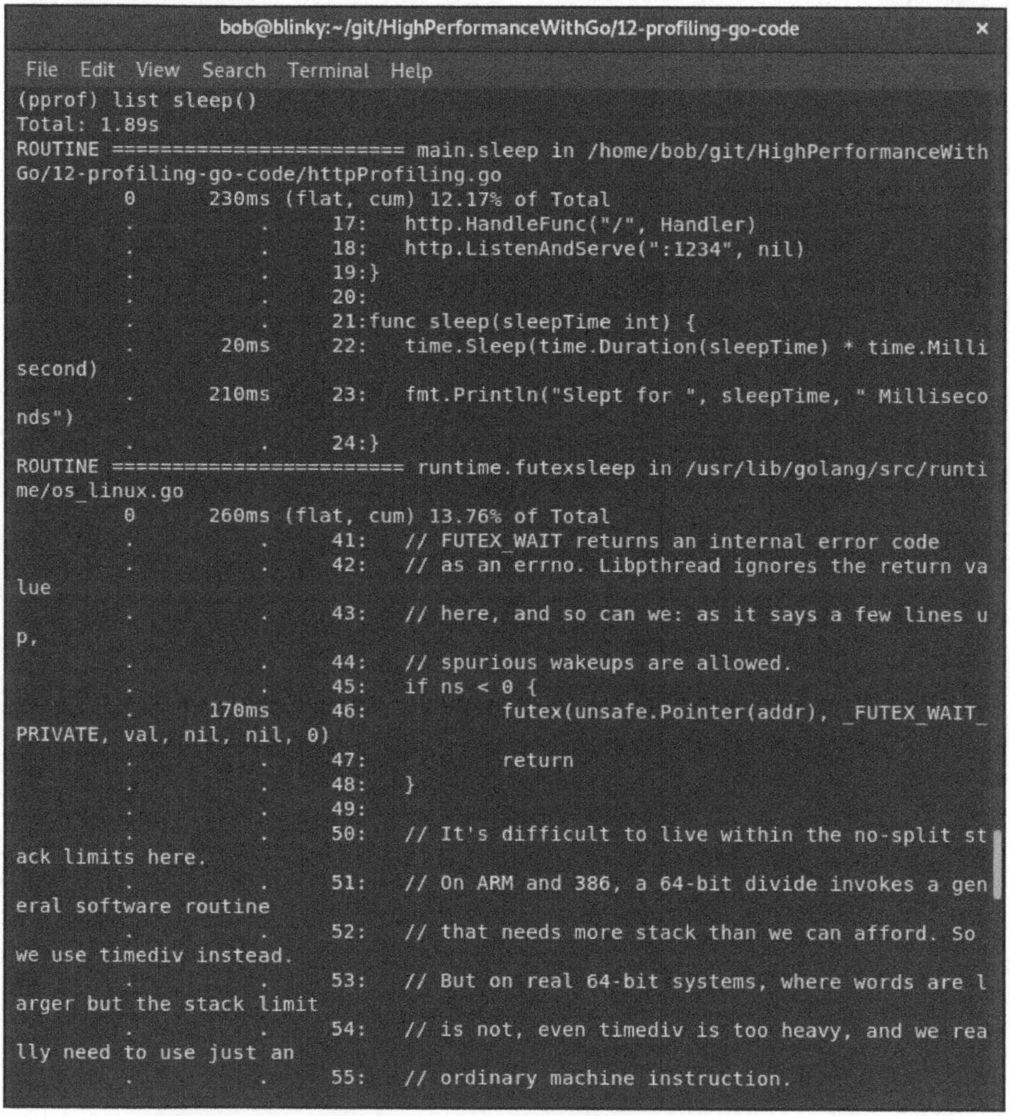

```
bob@blinky:~/git/HighPerformanceWithGo/12-profiling-go-code                    ×

 File  Edit  View  Search  Terminal  Help
(pprof) list sleep()
Total: 1.89s
ROUTINE ======================== main.sleep in /home/bob/git/HighPerformanceWith
Go/12-profiling-go-code/httpProfiling.go
         0      230ms (flat, cum) 12.17% of Total
         .          .         17:    http.HandleFunc("/", Handler)
         .          .         18:    http.ListenAndServe(":1234", nil)
         .          .         19:}
         .          .         20:
         .          .         21:func sleep(sleepTime int) {
         .        20ms        22:    time.Sleep(time.Duration(sleepTime) * time.Milli
second)
         .       210ms        23:    fmt.Println("Slept for ", sleepTime, " Milliseco
nds")
         .          .         24:}
ROUTINE ======================== runtime.futexsleep in /usr/lib/golang/src/runti
me/os_linux.go
         0      260ms (flat, cum) 13.76% of Total
         .          .         41:    // FUTEX_WAIT returns an internal error code
         .          .         42:    // as an errno. Libpthread ignores the return va
lue
         .          .         43:    // here, and so can we: as it says a few lines u
p,
         .          .         44:    // spurious wakeups are allowed.
         .          .         45:    if ns < 0 {
         .       170ms        46:          futex(unsafe.Pointer(addr), _FUTEX_WAIT_
PRIVATE, val, nil, nil, 0)
         .          .         47:          return
         .          .         48:    }
         .          .         49:
         .          .         50:    // It's difficult to live within the no-split st
ack limits here.
         .          .         51:    // On ARM and 386, a 64-bit divide invokes a gen
eral software routine
         .          .         52:    // that needs more stack than we can afford. So
we use timediv instead.
         .          .         53:    // But on real 64-bit systems, where words are l
arger but the stack limit
         .          .         54:    // is not, even timediv is too heavy, and we rea
lly need to use just an
         .          .         55:    // ordinary machine instruction.
```

Being able to break down the work we are doing by profiling into segmentable chunks can tell us a lot about the direction we need to take our development in from a utilization perspective.

In the next section, we will see what memory profiling is.

Briefing on memory profiling

We can perform similar actions to the CPU testing that we did in the previous section with memory. Let's take a look at another method to handle profiling, using the testing functionality. Let's use an example that we created back in Chapter 2, *Data Structures and Algorithms*—the o-logn function. We can use the benchmark that we have already created for this particular function and add some memory profiling to this particular test. We can execute the go test -memprofile=heap.dump -bench command.

We will see a similar output to what we saw in Chapter 2, *Data Structures and Algorithms*:

```
bob@blinky:~/git/HighPerformanceWithGo/2-data-structures-and-algorithms/BigO-notation-o-logn  ×

File   Edit   View   Search   Terminal   Help
[bob@blinky BigO-notation-o-logn]$ go test -memprofile=heap.dump -bench .
goos: linux
goarch: amd64
BenchmarkBinarySearchTimings10-8              50000000              21.8 ns/op
BenchmarkBinarySearchTimings100-8             50000000              31.0 ns/op
BenchmarkBinarySearchTimings200-8             50000000              34.1 ns/op
BenchmarkBinarySearchTimings300-8             30000000              38.2 ns/op
BenchmarkBinarySearchTimings1000-8            30000000              41.6 ns/op
BenchmarkBinarySearchTimings2000-8            30000000              44.6 ns/op
BenchmarkBinarySearchTimings3000-8            30000000              46.7 ns/op
BenchmarkBinarySearchTimings5000-8            30000000              52.4 ns/op
BenchmarkBinarySearchTimings10000-8           30000000              54.1 ns/op
BenchmarkBinarySearchTimings100000-8          20000000              64.3 ns/op
PASS
ok      /home/bob/git/HighPerformanceWithGo/2-data-structures-and-algorithms/Bi
gO-notation-o-logn      14.517s
[bob@blinky BigO-notation-o-logn]$
```

The only difference is that now we'll have the heap profile from this test. If we view it with the profiler, we'll see data about the heap usage rather than the CPU usage. We'll also be able to see the memory allocation for each of our functions in that program. The following diagram illustrates this:

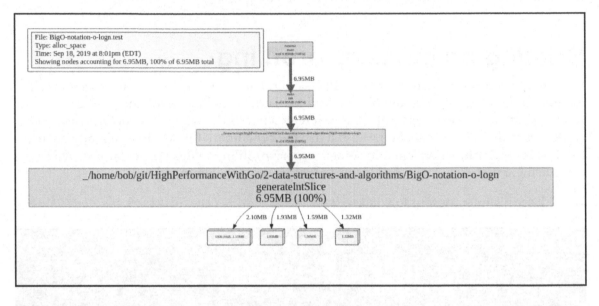

This is helpful, as it enables us to see the generated heap sizes for each of the parts of this code. We can also take a look at the top cumulative memory allocations:

```
bob@blinky:~/git/HighPerformanceWithGo/2-data-structures-and-algorithms/BigO-notation-o-logn  ×

File  Edit  View  Search  Terminal  Help
(pprof) top 5 -cum
Showing nodes accounting for 6.95MB, 100% of 6.95MB total
      flat  flat%   sum%        cum   cum%
   6.95MB   100%   100%     6.95MB   100%  /home/bob/git/HighPerformanceWithGo
/2-data-structures-and-algorithms/BigO-notation-o-logn.generateIntSlice
        0     0%   100%     6.95MB   100%  /home/bob/git/HighPerformanceWithGo
/2-data-structures-and-algorithms/BigO-notation-o-logn.init
        0     0%   100%     6.95MB   100%  main.init
        0     0%   100%     6.95MB   100%  runtime.main
(pprof)
```

As our programs grow more complex, being able to understand the state of the memory utilization becomes more and more important. In the next section, we will discuss how to extend our profiling capabilities with upstream `pprof`.

Extended capabilities with upstream pprof

If we want to be able to use additional functionality by default, we can use the upstream `pprof` binary in order to extend the views we have with our profiles:

1. We can retrieve this with an invocation of `go get` `github.com/google/pprof`. The `pprof` tool has a couple different invocation methods. We can use the report generation method to generate a file in the requested format (currently supported are the `.dot`, `.svg`, `.web`, `.png`, `.jpg`, `.gif`, and `.pdf` formats). We can also use the interactive terminal format in a similar way to what we did in the previous sections about CPU and memory profiling. The last and most commonly used method is using the HTTP server. This method involves hosting an HTTP server that includes much of the pertinent output in an easily digestible format.

2. Once we have retrieved the binary via `go get`, we can invoke it with a web interface, looking at an output that we generated previously: `pprof -http=:1234 profile.dump`.

3. We can then visit the newly available UI and see the features and functionality that were not built into the default `pprof` tool. A couple of the key highlights available from this tool are as follows:
   - A regex searchable form field to help with searching for necessary profiling elements
   - A drop-down view menu for easy viewing of the different profiling tools available
   - A sample dropdown to display the samples from the profile
   - A refine filter for hiding/showing different parts of the request flow

Having all of these tools at our disposal for profiling helps to make the profiling process more streamlined. If we want to take a look at the time that is taken to run anything with a `fmt` in the name of the call, we can use the sample view with the regex filter, and it'll highlight the `fmt` calls, as we can see in the following screenshot:

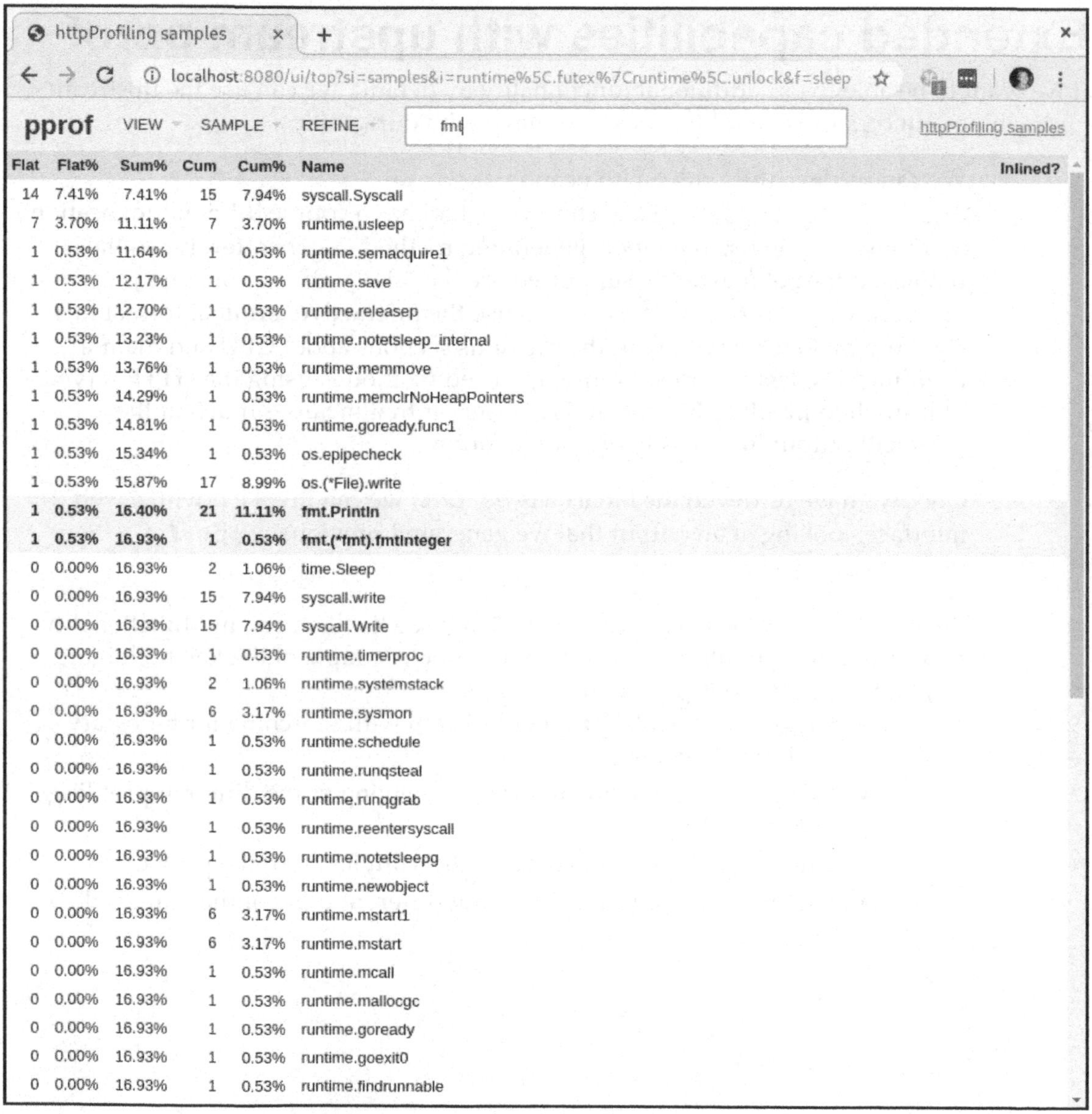

Flat	Flat%	Sum%	Cum	Cum%	Name	Inlined?
14	7.41%	7.41%	15	7.94%	syscall.Syscall	
7	3.70%	11.11%	7	3.70%	runtime.usleep	
1	0.53%	11.64%	1	0.53%	runtime.semacquire1	
1	0.53%	12.17%	1	0.53%	runtime.save	
1	0.53%	12.70%	1	0.53%	runtime.releasep	
1	0.53%	13.23%	1	0.53%	runtime.notetsleep_internal	
1	0.53%	13.76%	1	0.53%	runtime.memmove	
1	0.53%	14.29%	1	0.53%	runtime.memclrNoHeapPointers	
1	0.53%	14.81%	1	0.53%	runtime.goready.func1	
1	0.53%	15.34%	1	0.53%	os.epipecheck	
1	0.53%	15.87%	17	8.99%	os.(*File).write	
1	0.53%	16.40%	21	11.11%	**fmt.Println**	
1	0.53%	16.93%	1	0.53%	**fmt.(*fmt).fmtInteger**	
0	0.00%	16.93%	2	1.06%	time.Sleep	
0	0.00%	16.93%	15	7.94%	syscall.write	
0	0.00%	16.93%	15	7.94%	syscall.Write	
0	0.00%	16.93%	1	0.53%	runtime.timerproc	
0	0.00%	16.93%	2	1.06%	runtime.systemstack	
0	0.00%	16.93%	6	3.17%	runtime.sysmon	
0	0.00%	16.93%	1	0.53%	runtime.schedule	
0	0.00%	16.93%	1	0.53%	runtime.runqsteal	
0	0.00%	16.93%	1	0.53%	runtime.runqgrab	
0	0.00%	16.93%	1	0.53%	runtime.reentersyscall	
0	0.00%	16.93%	1	0.53%	runtime.notetsleepg	
0	0.00%	16.93%	1	0.53%	runtime.newobject	
0	0.00%	16.93%	6	3.17%	runtime.mstart1	
0	0.00%	16.93%	6	3.17%	runtime.mstart	
0	0.00%	16.93%	1	0.53%	runtime.mcall	
0	0.00%	16.93%	1	0.53%	runtime.mallocgc	
0	0.00%	16.93%	1	0.53%	runtime.goready	
0	0.00%	16.93%	1	0.53%	runtime.goexit0	
0	0.00%	16.93%	1	0.53%	runtime.findrunnable	

Being able to filter according to these values can be helpful in narrowing the scope of your ill-performing function.

Comparing multiple profiles

One of the really nice features of profiling is that you can compare profiles with one another. If we have two separate measurements from the same program, we can determine whether or not the change we made is having a positive impact on the system. Let's augment our HTTP sleep timing function a little bit:

1. Let's add a few extra imports:

```
package main

import (
  "fmt"
  "net/http"
  _ "net/http/pprof"
  "strconv"
  "time"
)
```

2. Next, we'll augment our handler to take a query string parameter for time:

```
func main() {
    Handler := func(w http.ResponseWriter, r *http.Request) {
        sleepDuration := r.URL.Query().Get("time")
        sleepDurationInt, err := strconv.Atoi(sleepDuration)
        if err != nil {
            fmt.Println("Incorrect value passed as a query string
for time")
            return
        }
        sleep(sleepDurationInt)
        fmt.Fprintf(w, "Slept for %v Milliseconds", sleepDuration)
    }
    http.HandleFunc("/", Handler)
    http.ListenAndServe(":1234", nil)
}
```

3. We'll leave our sleep function exactly the same:

```
func sleep(sleepTime int) {
    time.Sleep(time.Duration(sleepTime) * time.Millisecond)
    fmt.Println("Slept for ", sleepTime, " Milliseconds")
}
```

4. Now that we have this extra functionality, we can take multiple profiles with different timings just by passing a query parameter to our HTTP handler:

   - We can run our new timed profiling tool:

   ```
   go run timedHttpProfiling.go
   ```

   - In another Terminal, we can start our profiling tool:

   ```
   curl -s "localhost:1234/debug/pprof/profile?seconds=20" >
   5-millisecond-profile.dump
   ```

   - We can then make many requests for our new resource:

   ```
   ab -n 10000 -c 10 http://localhost:1234/?time=5
   ```

   - We can then gather a second profile:

   ```
   curl -s "localhost:1234/debug/pprof/profile?seconds=20" >
   10-millisecond-profile.dump
   ```

   - Then we make a second request for our new resource, generating a second profile:

   ```
   ab -n 10000 -c 10 http://localhost:1234/?time=10
   ```

5. We now have two separate profiles available, which are stored in `5-millisecond-profile.dump` and `10-millisecond-profile.dump`. We can compare these using the same tools as before, setting a base profile and a secondary profile. The following screenshot illustrates this:

```
                  bob@blinky:~/git/HighPerformanceWithGo/12-profiling-go-code        ✕

  File  Edit  View  Search  Terminal  Help
[bob@blinky 12-profiling-go-code]$ pprof -base 5-millisecond-profile.dump 10-mil
lisecond-profile.dump
File: timedHttpProfiling
Type: cpu
Time: Sep 19, 2019 at 6:03pm (EDT)
Duration: 40s, Total samples = 3.30s ( 8.25%)
Entering interactive mode (type "help" for commands, "o" for options)
(pprof) top10 -cum
Showing nodes accounting for -0.22s, 6.67% of 3.30s total
Dropped 10 nodes (cum <= 0.02s)
Showing top 10 nodes out of 306
      flat  flat%   sum%        cum   cum%
    -0.14s  4.24%  4.24%     -0.14s  4.24%  runtime.usleep
    -0.13s  3.94%  8.18%     -0.13s  3.94%  runtime.futex
     0.01s   0.3%  7.88%     -0.12s  3.64%  net/http.(*conn).serve
         0     0%  7.88%     -0.12s  3.64%  runtime.futexwakeup
         0     0%  7.88%     -0.11s  3.33%  runtime.notewakeup
     0.01s   0.3%  7.58%     -0.09s  2.73%  runtime.systemstack
         0     0%  7.58%      0.08s  2.42%  internal/poll.(*FD).Accept
    -0.01s   0.3%  7.88%      0.08s  2.42%  net.(*netFD).accept
     0.06s  1.82%  6.06%      0.08s  2.42%  syscall.Syscall
    -0.02s  0.61%  6.67%     -0.07s  2.12%  net/textproto.(*Reader).ReadMIMEHead
er
(pprof) █
```

Comparing profiles allows us to understand how changes impact our systems.

Let's move on to flame graphs in the next section.

Interpreting flame graphs within pprof

One of the most helpful/useful tools in the upstream `pprof` package is the flame graph. A flame graph is a fixed-rate sampling visualization that can help to determine hot codepaths in a profile. As your programs get more and more complex, the profiles become larger and larger. It will often become difficult to know exactly what codepath is eating up the most CPU, or, as I often like to call it, *the long pole in the tent*.

Flame graphs were originally developed by Brendan Gregg at Netflix to solve a MySQL CPU utilization problem. The advent of this visualization has helped many programmers and system administrators determine what the source of latency is in their program. The `pprof` binary produces an icicle-style (flames pointing downward) flame graph. In a flame graph, we have data visualized in a specific frame:

- The *x* axis is the collection of all of the samples from our request
- The y axis shows the number of frames that are on the stack, also often known as the stack depth
- The width of the box shows the total amount of CPU time a particular function call used

These three things visualized together helps to determine which part of the program introduces the most latency. You can visit the flame graph section of the `pprof` profile at `http://localhost:8080/ui/flamegraph`. The following image shows an example of such a flame graph:

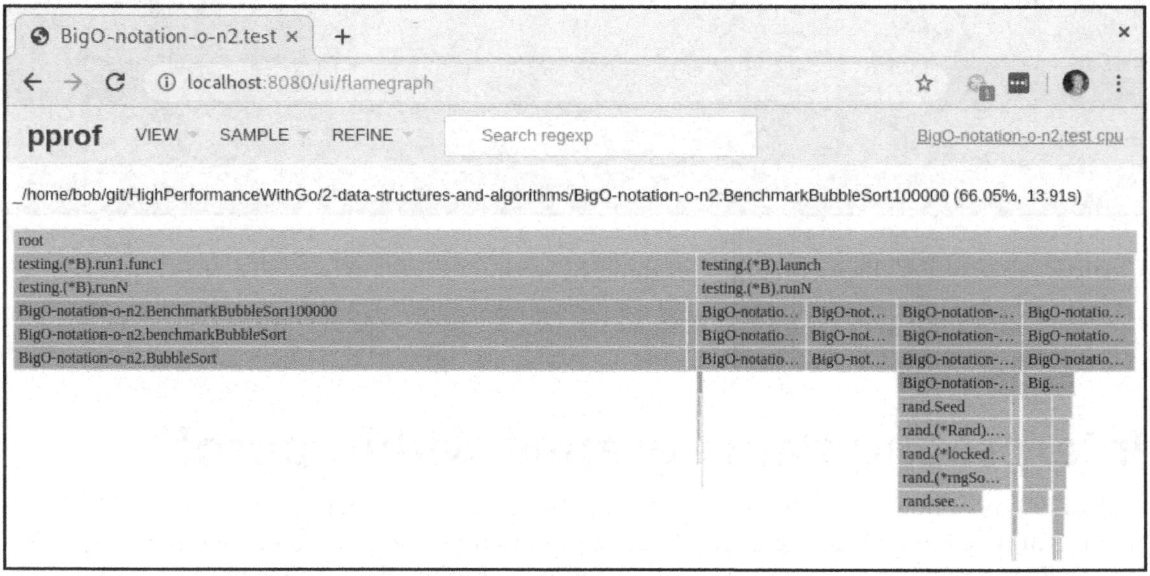

If we look at our `bubbleSort` example from `Chapter 2`, *Data Structures and Algorithms*, we can see the breakdown of the different bits that take up CPU time in our tests. In the interactive web mode, we can hover over each of these samples and validate their duration and percentage execution time.

In the upcoming section, we will see how to detect memory leaks in Go.

Detecting memory leaks in Go

As discussed in the *Memory object allocation* section of `Chapter 8`, *Memory Management in Go*, we have a myriad of tools at our disposal to view the current memory statistics for our currently executing program. In this chapter, we will also learn about profiling using the pprof tool. One of the more common Go memory leaks is the unbounded creation of goroutines. This happens frequently when you overload an unbuffered channel or you have an abstraction with a lot of concurrency spawning new goroutines that don't finish. Goroutines have a very small footprint and systems can often spawn a very large number of them, but they eventually have an upper bound that becomes taxing to find when trying to troubleshoot your program in a production environment.

In the following example, we are going to look at an unbuffered channel that has a leaky abstraction:

1. We start by initializing our package and importing our necessary dependencies:

```
package main

import (
 "fmt"
 "net/http"

 _ "net/http/pprof"
 "runtime"
 "time"
)
```

2. In our main function, we handle HTTP listening to and serving the `leakyAbstraction` function. We are serving this over HTTP in order to make it simple to see the number of goroutines grow:

```
func main() {
 http.HandleFunc("/leak", leakyAbstraction)
 http.ListenAndServe("localhost:6060", nil)
}
```

3. In our `leakyAbstraction` function, we first initialize an unbuffered string channel. We then endlessly iterate through a for loop, writing the number of goroutines to the HTTP response writer and writing the result of our `wait()` function to the channel:

```
func leakyAbstraction(w http.ResponseWriter, r *http.Request) {
 ch := make(chan string)
```

```
    for {
        fmt.Fprintln(w, "Number of Goroutines: ",
runtime.NumGoroutine())
        go func() { ch <- wait() }()
    }
}
```

4. Our `wait()` function sleeps for five microseconds and returns a string:

```
func wait() string {
    time.Sleep(5 * time.Microsecond)
    return "Hello Gophers!"
}
```

These functions together will spawn goroutines until the runtime is no longer able to do so and dies. We can test this by running our server by executing the following command:

go run memoryLeak.go

After the server is running, in a separate Terminal window, we can make a request to our server with the following command:

curl localhost:6060/leak

The `curl` command will print the number of goroutines generated until the server is killed:

```
Number of Goroutines:  4325392          [bob@blinky memoryLeakTest]$ go run memoryLeak.go
Number of Goroutines:  4325393          signal: killed
Number of Goroutines:  4325394          [bob@blinky memoryLeakTest]$
Number of Goroutines:  4325395
Number of Goroutines:  4325396
Number of Goroutines:  4325397
Number of Goroutines:  4325398
Number of Goroutines:  4325399
Number of Goroutines:  4325400
Number of Goroutines:  4325401
Number of Goroutines:  4325402
Number of Goroutines:  4325403
Number of Goroutines:  4325404
Number of Goroutines:  4325405
Number of Goroutines:  4325406
Number of Goroutines:  4325407
Number of Goroutines:  4325408
Number of Goroutines:  4325409
Number of Goroutines:  4325410
Number of Goroutines:  4325411
Number of Goroutines:  4325412
Number of Goroutines:  4325413
curl: (18) transfer closed with outstanding read data remaining
Number [bob@blinky memoryLeakTest]$
```

 Please note that this request may take a while depending on the specifications of your system. This is okay—it illustrates the number of goroutines that your program has available for use.

Using the techniques we learn in this chapter, we will be able to further debug memory issues like this one with pprof, but understanding the underlying problems will help us to avoid memory issues.

This example was written in order to explicitly show a memory leak, but if we wanted to make this executable not leak goroutines, we'd have to fix two things:

- Our unbounded for loop should most likely have a bound
- We could add a buffered channel in order to make sure we have the ability to process all the spawned goroutines that come in through the channel

Summary

In this chapter, we have learned about profiles—what profiles are and how to generate profiles using pprof. You also learned how to analyze profiles using different methodologies, how to compare profiles, and how to read flame graphs for performance. Being able to perform this action in a production environment will help you to maintain stability, improve performance, and give your end user a better end user experience. In the next chapter, we will discuss another methodology of analyzing code—tracing.

13
Tracing Go Code

Tracing Go programs is a fantastic way to check the interoperability between functions and services within your Go program. Tracing allows you to pass context through your system and evaluate where you are being held up, whether it's by a third-party API call, a slow messaging queue, or an $O(n^2)$ function. Tracing will help you to find where this bottleneck resides. In this chapter, we're going to learn the following:

- The process of implementing tracing
- The process of sampling with tracing
- The process of interpreting tracing
- The process of comparing traces

Being able to implement tracing and interpret the results will help developers to understand and troubleshoot their distributed systems.

Implementing tracing instrumentation

Go's concurrency model uses goroutines, and is very powerful. One of the drawbacks of having high concurrency is that you will experience difficulty when you attempt to debug that high-concurrency model. To avoid this difficulty, the language creators created `go tool trace`. They then distributed this in Go version 1.5 in order to be able to investigate and resolve concurrency issues. The Go tracing tool hooks into the goroutine scheduler so that it can produce meaningful information about goroutines. Some of the implementation details that you may want to investigate with Go tracing include the following:

- Latency
- Contention of resources
- Poor parallelism
- I/O-related events

- Syscalls
- Channels
- Locks
- **Garbage Collection (GC)**
- Goroutines

Troubleshooting all of these issues will help you to build a more resilient distributed system. In the next section, we are going to discuss the tracing format and how it's applicable to Go code.

Understanding the tracing format

Go traces can have lots of information and can capture a lot of requests per second. The traces are therefore captured in a binary format. The structure of the trace output is static. In the following output, we can see that the traces follow a specific pattern—they are defined, and events are categorized with a hex prefix and some information about the specific trace event. Looking at this trace format will help us to understand how the events of our traces are stored and retrieved with the tooling that the Go team has made available to us:

```
Trace = "gotrace" Version {Event} .

Event = EventProcStart | EventProcStop | EventFreq | EventStack |
EventGomaxprocs | EventGCStart | EventGCDone | EventGCScanStart |
EventGCScanDone | EventGCSweepStart | EventGCSweepDone | EventGoCreate |
EventGoStart | EventGoEnd | EventGoStop | EventGoYield | EventGoPreempt |
EventGoSleep | EventGoBlock | EventGoBlockSend | EventGoBlockRecv |
EventGoBlockSelect | EventGoBlockSync | EventGoBlockCond | EventGoBlockNet
| EventGoUnblock | EventGoSysCall | EventGoSysExit | EventGoSysBlock |
EventUser | EventUserStart | EventUserEnd .

EventProcStart = "\x00" ProcID MachineID Timestamp .
EventProcStop = "\x01" TimeDiff .
EventFreq = "\x02" Frequency .
EventStack = "\x03" StackID StackLen {PC} .
EventGomaxprocs = "\x04" TimeDiff Procs .
EventGCStart = "\x05" TimeDiff StackID .
EventGCDone = "\x06" TimeDiff .
EventGCScanStart= "\x07" TimeDiff .
EventGCScanDone = "\x08" TimeDiff .
EventGCSweepStart = "\x09" TimeDiff StackID .
EventGCSweepDone= "\x0a" TimeDiff .
EventGoCreate = "\x0b" TimeDiff GoID PC StackID .
```

```
EventGoStart = "\x0c" TimeDiff GoID .
EventGoEnd = "\x0d" TimeDiff .
EventGoStop = "\x0e" TimeDiff StackID .
EventGoYield = "\x0f" TimeDiff StackID .
EventGoPreempt = "\x10" TimeDiff StackID .
EventGoSleep = "\x11" TimeDiff StackID .
EventGoBlock = "\x12" TimeDiff StackID .
EventGoBlockSend= "\x13" TimeDiff StackID .
EventGoBlockRecv= "\x14" TimeDiff StackID .
EventGoBlockSelect = "\x15" TimeDiff StackID .
EventGoBlockSync= "\x16" TimeDiff StackID .
EventGoBlockCond= "\x17" TimeDiff StackID .
EventGoBlockNet = "\x18" TimeDiff StackID .
EventGoUnblock = "\x19" TimeDiff GoID StackID .
EventGoSysCall = "\x1a" TimeDiff StackID .
EventGoSysExit = "\x1b" TimeDiff GoID .
EventGoSysBlock = "\x1c" TimeDiff .
EventUser = "\x1d" TimeDiff StackID MsgLen Msg .
EventUserStart = "\x1e" TimeDiff StackID MsgLen Msg .
EventUserEnd = "\x1f" TimeDiff StackID MsgLen Msg .
```

 More information about the Go execution tracer can be found in the
original specification document by Dmitry Vyukov, published at `https:/
/docs.google.com/document/u/1/d/1FP5apqzBgr7ahCCgFO-
yoVhk4YZrNIDNf9RybngBc14/pub`.

Being able to see all these elements of a trace can help us to understand how to break traces
down into atomic chunks. In the next section, we'll be discussing trace collection.

Understanding trace collection

Being able to collect traces is integral to implementing tracing in your distributed system. If
we don't aggregate these traces somewhere, we won't be able to make sense of them at
scale. There are three methods with which we can collect trace data:

- Manually invoking the tracing of the data by calling `trace.Start` and
  `trace.Stop`
- Using the test flag `-trace=[OUTPUTFILE]`
- Instrumenting the `runtime/trace` package

In order to understand how to implement tracing around your code, let's take a look at a simple example program:

1. We first instantiate our package and import the necessary packages:

```
package main

import (
    "os"
    "runtime/trace"
)
```

2. We then invoke our `main` function. We write the trace output to a file, `trace.out`, which we will use later:

```
func main() {

    f, err := os.Create("trace.out")
    if err != nil {
        panic(err)
    }

    defer f.Close()
```

3. Next, we implement the trace that we want to use in our program and we defer the end of the trace until the return of the function:

```
err = trace.Start(f)
if err != nil {
    panic(err)
}

defer trace.Stop()
```

4. We then write the code that we want to implement. Our example here is just a simple pass of the string `"Hi Gophers"` across a channel in an anonymous function:

```
ch := make(chan string)
go func() {
    ch <- "Hi Gophers"
}()
<-ch
}
```

Now that we have our trace implemented around our (admittedly simple) program, we need to execute our program to produce a trace output:

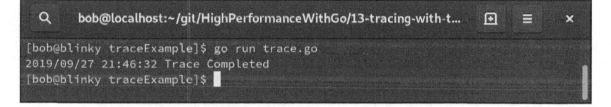

5. To view traces, you may need to install additional packages. For the Fedora system I'm testing on, I had to install an additional `golang-misc` package: `sudo dnf install golang-misc`.
6. After you create a trace, you can open the trace that you created using the `go tool trace trace.out` command.

This makes it possible for you to start the HTTP server that will serve the trace output. We can see this output in the following screenshot:

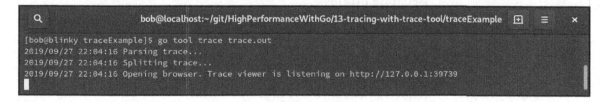

We can see the resulting trace output in a Chrome browser. It's important to mention that we need to use a compatible browser, namely Chrome. At the time of writing this book, Firefox will produce a blank page for a trace output. Here is the output of the trace in a Chrome browser:

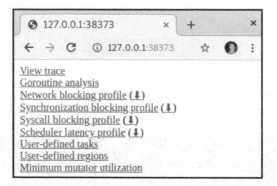

This HTML page gives you a bunch of different useful output choices. Let's look at them one by one in the following table:

Link	Description
View trace	View the GUI trace output.
Goroutine analysis	Displays distinct goroutine information.
Network blocking profile	Displays network blocking; can create a separate profile.
Synchronization blocking profile	Displays synchronization blocking; can create a separate profile.
Syscall blocking profile	Displays syscall blocking; can create a separate profile.
Scheduler latency profile	Shows all the latency associated with the scheduler; can create a separate profile.
User-defined tasks	Allows for the viewing of the task data type; used for tracing a user-defined, logical operation. This is called using the format `trace.NewTask()`.
User-defined regions	Allows for the viewing of the region data type; used for tracing a region of code. This is called using the format `trace.WithRegion()`.
Minimum mutator utilization	Creates a visual plot of where and when the garbage collector is stealing work from your program. This helps you know whether or not your production service is GC-bound.

We can start by looking at the trace in our web browser:

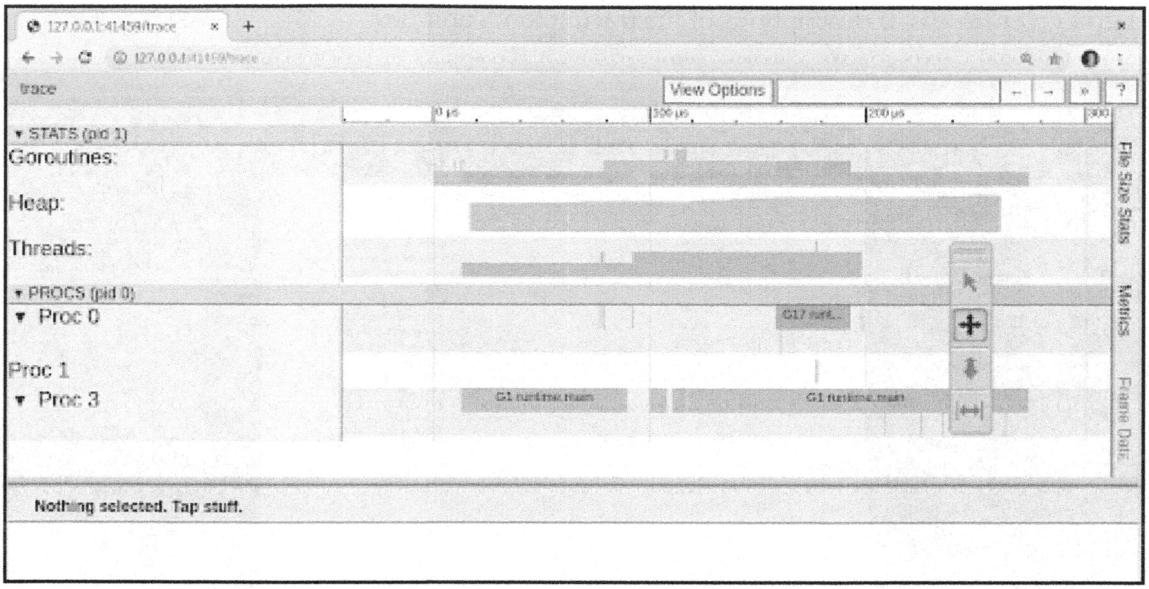

One of the first things we can do when we look at these traces is to look at the help menu, available in the question mark box in the top-right corner of the screen. This information menu gives us lots of descriptions of the tracing tool's abilities:

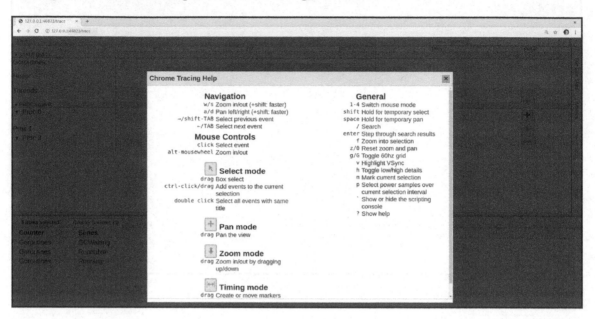

Being able to quickly and effectively move about in the tracing window will help you to look through the trace very quickly. This can be exceptionally helpful when you are trying to troubleshoot a production problem quickly.

Movement in the tracing window

Using the classic *WASD* movement keys (inspired by lots of first-person role-playing video games), we can move around the trace. The movement keys are described as follows:

- The *W* key zooms into the trace's timing window.
- The *S* key zooms out.

- The *A* key goes backward in time.
- The *D* key moves forward in time. We can also go backward and forward in time by clicking and dragging the mouse.

Using the mouse pointer selector or clicking on the number keys allows us to manipulate timing information. The keypad changes are listed in the following bullet points:

- The *1* key lets us select the part of the trace that we'd like to inspect
- The *2* key allows us to pan
- The *3* key invokes the zoom functionality
- The *4* key allows us to select a specific timing

We can now use the / key to search through the trace and the *Enter* key to step through the results.

We also have file-size stats, metrics, frame data, and input latency windows that are available on the right-hand side of the screen. When clicked, these buttons will open a popup that will tell you more details about each of these particular statistics within the trace.

If we click on the blue area in the goroutines row in the trace, we can take a look at some of the available stats we have for our goroutines:

- The GCWaiting, which is the amount of garbage collection runs that are waiting (currently with a value of 0)
- The number of runnable goroutines (currently with a value of 1)
- The number of running goroutines (currently with a value of 1)

We can see a sampling of the available stats for our goroutines in the following screenshot:

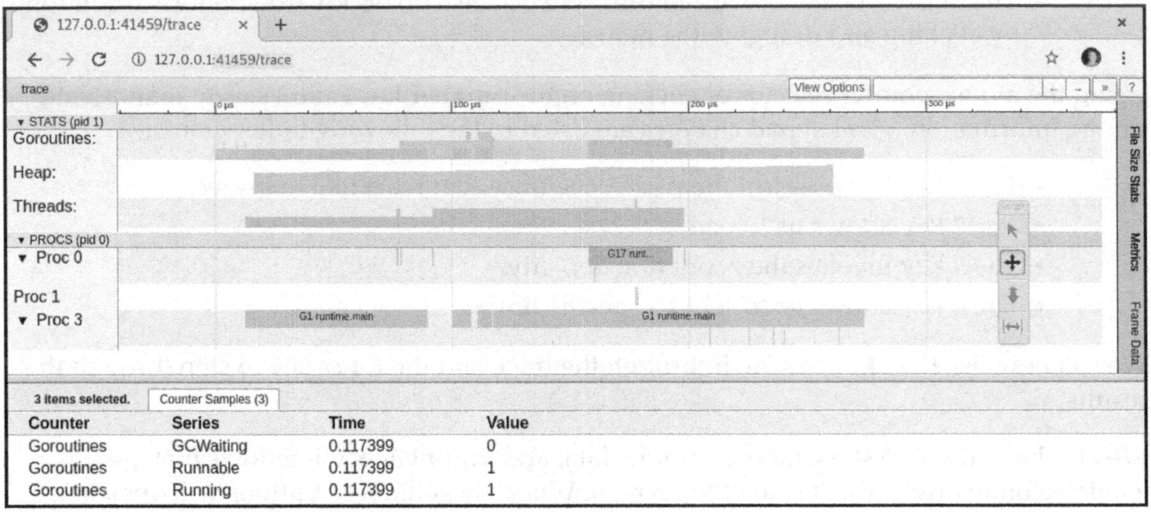

The goroutine information can be helpful for the end user debugging the program. Watching goroutines in the Go trace tool can help us to determine when a goroutine is fighting for contention. It may be waiting on a channel to clear, it might be blocked by a syscall, or it might be blocked by the scheduler. If there are many goroutines in a waiting state, that means the program might be creating too many goroutines. This could cause the scheduler to be overallocated. Having access to all of this information can help us to make an informed decision on how to better write our program to utilize goroutines more effectively.

Clicking on the orange bar in the **Heap** row will display the heap information:

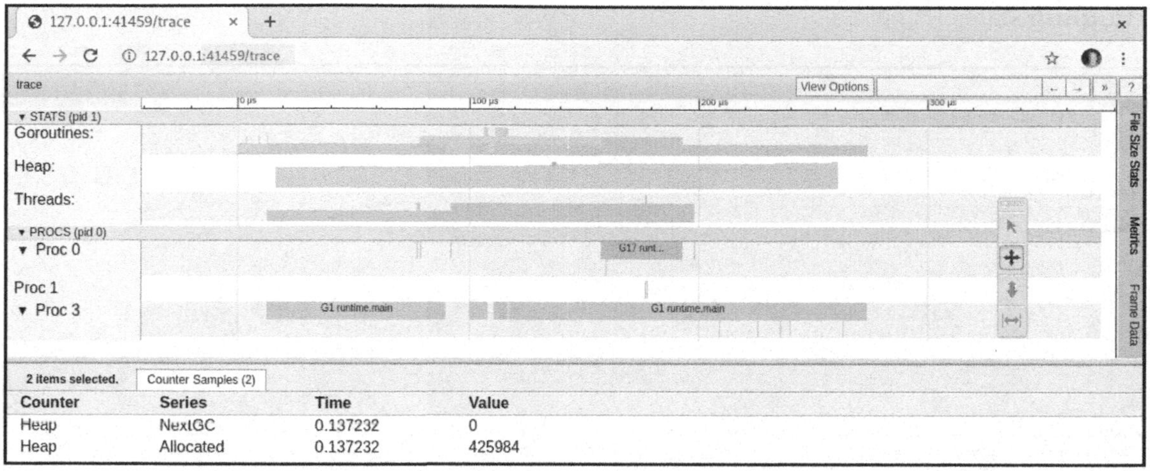

At the time selected (**0.137232**), we can see that we have **425984** bytes, or approximately 425 KB, allocated to the heap. Knowing the amount of memory currently allocated to the heap can tell us whether or not we have memory contention in our program. Profiling (as we learned in Chapter 12, *Profiling Go Code*) is usually a better methodology for looking at heap information, but having a general understanding of the allocation within the trace context can often be helpful.

We can look at the thread information next. Clicking on an active thread (the magenta block in the **Threads** row of the trace) will show you the number of threads in **InSyscall** and **Running** states:

It can be helpful to know the number of OS threads that are running and how many are currently being blocked by syscalls.

Next, we can take a look at each of the individual processes running. Clicking on the process will tell you all of the details that are shown in the following screenshot. If you hover over one of the events at the bottom pane of the trace, you will be able to see how the processes are tied together, denoted by the red arrow in the following screenshot:

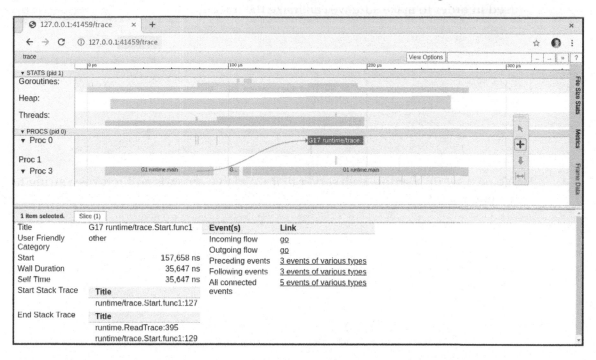

Knowing the end-to-end flow of your processes can often help you diagnose problem processes. In the next section, we'll learn how to explore pprof-like traces.

Exploring pprof-like traces

The Go tool trace can also generate four different types of traces that may be pertinent to your troubleshooting needs:

- `net`: A network-blocking profile
- `sync`: A synchronization-blocking profile
- `syscall`: A syscall-blocking profile
- `sched`: A scheduler-latency profile

Let's take a look at an example of how to use these tracing profiles on a web server:

1. First, we initialize our `main` and import the necessary packages. Note the blank identifier for the explicit package name within `_ "net/http/pprof"`. This is used in order to make sure we can make the tracing call:

```
package main


import (
    "io"
    "net/http"
    _ "net/http/pprof"
    "time"
)
```

2. We next set up a simple web server that waits five seconds and returns a string to the end user:

```
func main() {

    handler := func(w http.ResponseWriter, req *http.Request) {
        time.Sleep(5 * time.Second)
        io.WriteString(w, "Network Trace Profile Test")
    }

    http.HandleFunc("/", handler)
    http.ListenAndServe(":1234", nil)
}
```

3. After we run our server by executing `go run netTracePprof.go`, we can take a trace: `curl localhost:1234/debug/pprof/trace?seconds=10 > trace.out`. We can see the output of our `curl` in the following screenshot:

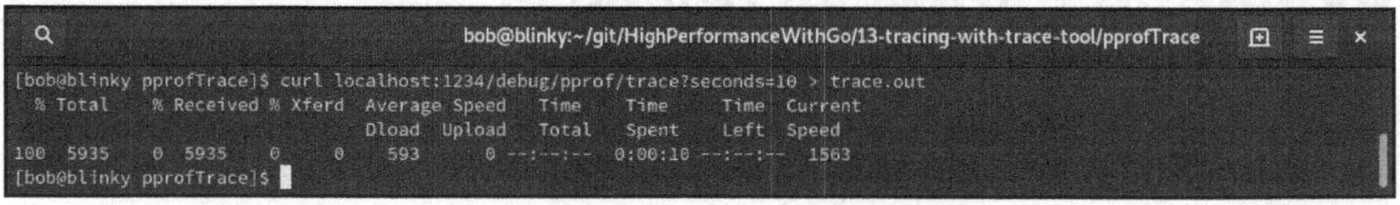

4. Concurrently, in another Terminal, we can make a request for the / path on our sample webserver: `curl localhost:1234/`. We will then be returned with a `trace.out` file in the directory in which we ran the trace. We can then open our trace using `go tool trace trace.out`. We will then see our tracing result. Utilizing the network-blocking profile in the resulting HTTP page, we can see a trace of the network-blocking profile:

As expected, we see a five-second wait, as this is the waiting timing that we added into our handler function for this particular web request. If we want to, we can download this profile and look at it in the upstream `pprof` tool that we discussed in `Chapter 12`, *Profiling Go Code*. In the trace HTML window, there's a download button next to the web profile:

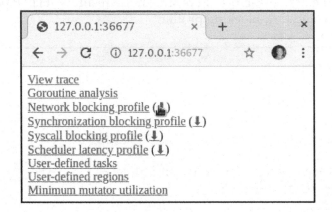

After we have downloaded this profile, we can take a look at it using the upstream `pprof` tool we installed in `Chapter 12`, *Profiling Go Code*:

```
$ pprof -http=:1235 ~/Downloads/io.profile
```

We can then look at things like the flame graph:

We can see the peek UI in the following screenshot:

Both the flame graph and the peek UI help to make these complex debugging views a little bit more concise. In the next section, we shall see what distributed tracing in Go is.

Go distributed tracing

Implementing and investigating individual traces for Go programs can be a fruitful endeavor, giving a lot of output with respect to the data that results in requests to our programs. As enterprises have more and more distributed code bases with many more intricate calls that all interoperate with one another, tracing individual calls becomes untenable in the long run. There have been two projects that have tried to help with distributed tracing for Go, and these are the OpenCensus Go library and the OpenTelemetry library:

- `opencensus-go`: https://github.com/census-instrumentation/opencensus-go
- `opentracing-go`: https://github.com/opentracing/opentracing-go

The maintainers of these projects have decided to converge these two projects and begin working on one code base, named OpenTelemetry. This new code base will allow for a simplified integration of distributed tracing across many languages and infrastructures. You can read more about the Go implementation of OpenTelemetry at https://github.com/open-telemetry/opentelemetry-go.

At the time of writing this book, OpenTelemetry is not yet ready for production use. OpenTelemetry will provide backward compatibility with both OpenCensus and OpenTracing, and will also provide security patches. In the next section of the book, we'll look at how we can implement Go programs with OpenCensus. In the future, implementing your program with OpenTelemetry should be relatively straightforward using the strategies that we are going to talk about when we look at implementing tracing with OpenCensus.

In the following section, we will see how to implement OpenCensus for our application.

Implementing OpenCensus for your application

Let's use a practical example for OpenCensus tracing in an application. To get started, we need to make sure that we have Docker installed on our machine. You should be able to use the installation documents at `https://docs.docker.com/` in order to be certain that Docker is installed and runs correctly on your machine. Once this is completed, we can get going with creating, implementing, and viewing a sample application. Once we have Docker installed, we can pull important images for our instrumentation. In our example, we will use Redis (a key–value store) to store key–value events in our application and Zipkin (a distributed tracing system) to view these traces.

Let's pull our dependencies for this project:

1. Redis, which is a key–value store that we are going to use in our sample application:

   ```
   docker pull redis:latest
   ```

2. Zipkin, which is a distributed trace system:

   ```
   docker pull openzipkin/zipkin
   ```

3. We will stand up our Redis server and let it run in the background:

   ```
   docker run -it -d -p 6379:6379 redis
   ```

4. We will do the same thing for our Zipkin server:

   ```
   docker run -it -d -p 9411:9411 openzipkin/zipkin
   ```

Once we have all of our dependencies installed and ready, we can start writing our application:

1. First, we'll instantiate our `main` package and add our necessary imports:

```
package main

import (

    "context"
    "log"
    "net/http"
    "time"

    "contrib.go.opencensus.io/exporter/zipkin"
    "go.opencensus.io/trace"
    "github.com/go-redis/redis"
    openzipkin "github.com/openzipkin/zipkin-go"
    zipkinHTTP "github.com/openzipkin/zipkin-go/reporter/http"
)
```

2. Our `tracingServer` function defines a few things:
    - We set up a new Zipkin endpoint.
    - We initialize a new HTTP reporter, which is the endpoint to which we send spans.
    - We set up a new exporter, which returns a `trace.Exporter` (this is how we upload spans to the Zipkin server).
    - We register our exporter to the tracing handlers.
    - We apply a configuration for a sampling rate. In this example, we set up our example to always trace, but we could make this a smaller percentage of our requests:

```
func tracingServer() {

    l, err := openzipkin.NewEndpoint("oc-zipkin",
"192.168.1.5:5454")

    if err != nil {
        log.Fatalf("Failed to create the local zipkinEndpoint: %v",
err)

    }

    r :=
```

```
zipkinHTTP.NewReporter("http://localhost:9411/api/v2/spans")
    z := zipkin.NewExporter(r, l)
    trace.RegisterExporter(z)
    trace.ApplyConfig(trace.Config{DefaultSampler:
trace.AlwaysSample()})

}
```

3. In our `makeRequest` function, we do the following:
    - Create a new span
    - Make a request to a given HTTP URL
    - Set a sleep timeout to simulate additional latency
    - Annotate our span
    - Return a response status

```
func makeRequest(ctx context.Context, url string) string {
    log.Printf("Retrieving URL")
    _, span := trace.StartSpan(ctx, "httpRequest")
    defer span.End()
    res, _ := http.Get(url)
    defer res.Body.Close()
    time.Sleep(100 * time.Millisecond)
    log.Printf("URL Response : %s", res.Status)
    span.Annotate([]trace.Attribute{
        trace.StringAttribute("URL Response Code", res.Status),
    }, "HTTP Response Status Code:"+res.Status)
    time.Sleep(50 * time.Millisecond)
    return res.Status
}
```

4. In our `writeToRedis` function, we do the following:
    - Start a new span
    - Connect to our local Redis server
    - Set a specific key–value pair

```
func writeToRedis(ctx context.Context, key string, value string) {

    log.Printf("Writing to Redis")
    _, span := trace.StartSpan(ctx, "redisWrite")
    defer span.End()
    client := redis.NewClient(&redis.Options{
        Addr: "localhost:6379",
        Password: "",
        DB: 0,
    })
```

```
    err := client.Set(key, value, 0).Err()
    if err != nil {
        panic(err)
    }
}
```

5. We then bring this all together using our `main` function:

```
func main() {

    tracingServer()
    ctx, span := trace.StartSpan(context.Background(), "main")
    defer span.End()
    for i := 0; i < 10; i++ {
        url := "https://golang.org/"
        respStatus := makeRequest(ctx, url)
        writeToRedis(ctx, url, respStatus)
    }
}
```

6. After we've invoked our program by executing `go run ocZipkin.go`, we can then take a look at our Zipkin server. If we select one of the traces that are in our trace list, we can see the traces that we've created:

If we click on one of the spans, we can investigate it further:

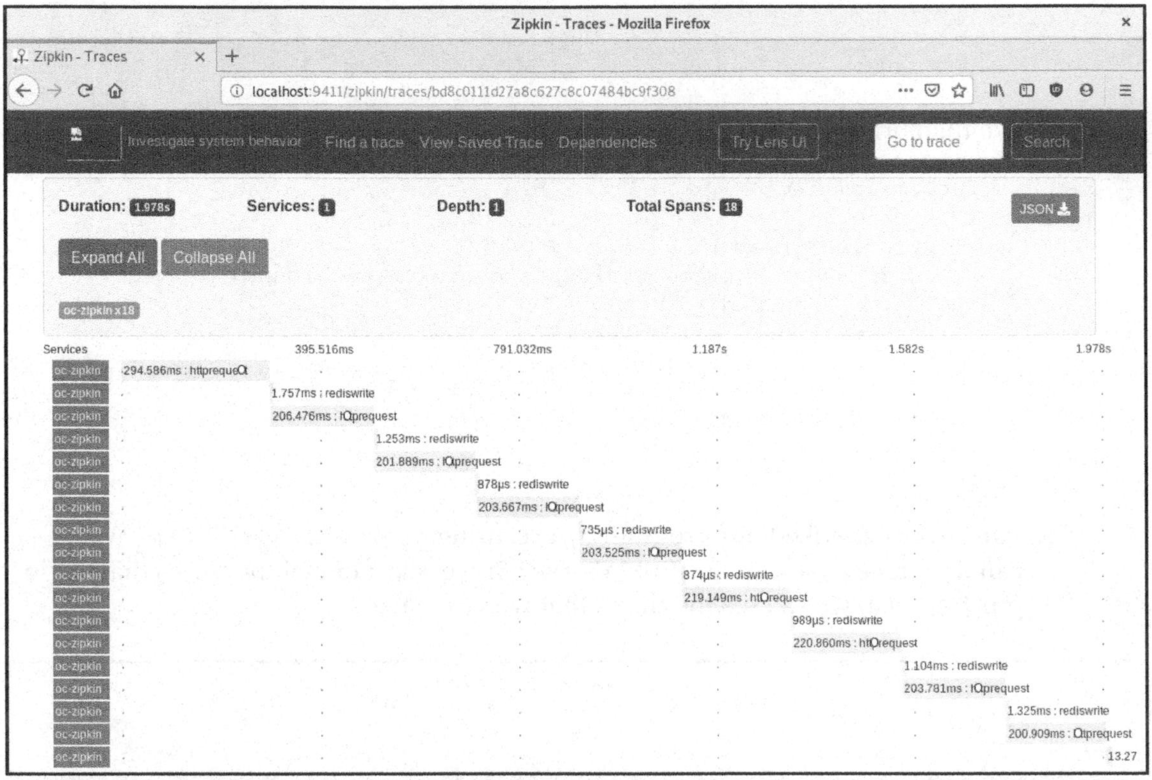

We can see the calls to the `httprequest` and `rediswrite` functions that are in our code. As we start to implement more spans around our code, we will get larger and larger traces that will help us diagnose where our code has the most amount of latency.

If we click on one of the individual elements in the trace, we can see the annotations that we wrote in our code:

#### Chapter 13

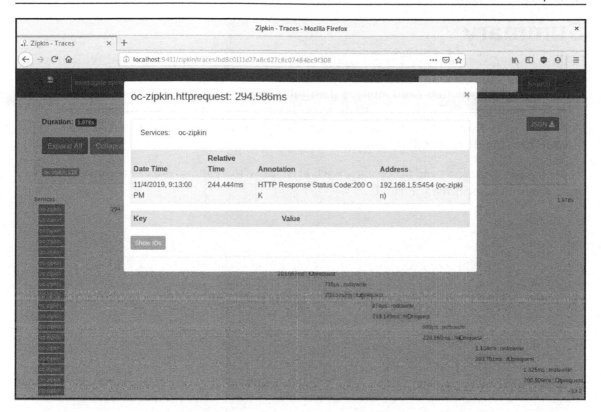

Annotations can be useful if we are trying to understand a particular behavior for an end user. We can also see the details of `traceId`, `spanId`, and `parentId`.

Summary

In this chapter, we learned all about traces. We learned how to implement individual traces on particular pieces of code and analyze them to understand their behavior. We also learned how to implement and analyze distributed traces to understand problems in our distributed system. Being able to use these skills will help you to debug distributed systems, and in turn, help to lower the **mean time-to-resolution** (**MTTR**) while troubleshooting distributed systems.

In Chapter 14, *Clusters and Job Queues*, we'll learn how to evaluate clusters and job queues for performance optimizations.

14
Clusters and Job Queues

Clustering and job queues in Go are good ways to get distributed systems to work synchronously and deliver a consistent message. Distributed computing is difficult and it becomes very important to watch for potential performance optimizations within both clustering and job queues.

In this chapter, we will learn about the following topics:

- Clustering with hierarchical and centroid algorithms
- Goroutines as queues
- Buffered channels as job queues
- Implementing third-party queuing systems (Kafka and RabbitMQ)

Learning about different clustering systems can help you identify large groups of data and how to accurately classify them in your datasets. Learning about queueing systems will help you move large amounts of information from your data structures into specific queueing mechanisms in order to pass large amounts of data to different systems in real time.

Clustering in Go

Clustering is a methodology that you can use in order to search for consistent groups of data within a given dataset. Using comparison techniques, we can look for groups of items within the dataset that contain similar characteristics. These individual datapoints are then divided into clusters. Clustering is commonly used in order to solve multi-objective problems.

There are two general classifications of clustering, both of which have distinct subclassifications:

- **Hard clustering**: The datapoints within the dataset are either explicitly a part of a cluster or not explicitly part of a cluster. Hard clustering can be further classified as follows:
    - **Strict partitioning**: An object can belong to exactly one cluster.
    - **Strict partitioning with outliers**: Strict partitioning, which also includes a concept that objects can be classified as outliers (meaning they belong to no cluster).
    - **Overlapping clustering**: Individual objects can be associated with one or more clusters.
- **Soft clustering**: Datapoints are assigned a probability that they are associated with a particular cluster based on explicit criteria. They can be further classified as follows:
    - **Subspace**: Clusters use a two-dimensional subspace in order to be further classified into two dimensions.
    - **Hierarchical**: Clustering using a hierarchical model; an object that is associated with a child cluster is also associated with the parent clusters.

There are also many different algorithm types that are used for clustering. Some examples are shown in the following table:

Name	Definition
Hierarchical	Used to attempt to build a hierarchy of clusters. Usually based on a top-down or a bottom-up approach, attempting to segment datapoints either from one to many clusters (top-down) or many to few clusters (bottom-up).
Centroid	Used to find a specific point location that acts as the center of a cluster.
Density	Used to look for places in the dataset that have dense regions of datapoints.
Distribution	Used to utilize distribution models to order and classify datapoints within a cluster.

In this book, we're going to focus on hierarchical and centroid algorithms as they are commonly used in computer science (namely in machine learning).

K-nearest neighbors

Hierarchical clustering is a clustering method in which an object that is associated with a child cluster is also associated with the parent clusters. The algorithm begins with all of the individual datapoints in the data struct being assigned to individual clusters. The nearest clusters to one another merge. This pattern continues until all the datapoints have an association with another datapoint. Hierarchical clustering is often displayed using a charting technique called a **dendrogram**. Hierarchical clustering is $O(n^2)$, so it's not typically used for large datasets.

The **K-nearest neighbors** (**KNN**) algorithm is a hierarchical algorithm often used in machine learning. One of the most popular ways to find KNN data in Go is with the `golearn` package. A classic KNN example that gets used as a machine learning example is the classification of iris flowers, which can be seen at `https://github.com/sjwhitworth/golearn/blob/master/examples/knnclassifier/knnclassifier_iris.go`.

Given a dataset with sepal and petal lengths and widths, we can see calculated data about this dataset:

```
bob@blinky:~/git/golearn/examples/knnclassifier                        ×

 File  Edit  View  Search  Terminal  Help
[bob@blinky knnclassifier]$ go run knnclassifier_iris.go
Instances with 88 row(s) 1 attribute(s)
Attributes:
*       CategoricalAttribute("Species", [Iris-setosa Iris-versicolor Iris-virgin
ica])

Data:
        Iris-setosa
        Iris-virginica
        Iris-virginica
        Iris-versicolor
        Iris-setosa
        Iris-virginica
        Iris-setosa
        Iris-versicolor
        Iris-setosa
        Iris-setosa
        Iris-versicolor
        Iris-versicolor
        Iris-versicolor
        Iris-setosa
        Iris-virginica
        Iris-setosa
        Iris-setosa
        Iris-setosa
        Iris-virginica
        Iris-versicolor
        Iris-setosa
        Iris-setosa
        Iris-versicolor
        Iris-versicolor
        Iris-virginica
        Iris-virginica
        Iris-setosa
        Iris-virginica
        Iris-versicolor
        Iris-versicolor
        ...
58 row(s) undisplayed
Reference Class True Positives  False Positives True Negatives  Precision
Recall  F1 Score
--------------- --------------- --------------- --------------- ----------
------  --------
Iris-virginica  27              1               58              0.9643
0.9310  0.9474
Iris-versicolor 28              2               57              0.9333
0.9655  0.9492
Iris-setosa     30              0               58              1.0000
1.0000  1.0000
Overall accuracy: 0.9659

[bob@blinky knnclassifier]$
```

We can see the calculated accuracy in this prediction model. In the preceding output, we have the following descriptors:

Descriptor	Definition
Reference Class	A title associated with the output.
True Positives	The model correctly predicts a positive response.
False Positives	The model incorrectly predicts a positive response.
True Negatives	The model correctly predicts a negative response.
Precision	Ability to not label an instance positive that's actually negative.
Recall	A ratio of *True Positives / (Sum of True Positives + False Negatives)*.
F1 Score	The weighted harmonic mean of precision and recall. This value is somewhere between 0.0 and 1.0, with 1.0 being the best possible outcome for this value.

Last but certainly not least, we have an overall accuracy, which tells us how accurately our algorithm predicted our outcomes.

K-means clustering

K-means clustering is one of the most commonly utilized clustering algorithms in machine learning. K-means attempts to identify the underlying patterns of datapoints in a dataset. In K-means, we define k as the number of centroids (the center of an object with uniform density) that our cluster has. Then, we categorize the different datapoints with respect to those centroids.

We can use the K-means library, which can be found at https://github.com/muesli/kmeans, in order to perform K-means clustering on a dataset. Let's take a look:

1. First, we instantiate the main package and import our required packages:

```
package main

import (
  "fmt"
  "log"
  "math/rand"

  "github.com/muesli/clusters"
  "github.com/muesli/kmeans"
)
```

2. Next, we create a random two-dimensional dataset with the `createDataset` function:

```
func createDataset(datasetSize int) clusters.Observations {
    var dataset clusters.Observations
    for i := 1; i < datasetSize; i++ {
        dataset = append(dataset, clusters.Coordinates{
            rand.Float64(),
            rand.Float64(),
        })
    }
    return dataset
}
```

3. Next, we create a function that allows us to print our data for consumption:

```
func printCluster(clusters clusters.Clusters) {
    for i, c := range clusters {
        fmt.Printf("\nCluster %d center points: x: %.2f y: %.2f\n", i,
c.Center[0], c.Center[1])
        fmt.Printf("\nDatapoints assigned to this cluster: : %+v\n\n",
c.Observations)
    }
}
```

In our `main` function, we define our cluster size, our dataset size, and our threshold size.

4. Now, we can create a new random 2D dataset and perform K-means clustering on that dataset. We plot the result and print our clusters as follows:

```
func main() {

    var clusterSize = 3
    var datasetSize = 30
    var thresholdSize = 0.01
    rand.Seed(time.Now().UnixNano())
    dataset := createDataset(datasetSize)
    fmt.Println("Dataset: ", dataset)

    km, err := kmeans.NewWithOptions(thresholdSize,
kmeans.SimplePlotter{})
    if err != nil {
        log.Printf("Your K-Means configuration struct was not
initialized properly")
    }

    clusters, err := km.Partition(dataset, clusterSize)
```

```
    if err != nil {
        log.Printf("There was an error in creating your K-Means
    relation")
    }

    printCluster(clusters)
}
```

After we execute this function, we will be able to see our datapoints grouped together in their respective clusters:

In our results, we can see the following:

- Our initial (randomly generated) 2D dataset
- Our three defined clusters
- The associated datapoints that are assigned to each cluster

This program also generates `.png` images of each step of clustering. The one that was created last is a visualization of the clustering of the datapoints:

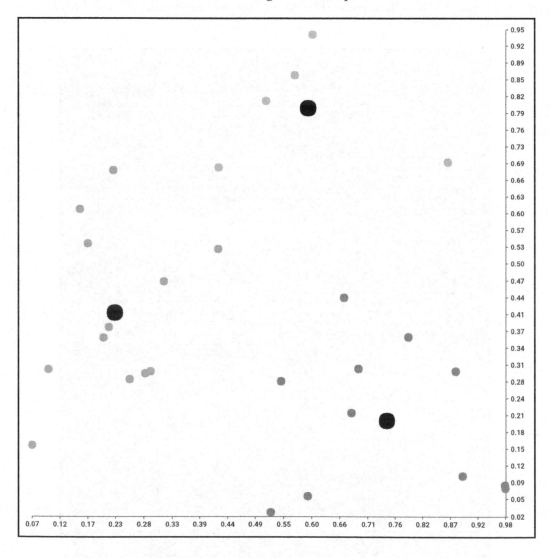

K-means clustering is a very good algorithm to use if you want to group a large dataset into smaller groups. It has an O notation of $O(n)$, so it is often practical to use for large datasets. Practical applications of K-means clustering may include two-dimensional datasets for the following:

- Identifying crime-prone areas on a map using GPS coordinates
- Identifying clustering of pages for on-call developers
- Identifying athlete performance characteristics based on step output compared to the number of rest days

In the next section, let's explore job queues in Go.

Exploring job queues in Go

Job queues are frequently used to process units of work in a computer system. They are often used to schedule both synchronous and asynchronous functions. While working with larger datasets, there can be data structures and algorithms that take quite a bit of time to process. Either the system is processing a very large segment of data, the algorithm that is being applied to the dataset is very complex, or there's a combination of the two. Being able to add these jobs to a job queue and perform them in a different order or at different times can be very helpful to maintain the stability of a system and give an end user a better experience. Job queues are also frequently used for asynchronous jobs since the time when the job completes isn't as impactful for the end user. The job system can also prioritize the jobs in a priority queue if one is implemented. This allows the system to process the most important jobs first, followed by the jobs that don't have as much of an explicit deadline.

Goroutines as job queues

Perhaps you don't need a job queue for your particular task. Using a goroutine for a task is often sufficient. Let's say that we want to send an email asynchronously during some particular task. We can send this email using a goroutine within our function.

For this example, I'm going to send an email via Gmail. To do so, you may need to allow less secure app access for email authentication to work (`https://myaccount.google.com/lesssecureapps?pli=1`). This is not recommended to do in the long term; it's just a simple way to show a real-world email interaction. If you're interested in building a more robust email solution, you can use the Gmail API at `https://developers.google.com/gmail/api/quickstart/go`. Let's get started:

1. First, we'll instantiate our `main` package and import the necessary packages into our sample program:

```
package main

import (
  "log"
  "time"

  "gopkg.in/gomail.v2"
)
```

2. Then, we will create our `main` function, which will do the following:
   - Log a `Doing Work` line (representative of doing other things in our function).
   - Log a `Sending Emails` line (representative of the time where the email is added to the goroutine).
   - Spawn a goroutine to send the email.
   - Sleep to ensure the goroutine completes (we could use a `WaitGroup` here too if we'd like):

```
func main() {

    log.Printf("Doing Work")
    log.Printf("Sending Emails!")
    go sendMail()
    time.Sleep(time.Second)
    log.Printf("Done Sending Emails!")
}
```

In our `sendMail` function, we take in a recipient, set the proper email headers we need to send our email, and send it using the `gomail` dialer. You'll need to change the `sender`, `recipient`, `username`, and `password` variables if you'd like to see this program execute successfully:

```
func sendMail() {
    var sender = "USERNAME@gmail.com"
```

```
    var recipient = "RECIPIENT@gmail.com"
    var username = "USERNAME@gmail.com"
    var password = "PASSWORD"
    var host = "smtp.gmail.com"
    var port = 587

    email := gomail.NewMessage()
    email.SetHeader("From", sender)
    email.SetHeader("To", recipient)
    email.SetHeader("Subject", "Test Email From Goroutine")
    email.SetBody("text/plain", "This email is being sent from a
Goroutine!")

    dialer := gomail.NewDialer(host, port, username, password)
    err := dialer.DialAndSend(email)
    if err != nil {
        log.Println("Could not send email")
        panic(err)
    }
}
```

We can see from our resulting output that we are able to effectively do some work and send
an email:

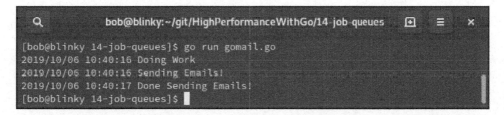

It's been noted as a core tenant in this book that the most performant method to perform a
task can often be the simplest one. If you don't need to build a new job-queueing system to
perform a simple task, you should avoid it. At larger companies, there are often dedicated
teams to maintaining job queue systems for large-scale data. They are expensive from both
performance and cost perspectives. They are often important to manage large-scale data
systems, but I feel as if I'd be remiss if I didn't mention that you should take careful
consideration before you add a distributed job queue to your technology stack.

Buffered channels as job queues

Go's buffered channels are a perfect example of a worker queue. As we learned in `Chapter 3`, *Understanding Concurrency*, buffered channels are channels that have a bounded size. They are typically more performant than their unbounded counterpart. They are useful for retrieving values from an explicit number of goroutines you've launched. Because they are **first in first out (FIFO)** queuing mechanisms, they can be effectively used as a fixed-size queuing mechanism, and we can process requests in the order that they came in. We can write a simple job queue using a buffered channel. Let's take a look:

1. We start by instantiating our `main` package, importing our required libraries, and setting our constants:

```
package main

import (
  "log"
  "net/http"
)

const queueSize = 50
const workers = 10
const port = "1234"
```

2. Then, we create a `job` struct. This keeps track of the job name and the payload, as shown in the following code block:

```
type job struct {
  name string
  payload string
}
```

3. Our `runJob` function just prints a success message. This is where we could add more intense work if we were so inclined:

```
func runJob(id int, individualJob job) {
  log.Printf("Worker %d: Completed: %s with payload %s", id,
individualJob.name, individualJob.payload)
}
```

Our main function creates a `jobQueue` channel of a defined `queueSize`. Then, it iterates through the workers and spawns goroutines for each of the workers. Lastly, it iterates through the job queue and runs the necessary jobs:

```
func main() {
  jobQueue := make(chan job, queueSize)
```

```
            for i := 1; i <= workers; i++ {
                go func(i int) {
                    for j := range jobQueue {
                        runJob(i, j)
                    }
                }(i)

            }
```

We also have an HTTP handler function here to take requests from an external source (in our case, it's going to be a simple cURL request, but you could have many different requests from external systems):

```
    http.HandleFunc("/", func(w http.ResponseWriter, r *http.Request) {
        submittedJob := job{r.FormValue("name"),
    r.FormValue("payload")}
        jobQueue <- submittedJob
    })

    http.ListenAndServe(":"+port, nil)
}
```

4. After this, we start the job queue and execute a request to test the command:

```
for i in {1..15}; do curl localhost:1234/ -d id=$i -d name=job$i -d
payload="Hi from Job $i"; done
```

The following screenshot shows a resulting set that shows the different workers completing the different jobs:

Note that the individual workers picked up the jobs as they were able to. This is helpful as we continue to grow our system, which requires these jobs.

Integrating job queues

There are times where we may not want to use built-in Go queueing systems. Perhaps we already have a pipeline that contains other message-queueing systems or perhaps we know that we are going to have to maintain a very large data ingress. Two systems that are commonly used for this task are Apache Kafka and RabbitMQ. Let's take a quick look at how to integrate with both of these systems using Go.

Kafka

Apache Kafka is referred to as a *distributed streaming system*, which is just another way of saying a distributed job queue. Kafka, which is written in Java, uses the idea of a publish/subscribe model for message queueing. It's often used for writing real-time streaming data pipelines.

We'll assume you have a Kafka instance set up already. If you don't, you can use the following bash script to get a quick Kafka instance:

```
#!/bin/bash
rm -rf kafka_2.12-2.3.0
wget -c http://apache.cs.utah.edu/kafka/2.3.0/kafka_2.12-2.3.0.tgz
tar xvf kafka_2.12-2.3.0.tgz
./kafka_2.12-2.3.0/bin/zookeeper-server-start.sh
kafka_2.12-2.3.0/config/zookeeper.properties &
./kafka_2.12-2.3.0/bin/kafka-server-start.sh
kafka_2.12-2.3.0/config/server.properties
wait
```

We can execute this bash script as follows:

```
./testKafka.sh
```

After we do this, we can run the `kafka` read and write Go programs to read and write from Kafka. Let's investigate each of these.

We can use the `writeToKafka.go` program to write to Kafka. Let's take a look:

1. First, we initialize our `main` package and import the required packages:

```
package main

import (
  "context"
  "fmt"
  "log"
  "time"

  "github.com/segmentio/kafka-go"
)
```

2. In our `main` function, we create a connection to Kafka, set a write deadline, and then we write messages to our Kafka topic/partition. In this case, it's just a simple message count from 1 to 10:

```
func main() {
    var topic = "go-example"
    var partition = 0
    var connectionType = "tcp"
    var connectionHost = "0.0.0.0"
    var connectionPort = ":9092"
    connection, err := kafka.DialLeader(context.Background(),
connectionType,
        connectionHost+connectionPort, topic, partition)
    if err != nil {
        log.Fatal(err)
    }
    connection.SetWriteDeadline(time.Now().Add(10 * time.Second))
    for i := 0; i < 10; i++ {
        connection.WriteMessages(
            kafka.Message{Value: []byte(fmt.Sprintf("Message : %v",
i))},
        )
    }
    connection.Close()
}
```

3. The `readFromKafka.go` program instantiates the `main` package and imports all the necessary packages, as follows:

```
package main
import (
    "context"
    "fmt"
    "log"
    "time"
    "github.com/segmentio/kafka-go"
)
```

4. Our `main` function then sets a Kafka topic and partition, followed by creating a connection, setting a connection deadline, and setting a batch size.

 More information about Kafka topics and partitions can be found at: http://kafka.apache.org/documentation/#intro_topics.

5. We can see that our `topic` and `partition` have been set as variables and that our connection has been instantiated:

```
func main() {

    var topic = "go-example"
    var partition = 0
    var connectionType = "tcp"
    var connectionHost = "0.0.0.0"
    var connectionPort = ":9092"

    connection, err := kafka.DialLeader(context.Background(),
connectionType,
        connectionHost+connectionPort, topic, partition)
    if err != nil {
        log.Fatal("Could not create a Kafka Connection")
    }
```

6. Then, we set a deadline on our connection and read our batches. Lastly, we close our connections:

```
    connection.SetReadDeadline(time.Now().Add(1 * time.Second))
    readBatch := connection.ReadBatch(500, 500000)

    byteString := make([]byte, 500)
    for {
      _, err := readBatch.Read(byteString)
```

```
        if err != nil {
            break
        }
        fmt.Println(string(byteString))
    }

    readBatch.Close()
    connection.Close()
}
```

7. After we execute our `readFromKafka.go` and `writeFromKafka.go` files, we can see the resulting output:

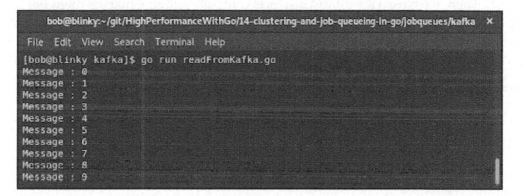

Our Kafka instance now has the messages that we sent from our `writeToKafka.go` program, which can now be consumed by our `readFromKafka.go` program.

To stop our Kafka and zookeeper services after we are finished with them, we can execute the following commands:

```
./kafka_2.12-2.3.0/bin/kafka-server-stop.sh
./kafka_2.12-2.3.0/bin/zookeeper-server-stop.sh
```

Many enterprises use Kafka as a message brokering system, so being able to understand how to read and write from these systems in Go can be helpful for creating things at scale in an enterprise setting.

RabbitMQ

RabbitMQ is a popular open source message broker written in Erlang. It uses a protocol called the **Advanced Message Queueing Protocol** (**AMQP**) in order to pass messages through its queueing system. Without further ado, let's set up a RabbitMQ instance and pass messages to and from it using Go:

1. First, we need to start up a RabbitMQ instance using Docker:

```
docker run -d --name rabbitmq -p 5672:5672 -p 15672:15672
rabbitmq:3-management
```

2. Then, we have a RabbitMQ instance, complete with the management portal, running on our host.

3. Now, we can use the Go AMQP library (`https://github.com/streadway/amqp`) in order to pass messages to and from our RabbitMQ system with Go.

We will start by creating a listener. Let's see this procedure step by step:

1. First, we instantiate the `main` package and import the necessary dependencies, as well as set the explicit variables:

```
package main

import (
  "log"

  "github.com/streadway/amqp"
)

func main() {
    var username = "guest"
    var password = "guest"
    var protocol = "amqp://"
    var host = "0.0.0.0"
    var port = ":5672/"
    var queueName = "go-queue"
```

2. Then, we create a connection to the `amqp` server:

```
connectionString := protocol + username + ":" + password + "@" +
host + port
connection, err := amqp.Dial(connectionString)
if err != nil {
  log.Printf("Could not connect to Local RabbitMQ instance on " +
host)
  }
```

```
defer connection.Close()

ch, err := connection.Channel()
if err != nil {
  log.Printf("Could not connect to channel")
}
defer ch.Close()
```

3. Next, we declare the queue that we are listening on and consume messages from the queue:

```
queue, err := ch.QueueDeclare(queueName, false, false, false,
false, nil)
if err != nil {
  log.Printf("Could not declare queue : " + queueName)
}

messages, err := ch.Consume(queue.Name, "", true, false, false,
false, nil)
if err != nil {
  log.Printf("Could not register a consumer")
}

listener := make(chan bool)

go func() {
  for i := range messages {
    log.Printf("Received message: %s", i.Body)
  }
}()

log.Printf("Listening for messages on %s:%s on queue %s", host,
port, queueName)
<-listener
}
```

4. Now, we can create the sending function. Again, we declare our package and import our dependencies, as well as set our variables:

```
package main

import (
  "log"

  "github.com/streadway/amqp"
)

func main() {
```

```
var username = "guest"
var password = "guest"
var protocol = "amqp://"
var host = "0.0.0.0"
var port = ":5672/"
var queueName = "go-queue"
```

5. We use the same connection methodology that we used in our listener. We might abstract this away in a production instance, but it was included here for ease of understanding:

```
connectionString := protocol + username + ":" + password + "@" +
host + port
connection, err := amqp.Dial(connectionString)
if err != nil {
  log.Printf("Could not connect to Local RabbitMQ instance on " +
host)
}
defer connection.Close()

ch, err := connection.Channel()
if err != nil {
  log.Printf("Could not connect to channel")
}
defer ch.Close()
```

6. Then, we declare the queue we'd like to use and publish a message body to that queue:

```
queue, err := ch.QueueDeclare(queueName, false, false, false,
false, nil)
if err != nil {
  log.Printf("Could not declare queue : " + queueName)
}

messageBody := "Hello Gophers!"
err = ch.Publish("", queue.Name, false, false,
  amqp.Publishing{
    ContentType: "text/plain",
    Body: []byte(messageBody),
  })
log.Printf("Message sent on queue %s : %s", queueName,
messageBody)
  if err != nil {
    log.Printf("Message not sent successfully on queue %s",
queueName, messageBody)
  }
}
```

7. After we've created both of these programs, we can test them out. We'll iterate over our message-sending program with a while true loop:

```
bob@blinky:~/git/HighPerformanceWithGo/14-clustering-and-job-queueing-in-go/jobqueues/rabbitMQ  ×

File  Edit  View  Search  Terminal  Help
[bob@blinky rabbitMQ]$ while true; do go run sendAmqpMessage.go; done
2019/10/24 16:26:07 Message sent on queue go-queue : Hello Gophers!
2019/10/24 16:26:07 Message sent on queue go-queue : Hello Gophers!
2019/10/24 16:26:08 Message sent on queue go-queue : Hello Gophers!
2019/10/24 16:26:08 Message sent on queue go-queue : Hello Gophers!
2019/10/24 16:26:08 Message sent on queue go-queue : Hello Gophers!
2019/10/24 16:26:09 Message sent on queue go-queue : Hello Gophers!
2019/10/24 16:26:09 Message sent on queue go-queue : Hello Gophers!
2019/10/24 16:26:09 Message sent on queue go-queue : Hello Gophers!
2019/10/24 16:26:10 Message sent on queue go-queue : Hello Gophers!
2019/10/24 16:26:10 Message sent on queue go-queue : Hello Gophers!
^C
[bob@blinky rabbitMQ]$
```

After we do this, we should see the messages coming into our receiver:

```
bob@blinky:~/git/HighPerformanceWithGo/14-clustering-and-job-queueing-in-go/jobqueues/rabbitMQ  ×

File  Edit  View  Search  Terminal  Help
[bob@blinky rabbitMQ]$ go run checkAmqpQueue.go
2019/10/24 16:26:02 Listening for messages on 0.0.0.0:5672 on queue go-queue
2019/10/24 16:26:07 Received message: Hello Gophers!
2019/10/24 16:26:07 Received message: Hello Gophers!
2019/10/24 16:26:08 Received message: Hello Gophers!
2019/10/24 16:26:08 Received message: Hello Gophers!
2019/10/24 16:26:08 Received message: Hello Gophers!
2019/10/24 16:26:09 Received message: Hello Gophers!
2019/10/24 16:26:09 Received message: Hello Gophers!
2019/10/24 16:26:10 Received message: Hello Gophers!
2019/10/24 16:26:10 Received message: Hello Gophers!
```

We can also see the output from this activity by looking at the RabbitMQ management portal, located at `http://0.0.0.0:15672`, using the username and password of guest by default:

This portal gives us all sorts of different information about the RabbitMQ job queue, from the number of messages queued, the publish/subscribe model state, and results about individual parts of the RabbitMQ system (connections, channels, exchanges, and queues). Understanding how this queueing system works will help you, should you ever need to communicate with a RabbitMQ queue.

Summary

In this chapter, we learned about clustering with hierarchical and centroid algorithms, goroutines as queues, buffered channels as job queues, and implementing third-party queuing systems (Kafka and RabbitMQ).

Learning about all of these clustering and job-queueing techniques will help make you better at using algorithms and distributed systems and solving computer science problems. In the next chapter, we are going to learn about how to measure and compare code quality across versions using the Prometheus exporter, APMs, SLIs/SLOs, and logging.

15
Comparing Code Quality Across Versions

After you've written, debugged, profiled, and monitored your Go code, you need to monitor your application in the long term for performance regressions. Adding new features to your code is useless if you can't continue to deliver a level of performance that other systems in your infrastructure depend on.

In this chapter, we will learn about the following topics:

- Utilizing the Go Prometheus exporter
- **Application performance monitoring (APM)** tools
- **Service-level indicators** and **service-level objectives (SLIs** and **SLOs)**
- Utilizing logging

Understanding these concepts should help drive you to write performant code over the longer term. When working on larger-scale projects, work often doesn't scale well. Having 10 times the number of engineers often does not guarantee 10 times the output. Being able to programmatically quantify code performance is important as software teams grow and features are added to products. Evangelizing performant code is something that is always taken in a positive light, and using some of the techniques described in this chapter will help you to improve your code performance in the long term, whether you're working in an enterprise setting or on a small open source project.

Go Prometheus exporter – exporting data from your Go application

One of the best ways to track long-term changes to your application is to use time-series data to monitor and alert us about important changes. Prometheus (`https://prometheus.io/`) is a great way to perform this task. Prometheus is an open source time-series monitoring tool that utilizes a pull model via HTTP in order to drive monitoring and alerting. It is written in Go and has first-class client libraries for Go programs. The following steps show a very simple implementation of the Go Prometheus HTTP library:

1. First, we instantiate our package and import our necessary libraries:

```
package main
import (
    "net/http"
    "github.com/prometheus/client_golang/prometheus/promhttp"

)
```

2. Then, in our `main` function, we instantiate a new server and have it serve a `NewServeMux` that returns a Prometheus handler (`promhttp.Handler()`):

```
func main() {
    mux := http.NewServeMux()
    mux.Handle("/metrics", promhttp.Handler())
    http.ListenAndServe(":1234", mux)
}
```

After we do this, we can see that we return values from the default Prometheus exporter. These are all well commented, and include the following:

- Go garbage collection information
- Goroutine information
- Go environment version
- Go memory statistics
- Go CPU utilization statistics
- HTTP handler statistics

3. We next build the binary for our Go service:

```
GOOS=linux go build promExporter.go
```

4. We next create a docker network for linking our services together:

```
docker network create prometheus
```

5. We then follow this by creating our Prometheus exporter service:

```
docker build -t promexporter -f Dockerfile.promExporter .
```

6. Next, we run our Prometheus exporter service on our Docker host:

```
docker run -it --rm --name promExporter -d -p 1234:1234 --net
prometheus promexporter
```

In the following screenshot, we can see a truncated output of this response. Excluded are the comments and the built-in Go statistics for brevity. You can see the key–value responses in the response from the server:

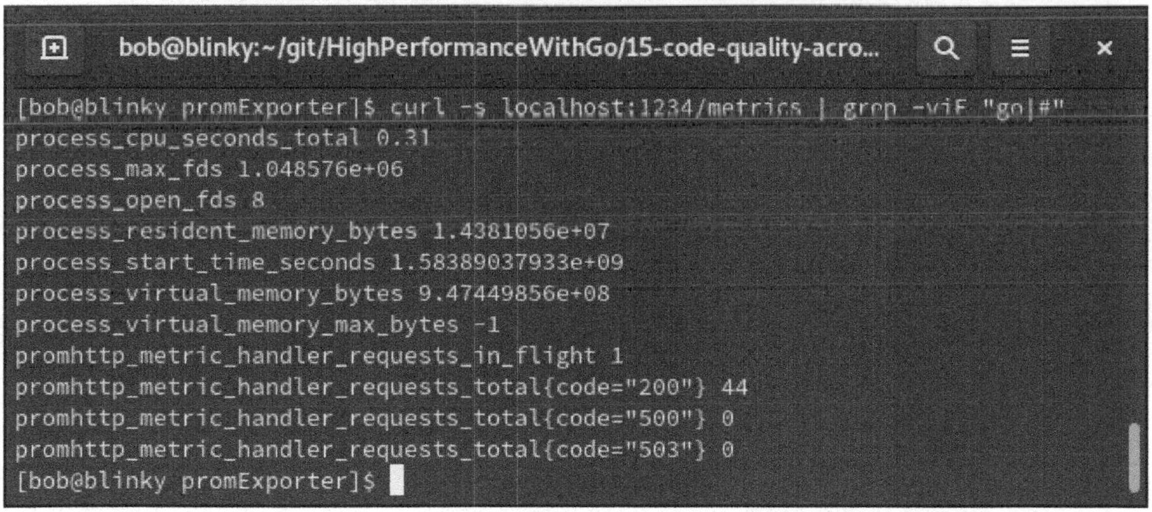

```
⊞   bob@blinky:~/git/HighPerformanceWithGo/15-code-quality-acro...    Q   ≡   ✕

[bob@blinky promExporter]$ curl -s localhost:1234/metrics | grep -viE "go|#"
process_cpu_seconds_total 0.31
process_max_fds 1.048576e+06
process_open_fds 8
process_resident_memory_bytes 1.4381056e+07
process_start_time_seconds 1.58389037933e+09
process_virtual_memory_bytes 9.47449856e+08
process_virtual_memory_max_bytes -1
promhttp_metric_handler_requests_in_flight 1
promhttp_metric_handler_requests_total{code="200"} 44
promhttp_metric_handler_requests_total{code="500"} 0
promhttp_metric_handler_requests_total{code="503"} 0
[bob@blinky promExporter]$ █
```

After we have set up this server, we can monitor it at a given cadence. We can run both our metrics service and Prometheus in containers and let them talk to each other. We can use a simple `prometheus.yml` definition for our Prometheus container:

```
[bob@blinky promExporter]$ cat prometheus.yml
global:
  scrape_interval:      10s
  evaluation_interval: 10s
  external_labels:
      monitor: 'metrics-example'
scrape_configs:
  - job_name: 'prometheus'
    static_configs:
      - targets: ['promExporter:1234']
[bob@blinky promExporter]$
```

You can replace `promExporter` within the `scrape_configs->static_configs->targets` portion of the YAML with an IP address or hostname if you'd like to use something besides your docker host for this.

7. After we have our binary build, we can create two separate Dockerfiles: one for the container that will contain our Prometheus exporter service and one that will contain our Prometheus service. Our Dockerfile for our Prometheus service takes the baseline Prometheus image and adds our YAML configuration to the appropriate place in our image. Our `Dockerfile.promservice` configuration is as follows:

```
FROM prom/prometheus
ADD prometheus.yml /etc/prometheus/
```

8. Once we have our `Dockerfile.promservice` created, we can build our Prometheus service:

```
docker build -t prom -f Dockerfile.promservice .
```

9. We can then run our Prometheus service on our Docker host:

```
docker run -it --rm --name prom -d -p 9090:9090 --net prometheus prom
```

Now we have a Prometheus instance running on our local environment.

10. After we have our Prometheus service up and running, we can go to `http://[IPADDRESS]:9090/` and we'll see our Prometheus instance:

11. We can validate that we are scraping our target by looking at the `/targets` path in the same URL:

12. Next, we can make a couple of requests to our host:

```
for i in {1..10}; do curl -s localhost:1234/metrics -o /dev/null;
done
```

13. Next, we can see the results of our `curl` in our Prometheus instance:

With these results, we can see the total number HTTP responses that we have served with a 200, 500, and 503 status code. Our example is simple, but we can use many different types of metrics here in order to validate any assumptions that we have. We will do a more involved metric-gathering example in our SLI/SLO example later in this chapter.

In the next section, we are going to talk about APM and how it can be used in maintaining a performant distributed system.

APM – watching your distributed system performance

There are many APM tools on the market today. They are frequently used to monitor the performance and reliability of software over time. Some of the products available for Go at the time of writing this book are as follows:

- **Elastic APM agent**: https://www.elastic.co/guide/en/apm/agent/go/current/index.html
- **New Relic APM**: https://newrelic.com/golang
- **Datadog**: https://docs.datadoghq.com/tracing/setup/go/
- **SignalFX**: https://docs.signalfx.com/en/latest/apm/apm-instrument/apm-go.html
- **AppDynamics** : https://www.appdynamics.com/supported-technologies/go
- **Honeycomb APM**: https://docs.honeycomb.io/getting-data-in/go/
- **AWS XRay**: https://docs.aws.amazon.com/xray/latest/devguide/xray-sdk-go.html
- **Google's suite of APM products**: https://cloud.google.com/apm/

Most of these tools are closed source and paid services. Aggregating distributed traces is a difficult value proposition. The vendors listed here (as well as some that are not mentioned) combine data storage, aggregation, and analysis in order to have a one-stop shop for APM. We can also use the OpenCensus/Zipkin open source example that we created in Chapter 13, *Tracing Go Code*, to perform distributed tracing in our system. Implementing spans around particular bits of our code base can help us to monitor long-term application performance.

Let's take a look at an example of Google's APM solutions. At the time of writing, Google Cloud offers 2.5 million span ingestions and 25 million span scans per month, which is more than adequate for an example.

Google Cloud environment setup

The first thing we need to do is to create a GCP project and retrieve the application credentials:

1. First, we'll log into https://console.cloud.google.com/. Once logged in, we can hit the project selector dropdown at the top of the page:

2. We can then create a new project for our particular application at the top right of
   the screen, as shown in the following screenshot:

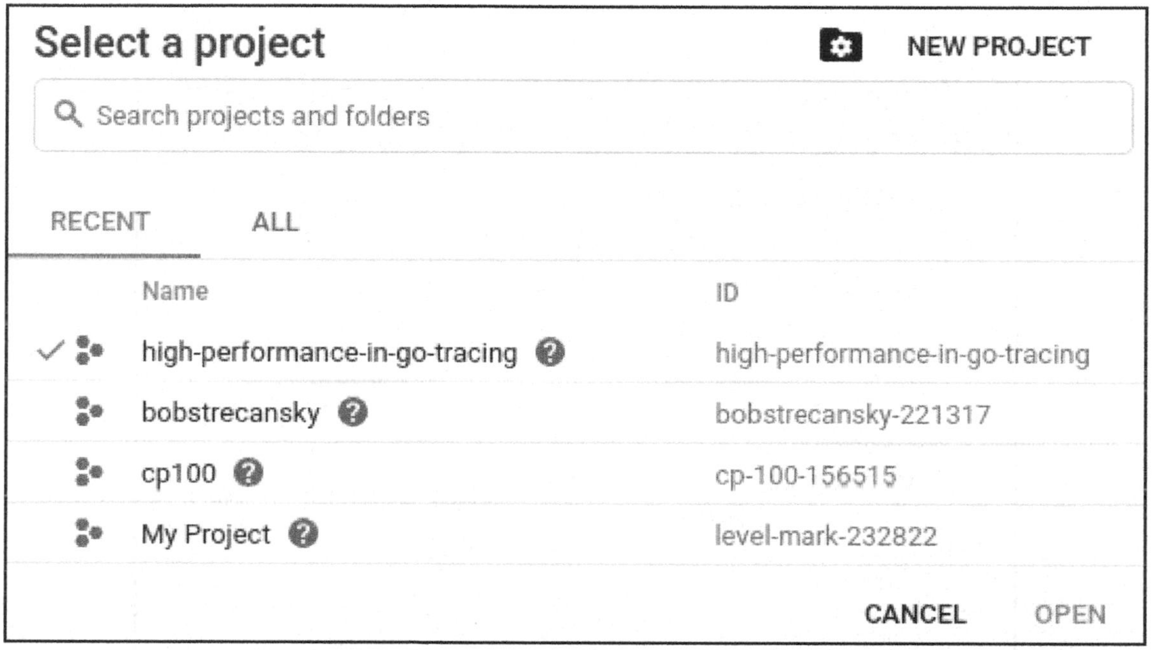

3. We can then visit the service account key page at `https://console.cloud.`
   `google.com/apis/credentials/serviceaccountkey`, which will let us create a
   service account key.

4. We can create a service account key for our application. Make sure you select the **Cloud Trace Agent**, as this is necessary for us to add traces to Google Cloud Trace. This is depicted in the following screenshot:

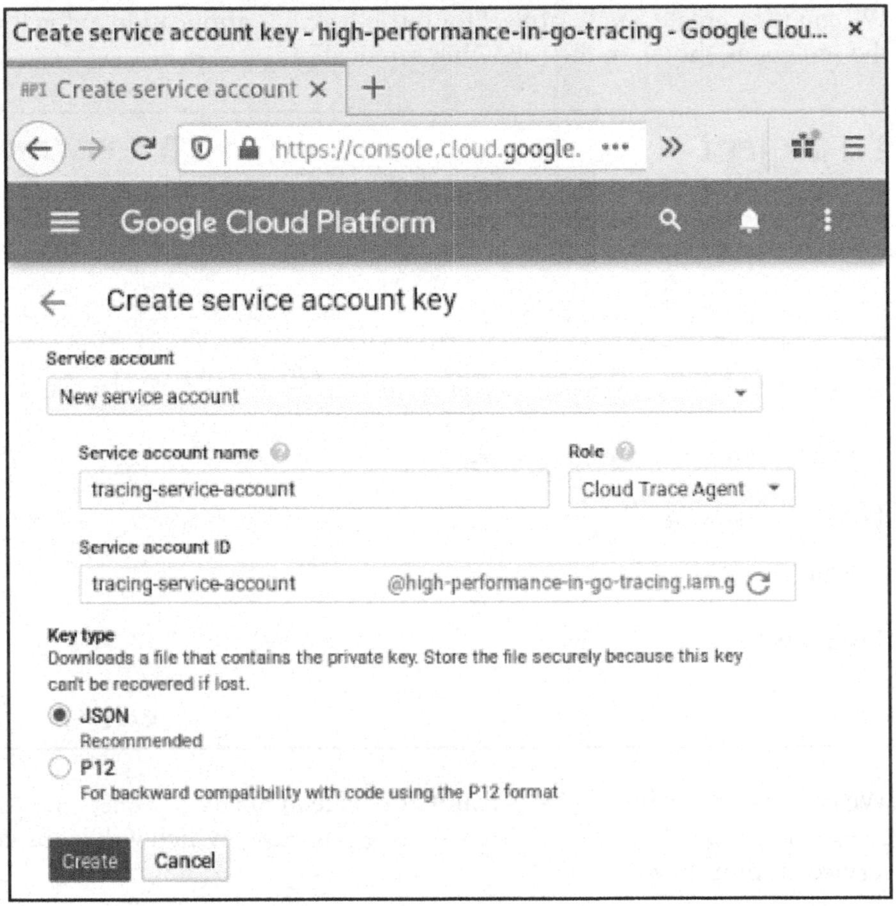

5. After we click **Create**, the browser will prompt us to download our new credentials. For reference, we will call this key `high-performance-in-go-tracing.json`. You can name your key whatever you like.

6. Once we have this key saved locally, we can turn it into an environment variable. In your Terminal, enter the following command:

```
export GOOGLE_APPLICATION_CREDENTIALS=/home/bob/service-accounts-private-key.json
```

This will save your service account credentials as a special environment variable, GOOGLE_APPLICATION_CREDENTIALS, which we will use in our next example.

Google Cloud Trace code

Once we have our application credentials all set up; we are off to the races to write our first trace that will be captured by our APM:

1. First, we instantiate the necessary packages and set a server host/port constant:

```
package main

import (
    "context"
    "fmt"
    "log"
    "net/http"
    "os"
    "time"

    "contrib.go.opencensus.io/exporter/stackdriver"

    "go.opencensus.io/trace"

)

const server = ":1234"
```

2. Next, in our init() function, we set up our StackDriver exporter and register our tracer to sample every web request that comes in. In production, we should probably sample fewer requests, as sampling adds additional latency to our requests:

```
func init() {

    exporter, err := stackdriver.NewExporter(stackdriver.Options{
        ProjectID: os.Getenv("GOOGLE_CLOUD_PROJECT"),
    })

    if err != nil {
        log.Fatal("Can't initialize GOOGLE_CLOUD_PROJECT environment
            variable", err)
    }
```

```
trace.RegisterExporter(exporter)
trace.ApplyConfig(trace.Config{DefaultSampler:
  trace.AlwaysSample()})

}
```

3. Next, we are going to have a sleep function that takes a context, sleeps, and writes a message to the end user. In this function, I am deferring the end of the span to the end of the function:

```
func sleep(ctx context.Context, w http.ResponseWriter, r
*http.Request) {
    _, span := trace.StartSpan(ctx, "sleep")
    defer span.End()
    time.Sleep(1 * time.Second)
    fmt.Fprintln(w, "Done Sleeping")
}
```

4. Our GitHub request function makes a request to `https://github.com` and returns the status to our end user. In this function, I'm explicitly calling the end of the span:

```
func githubRequest(ctx context.Context, w http.ResponseWriter, r
*http.Request) {
    _, span := trace.StartSpan(ctx, "githubRequest")
    defer span.End()
    res, err := http.Get("https://github.com")
    if err != nil {
        log.Fatal(err)
    }

    res.Body.Close()
    fmt.Fprintln(w, "Request to https://github.com completed with a
status of: ", res.Status)
    span.End()
}
```

Our main function sets up an HTTP handler function that performs the `githubRequest` and `sleep` functions:

```
func main() {

    h := http.HandlerFunc(func(w http.ResponseWriter, r *http.Request) {

        ctx, span := trace.StartSpan(context.Background(), "function/main")
        defer span.End()
        githubRequest(ctx, w, r)
        sleep(ctx, w, r)
    })

    http.Handle("/", h)
    log.Printf("serving at : %s", server)
    err := http.ListenAndServe(server, nil)

    if err != nil {
        log.Fatal("Couldn't start HTTP server: %s", err)
    }
}
```

5. After we execute our main function, we make a request to `localhost:1234` and see a response:

6. After this, we visit the Google Cloud console and select the trace that we made:

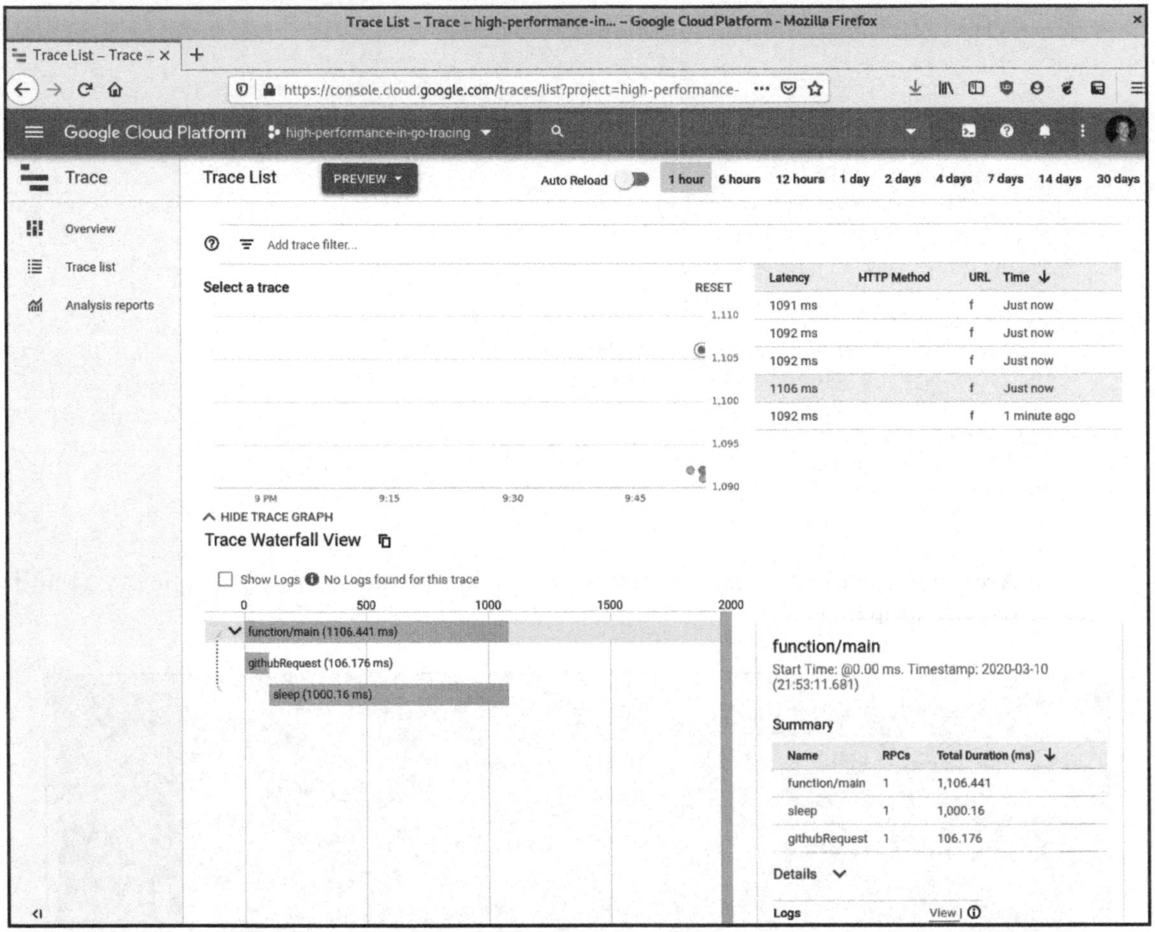

In this trace example, we can see all sorts of relevant details:

- All of the trace samples that have been taken (I added a bunch of different samples here to populate the fields).
- Our waterfall graph of the request flow. This is a bit small for our example with just the web request and the sleep, but as we pass context around in a distributed system, this graph quickly gets much bigger.
- The summary for each trace. If you click on one of the tracing bars in the graph, you can see more details about the particular trace.

Adding distributed tracing as an APM solution can be extremely helpful in determining the location of the web request that takes the most time. Finding real-life bottlenecks can often be much more practical than diving through logs. Google's APM also gives you the ability to run reports based on the traces you've made. After you have made more than 100 requests, you can execute an analysis report and see the results. The density distribution latency chart shows you where your request latencies lie in a graph. Our example should have mostly similar results, as we performed a long sleep and made one solitary request to an external service. We can see the density distribution graph in the following screenshot:

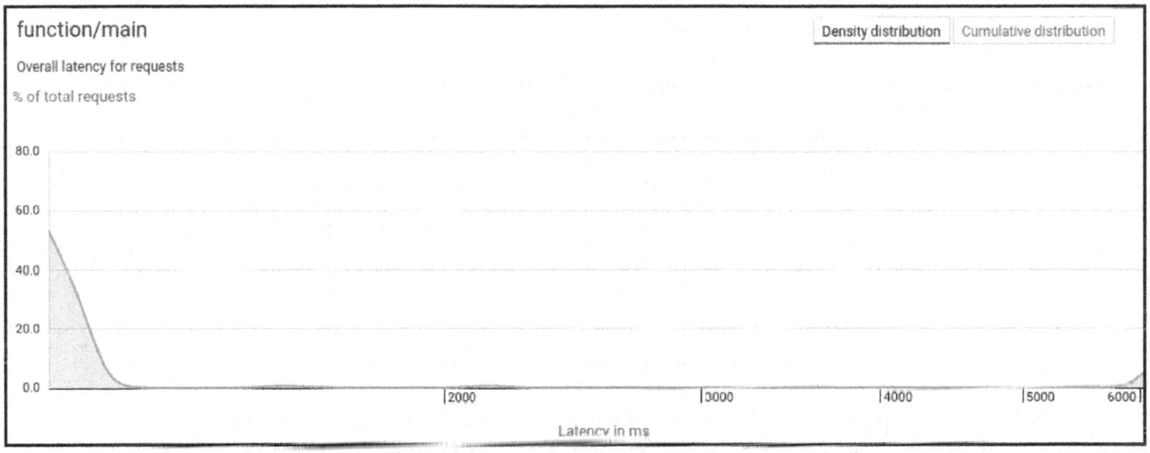

We can also look at the cumulative latency in this portal, which will show us the percentage of requests that are shorter than the value on the *x* axis:

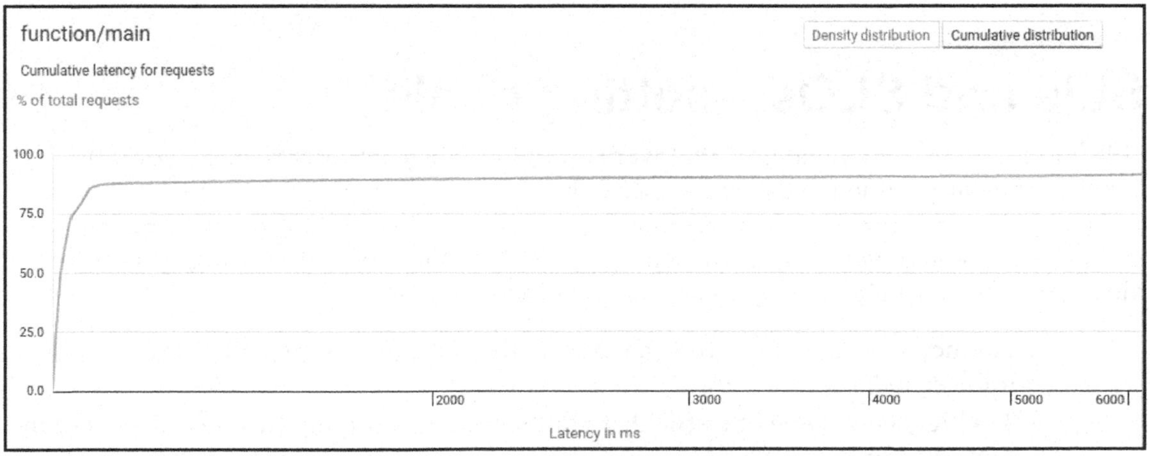

We can also see latency profiles with correlated requests:

Latency		
Request percentile	Latency	Sample Traces
25%	1,089 ms	1 2 3 4
50%	1,097 ms	1 2 3 4
75%	1,120 ms	1 2 3 4
90%	2,134 ms	1 2 3 4

Furthermore, we can also see the perceived bottlenecks within the distributed system:

Bottlenecks		
Request percentile	Bottleneck	Sample Traces
25%	999 ms on sleep	1
50%	1000 ms on sleep	1
75%	1001 ms on sleep 119 ms on githubRequest	1 1 2 3 4
90%	1133 ms on githubRequest	1 2 3 4

These analysis tools help us to deduce where we can make improvements in our distributed system. APMs help many companies to deliver performant applications to their customers. These tools are extra valuable because they look at performance through the lens of customer experience. In the next section, we will talk about setting goals with SLIs and SLOs.

SLIs and SLOs – setting goals

SLIs and SLOs are two paradigms that were brought to the computer science world by Google. They are defined in the SRE workbook (`https://landing.google.com/sre/sre-book/chapters/service-level-objectives/`) and are an excellent way to measure actionable items within your computing system. These measurements normally follow Google's four golden signals:

- **Latency**: The amount of time a request takes to complete (usually measured in milliseconds)
- **Traffic**: The volume of traffic that your service is receiving (usually measured in requests per second)

- **Errors**: The percentage of failed requests over total requests (usually measured with a percentage)
- **Saturation**: The measure of hardware saturation (usually measured by queued request counts)

These measurements can then be used to create one or more SLAs. These are frequently delivered to customers who expect a specific level of service from your application.

We can use Prometheus to measure these metrics. Prometheus has a bunch of different methodologies for counting things, including gauges, counters, and histograms. We will use all of these different tools to measure these metrics within our system.

To test our system, we'll use the hey load generator. This is a tool that is similar to ab, which we used in previous chapters, but it'll show our distribution a little better for this particular scenario. We can grab it by running the following command:

```
go get -u github.com/rakyll/hey
```

We are going to need to stand up our Prometheus service in order to read some of these values. If yours isn't still standing from our previous example, we can perform the following commands:

```
docker build -t slislo -f Dockerfile.promservice .
docker run -it --rm --name slislo -d -p 9090:9090 --net host slislo
```

This will get our Prometheus instance to stand up and measure requests:

1. Our code starts by instantiating the main package and importing the necessary Prometheus packages:

```
package main

import (
    "math/rand"
    "net/http"
    "time"

    "github.com/prometheus/client_golang/prometheus"
    "github.com/prometheus/client_golang/prometheus/promhttp"

)
```

2. We then gather our saturation, requests, and latency numbers in our `main` function. We use a gauge for saturation, a counter for requests, and a histogram for latency:

```
saturation := prometheus.NewGauge(prometheus.GaugeOpts{
   Name: "saturation",
   Help: "A gauge of the saturation golden signal",
})

requests := prometheus.NewCounterVec(
   prometheus.CounterOpts{
       Name: "requests",
       Help: "A counter for the requests golden signal",
   },
   []string{"code", "method"},
)

latency := prometheus.NewHistogramVec(
   prometheus.HistogramOpts{
       Name: "latency",
       Help: "A histogram of latencies for the latency golden
         signal",
       Buckets: []float64{.025, .05, 0.1, 0.25, 0.5, 0.75},
   },
   []string{"handler", "method"},
)
```

3. We then create our `goldenSignalHandler`, which randomly generates a latency from 0 to 1 seconds. For added visibility of our signals, if the random number is divisible by 4, we return a 404 error status, and if it's divisible by 5, we return a 500 error. We then return a response and log that the request has been completed.

Our `goldenSignalChain` ties these metrics together:

```
goldenSignalChain := promhttp.InstrumentHandlerInFlight
   (saturation,promhttp.InstrumentHandlerDuration
   (latency.MustCurryWith(prometheus.Labels{"handler": "signals"}),

          promhttp.InstrumentHandlerCounter(requests,
   goldenSignalHandler),
       ),
   )
```

4. We then register all of our measurements (saturation, requests, and latency) with Prometheus, handle our HTTP requests, and start our HTTP server:

```
prometheus.MustRegister(saturation, requests, latency)
http.Handle("/metrics", promhttp.Handler())
http.Handle("/signals", goldenSignalChain)
http.ListenAndServe(":1234", nil)
}
```

5. After we start our HTTP server by executing `go run SLISLO.go`, we can then make a `hey` request to our HTTP server. The output from our `hey` call is visible in the following screenshot. Remember that these are all random values and will be different if you execute this same test:

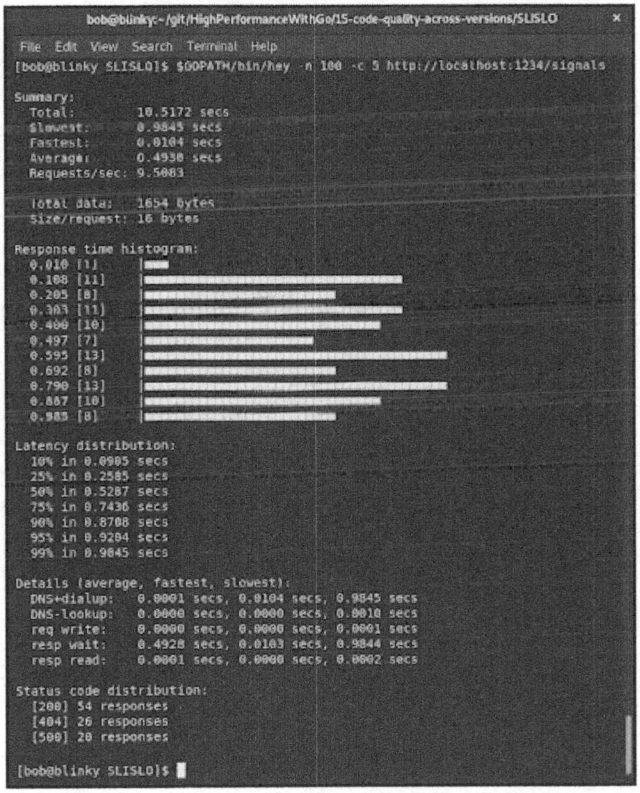

We can then take a look at our individual golden signals.

Measuring traffic

To measure our traffic, we can use the Prometheus query `sum(rate(requests[1m]))`.

We can measure the rate at any given interval. Configure this rate in a couple of different ways and see which is most conducive to your system's requirements.

Measuring latency

To measure latency, we can look at the `latency_bucket` Prometheus query. Our requests were lumped into a histogram with different latency numbers, and this query reflects that.

Measuring errors

To measure the number of errors in our system, we need to find the ratio of requests that had a successful response code to those that did not have a successful response code. We can find this with the following query `sum(requests {code!="200"}) / (sum(requests {code="200"})) + sum(requests {code!="200"})`.

This ratio is important to monitor. Computer systems fail and people make incorrect requests, but your ratio of 200 responses to non-200 responses should be relatively small.

Measuring saturation

We can measure saturation using the `saturation` **Prometheus** query. We want to validate that our system isn't saturated, and this query can help us to perform this action.

Grafana

We can encapsulate all of these golden signals into a Grafana dashboard. We can run Grafana locally by invoking:

```
docker run  -it --rm --name grafana -d -p 3000:3000 --net prometheus
grafana/grafana
```

We need to log into the Grafana portal by visiting
`http://localhost:3000` and using the default username and password
combination:
Username: admin
Password: admin

We can then set up a new password to our liking after we've logged in.

After we've logged in, we click **Add data source** at the top of the page and select
Prometheus on the next page. We then enter our local IP address and click **Save & Test**. If
all works as expected, we should see the **Data source is working** popup at the bottom of
the screen:

After we complete this, we visit `http://localhost:3000/dashboard/import`.

We then choose **Upload .json file** in the top-right corner, and we upload the JSON file that has been created for this dashboard at `https://github.com/bobstrecansky/` `HighPerformanceWithGo/blob/master/15-code-quality-across-versions/SLISLO/four_` `golden_signals_grafana_dashboard.json`.

After we have uploaded this JSON file, we import this data source, and we'll be able to see our **Request Rate**, **Duration Latency Buckets**, **Error Rate**, and **Saturation** charts, as shown in the following screenshot:

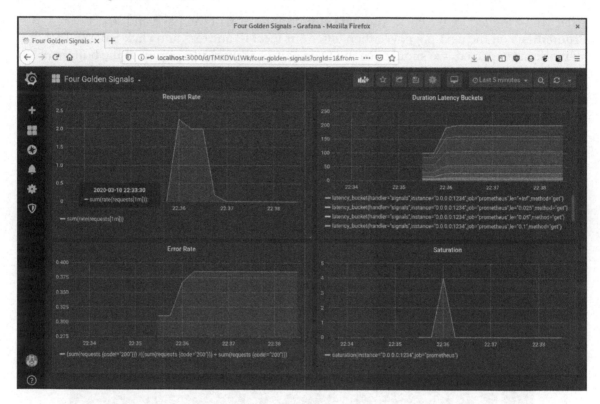

Having visibility into these statistics can be helpful in maintaining a stable system. After you have these statistics captured, you can use Prometheus Alertmanager to set alerts on thresholds you're interested in monitoring.

More information on configuring Alertmanager can be found at
`https://prometheus.io/docs/alerting/alertmanager/`.

In the next section, we will learn how to keep track of our data, also known as logging.

Logging – keeping track of your data

Logging, the act of recording events that occur in a system, is essential to creating performant software systems. Being able to record and validate events within a programming system is a great way to ensure that you're maintaining code quality across versions of your applications. Logs can often quickly show a bug in your software, and being able to consume that information in a quick fashion can often help lower your **mean time to recovery (MTTR)**.

There are many different logging packages for Go. A few of the most popular packages are as follows:

- The standard built-in log package provided by the Go maintainers
- **The Glog package**: `https://github.com/golang/glog`
- **Uber's Zap package**: `https://github.com/uber-go/zap`
- **The Zero Allocation JSON logger**: `https://github.com/rs/zerolog`
- **The Logrus package**: `https://github.com/sirupsen/logrus`

We are going to use the Zap package as our example, as benchmarks have shown. Using the standard library logger is often sufficient (if you've noticed, this is the package that I've used for logging in the book thus far). Having a structured logging package such as Zap available can make up for a pleasant experience because it offers a couple of features that the standard library logger doesn't offer out of the box, such as the following:

- Logging levels
- Structured logs (JSON in particular)
- Typed logs

It also performs best in comparison benchmarks among the loggers. Zap has two different types of logging available, the sugared logger and the structured logger. The structured logger is slightly more performant, whereas the sugared logger is more loosely typed. As this is a book about performance, we are going to take a look at the structured logger as it's more performant, but both logging options are more than adequate for production use.

Having a logger that has different logging levels is important because it allows you to determine which logs need dire attention and which logs are just returning information. This also lets you set a priority for your team depending on how urgent a fix is when you hit a logging inflection point.

Having logs that can be structured is helpful for ingestion into other systems. JSON logging is quickly becoming more and more popular because log aggregation tools such as the following accept JSON logging:

- The ELK Stack (ElasticSearch, Logstash, and Kibana)
- Loggly
- Splunk
- Sumologic
- Datadog
- Google Stackdriver Logging

As we saw with our APM solutions, we can utilize these logging services to aggregate large groupings of logs in a centralized location, whether it be on premise or in the cloud.

Having typed logs allows you to organize your logging data in a way that makes sense to your program or business. Maintaining consistency in your logging can allow for your system operators and site reliability engineers to more quickly diagnose problems, resulting in a shorter MTTR for production incidents.

Let's have a look at a logging example with Zap:

1. First, we instantiate our package and import the `time` package and the Zap logger:

```
package main

import (
    "time"
    "go.uber.org/zap"

)
```

2. We then set up a logging production configuration that will return logs to stdout (following the twelve-factor app process). These can often go to log routers such as Fluentd (https://www.fluentd.org/), and we can test all of the different log levels available in Zap:

```
func main() {

    c := zap.NewProductionConfig()
    c.OutputPaths = []string{"stdout"}
    logger, _ := c.Build()

    logger.Debug("We can use this logging level to debug. This
won't be printed, as the NewProduction logger only prints info and
above log levels.")

    logger.Info("This is an INFO message for your code. We can log
individual structured things here", zap.String("url",
"https://reddit.com"), zap.Int("connectionAttempts", 3),
zap.Time("requestTime", time.Now()))

    logger.Warn("This is a WARNING message for your code. It will
not exit your program.")

    logger.Error("This is an ERROR message for your code. It will
not exit your program, but it will print your error message -> ")

    logger.Fatal("This is a Fatal message for your code. It will
exit your program with an os.Exit(1).")

    logger.Panic("This is a panic message for your code. It will
exit your program. We won't see this execute because we have
already exited from the above logger.Fatal log message. This also
exits with an os.Exit(1)")

}
```

After we run our logger, we can see some pretty clean JSON output. We can also use a utility such as jq (`https://stedolan.github.io/jq/`) in order to make this easily consumable in your local environment:

```
[bob@blinky logging]$ go run logging.go | jq .
{
  "level": "info",
  "ts": 1584580455.4190106,
  "caller": "logging/logging.go:14",
  "msg": "This is an INFO message for your code.  We can log indiviual structure
d things here",
  "url": "https://reddit.com",
  "connectionAttempts": 3,
  "requestTime": 1584580455.419007
}
{
  "level": "warn",
  "ts": 1584580455.41905,
  "caller": "logging/logging.go:15",
  "msg": "This is a WARNING message for your code.  It will not exit your progra
m."
}
{
  "level": "error",
  "ts": 1584580455.4190664,
  "caller": "logging/logging.go:16",
  "msg": "This is an ERROR message for your code.  It will not exit your program
, but it will print your error message -> ",
  "stacktrace": "main.main\n\t/home/bob/git/HighPerformanceWithGo/15-code-qualit
y-across-versions/logging/logging.go:16\nruntime.main\n\t/usr/lib/golang/src/run
time/proc.go:203"
}
{
  "level": "fatal",
  "ts": 1584580455.4191012,
  "caller": "logging/logging.go:17",
  "msg": "This is a Fatal message for your code.  It will exit your program with
 an os.Exit(1).",
  "stacktrace": "main.main\n\t/home/bob/git/HighPerformanceWithGo/15-code-qualit
y-across-versions/logging/logging.go:17\nruntime.main\n\t/usr/lib/golang/src/run
time/proc.go:203"
}
exit status 1
[bob@blinky logging]$
```

As we mentioned, having a structured, leveled logger in your Go application will help you to troubleshoot more quickly and effectively.

Summary

In this chapter, we discussed the different methodologies of comparing code quality across versions:

- Utilizing the Go Prometheus exporter
- APM tools
- SLIs and SLOs
- Utilizing logging

Utilizing all of these techniques can help you to determine where your application isn't performing as it is expected to. Knowing these things can help you to iterate rapidly and produce the best software that you can.

Throughout the course of this book, you've learned about application performance and how it pertains to Go. I hope this book will help you to think about web performance while you are writing applications. Always keep performance in the forefront of your mind. Everyone enjoys performant applications, and hopefully this book will help you do your part as a developer in making them.

Other Books You May Enjoy

If you enjoyed this book, you may be interested in these other books by Packt:

Hands-On System Programming with Go
Alex Guerrieri

ISBN: 978-1-78980-407-2

- Explore concepts of system programming using Go and concurrency
- Gain insights into Golang's internals, memory models and allocation
- Familiarize yourself with the filesystem and IO streams in general
- Handle and control processes and daemons' lifetime via signals and pipes
- Communicate with other applications effectively using a network
- Use various encoding formats to serialize complex data structures
- Become well-versed in concurrency with channels, goroutines, and sync
- Use concurrency patterns to build robust and performant system applications

Hands-On Software Engineering with Golang
Achilleas Anagnostopoulos

ISBN: 978-1-83855-449-1

- Understand different stages of the software development life cycle and the role of a software engineer
- Create APIs using gRPC and leverage the middleware offered by the gRPC ecosystem
- Discover various approaches to managing package dependencies for your projects
- Build an end-to-end project from scratch and explore different strategies for scaling it
- Develop a graph processing system and extend it to run in a distributed manner
- Deploy Go services on Kubernetes and monitor their health using Prometheus

Leave a review - let other readers know what you think

Please share your thoughts on this book with others by leaving a review on the site that you bought it from. If you purchased the book from Amazon, please leave us an honest review on this book's Amazon page. This is vital so that other potential readers can see and use your unbiased opinion to make purchasing decisions, we can understand what our customers think about our products, and our authors can see your feedback on the title that they have worked with Packt to create. It will only take a few minutes of your time, but is valuable to other potential customers, our authors, and Packt. Thank you!

Index

A

Advanced Message Queueing Protocol (AMQP) 346
anonymous functions
  about 54, 55
  with respect, to closures 55, 56
AppDynamics
  reference link 360
application performance monitoring (APM)
  Google Cloud Trace code, writing 363, 365, 367, 368
  using 360
application
  OpenCensus, implementing for 322, 323, 325, 326, 327
array 90
associative containers
  about 99
  map 102
  multimap 103
  multiset 100
  set 99
AWS EC2 instances, with GPU
  URL 212
AWS XRay
  reference link 360

B

benchmark execution 26, 27, 28
benchmarking
  about 25, 26
  benefits 29
  drawbacks 29
  overview 21
  real-world benchmarking 29
benchstat package

reference link 29
Big O notation
  about 13, 30
  example 32
  O(1) – constant time 34, 35
  O(2n) – exponential time 41, 42, 43
  O(log n) – logarithmic time 35, 36, 37
  O(n log n) – quasilinear time 38, 40
  O(n) – linear time 37, 38
  O(n2) – quadratic time 40, 41
  reference link 13
binaries
  installing, with go install command 276, 277
binary search 47, 48, 88
binary trees 48, 49
BLAS 112
buffered channels
  about 66, 67, 68
  as job queues 340, 341
build directory
  cleaning 267, 268
build flags
  about 259, 260
  usages 259

C

C
  comparable performance 22
  writing, in Go 207
caching
  improvements 247
Cgo
  about 207
  example 209, 210
  URLs 208
channel internals 65
channels

about 22, 65
buffered channels 66, 67, 68
unbuffered channels 69, 70
closures
about 54
HTTP handlers 57, 58, 59
work, deferring 57
work, nesting 57
clustering
hard clustering 330
in Go 330
soft clustering 330
Cobra
resulting sets 171, 172
used, for configuration programming 168, 170
column vector 113
compiler flags 263, 264, 265
complete binary tree 49
comprehending inheritance
in Go 154, 155
comprehending methods
in Go 151, 152, 153, 154
Compressed Sparse Column (CSC) 130
Compressed Sparse Row (CSR) 130
constant time 34, 35
container adapters
about 95
priority queue 96, 97
queue 95
stack 98
containers
about 89
sequence containers 89
CPU profiling
about 287, 288, 290, 291, 292
reasons 283
CSC matrix 132
CSR matrix 130, 131
CUDA C++ program
starting 227, 228, 229, 230, 231, 232
CUDA toolkit package
download link 213
CUDA
about 215
on GCP 217

D

data structure operations 33
Datadog
reference link 360
debug package 249
dendrogram 331
dense matrices 127
deque 91
dequeuing 51
Dictionary of Keys (DOK) 128
distributed system performance 360
Docker CE
installing, on GCP 224, 225
Docker
for GPU-enabled programming 215, 216, 217
Go binaries, building 277, 279
DOK matrix 129
doubly linked list 49, 93

E

Elastic APM agent
reference link 360
ELF files
format 188
errors
about 369
measuring 372
Executable and Linkable Format (ELF) 186
exponential time 41, 42, 43

F

filename conventions 266
first in first out (FIFO) 50, 66, 95, 340
first-class functions 53
flame graphs
about 299
integrating, within pprof 299, 300
FloydHub
URL 212
Fluentd
URL 377
formatting
in Go 148
forward list 94

FreeOSMemory()
  reference link 204
full binary tree 49
function objects 104
functor 104, 105, 106

G

G struct 63
GC() function
  reference link 204
GCP's GPU offerings
  reference link 217
GCP
  Docker CE, installing on 224, 225
  NVIDIA Docker, installing on 225
GCTRACE 238, 240, 241
General-Purpose Graphics Processing Units
    (GPGPUs) 211
generators 82, 108
Go binaries
  building 258
  building, with Docker 277, 279
Go build cache 247
go build command 20
Go build
  about 259
  constraints 265, 266
  working 261, 262
Go clean 267, 268
Go code
  building 259
  profiling 283
Go distributed tracing 321, 322
Go execution tracer
  reference link 307
Go generate tool 161, 162
go get and go mod commands
  used, for retrieving package dependencies 269
go install command
  used, for installing binaries 276, 277
go list command 270, 272, 273, 274
Go modules 143, 144, 145, 146
Go performance
  ideology 21
Go Prometheus exporter

used, for exporting data from Go application
    354, 355, 356, 357, 358, 359
go run command
  used, for executing packages 274, 276
Go runtime library, functions
  about 249
  KeepAlive 250
  NumCPU 250
  ReadMemStats 251, 252
  reference link 249
Go runtime memory allocation 193
Go runtime
  exploring 236
  features 19
Go scheduler 61, 62
Go scheduler goroutine internals
  about 62
  G struct 63
  M struct 63
  P struct 63
go test
  used, for profiling implementation 284
Go testing package
  reference link 26
Go
  C, writing in 207
  history 17, 18
  in large-scale distributed systems 23
  readability, maintaining 138
  simplicity, maintaining 138
  standard library 18
  toolset 19, 20
GODEBUG
  about 236
  variables 236, 237
GOGC variable 241, 242, 243
GOMAXPROCS variable 243, 244
Gonum package
  reference link 112
Google Cloud environment
  setting up 360, 362
Google Cloud GPUs
  URL 212
Google's Suite of APM products
  reference link 360

goroutines
  about 22
  as job queues 337, 338
  exploring 61
  working 64
GOTRACEBACK variable 245, 246
goweight library
  reference link 199
GPU-accelerated computing 211, 213, 214
GPU
  VM, creating 218, 220, 221, 222
Grafana
  signals, encapsulating 372, 373

H

hard clustering 330
heap 191
heap sort 44, 45
Honeycomb APM
  reference link 360
host processes
  utilizing 215
HTML templating 174, 175
HTTP handlers
  with closures 57, 58, 59, 60, 61
HTTP pprof paths 287

I

insertion sort 44
instrumenting profiling
  in code, manually 285
interfaces
  in Go 150
internal iterators 106
internal packaging 142
iteration 77, 78, 80
iterator patterns
  benefits 77
  drawback 77
iterators
  about 106
  external iterators 107
  generators 108
  implicit iterator 108
  internal iterators 106

J

job queues
  in Go 337
  integrating 342
jq
  reference link 378

K

K-means clustering 333, 334, 336, 337
K-nearest neighbors (KNN) algorithm 331, 333
Kafka
  job queues, integrating 342, 343, 345
  URL 51
kind 157

L

last in first out (LIFO) 98
latency
  about 368
  measuring 372
limited memory situations 204
linear search 46
linear time 37, 38
link toolchain 166, 167, 168
linker flags 263, 264, 265
list 92
list of lists (LIL) matrix 129
logarithmic time 35, 36, 37
logging 375
logging packages, Go
  Glog package, reference link 375
  Logrus package, reference link 375
  Uber's Zap package, reference link 375
  Zero Allocation JSON logger, reference link 375
long term performance
  gauging 14

M

M struct 63
malloc
  reference link 193
map 102
Math Kernel Library (MKL) 112
matrices

about 115
operations 116
matrix addition 116, 117
matrix multiplication
about 121
practical example 122, 123
matrix structures
about 127
dense matrices 127
sparse matrices 127
matrix subtraction 117, 118, 119
matrix transposition
about 124, 125
practical example 126
max_element algorithm 86
memory allocation primer 193
memory leaks
detecting 301, 302, 303
Memory Management Unit (MMU) 184
memory object allocation 194, 195, 197, 199,
200, 202, 203
memory profiling
about 293, 294
reasons 284
memory utilization 190, 192
memory
allocating 184
MemStats values
reference link 253
merge sort 45
methods, for gauging long term performance
reference link 14
mheap
reference link 193
min_element algorithm 86
modern computers
memory 183
mspan 195
multimap 103
multiple profiles
comparing 297, 298
multiset 100

N

naming
in Go 146, 147
New Relic APM
reference link 360
Numba
URL 212
NVIDIA CUDA drivers
installing 224
reference link 223
NVIDIA Docker
installing, on GCP 225
NVIDIA's CUDA platform
URL 211

O

OpenCensus
implementing, for application 322, 323, 325,
326, 327
OpenCL
URL 211
OpenMP
URL 211
optimization levels 16, 17
optimization strategies
overview 14, 15, 16

P

P struct 63
package dependencies
retrieving, with go get and go mod commands
269
package
executing, with go run command 274, 276
naming 139
packaging
about 139
internal packaging 142
layout 140, 141
Paperspace
URL 212
perfect binary tree 49
performance
in computer science 12, 13

position-independent executables (PIE) 260
pprof-like traces
    exploring 317, 318, 319, 320, 321
pprof
    about 249
    flame graphs, integrating 299, 300
    instrumentation methodologies 284
    reference link 19
priority queue 96, 97
profiling
    about 283
    implementing, with go test 284
    running service code 286
programmer 108
Prometheus
    URL 247, 354
protobufs
    code results 165, 166
    generated code 162, 163
protocol buffers
    reference link 162
PyTorch
    URL 212

Q

quadratic time 40, 41
quasilinear time 38, 40
queues
    about 95
    exploring 50
queuing functions 50
queuing patterns 51
quick sort 46

R

RabbitMQ
    job queues, integrating 346, 348, 349, 350
    URL 51
race 249
Random Access Memory (RAM) 183
ranges
    over channels 68
readability
    maintaining, in Go 138
reflection, Go

about 156
    kinds 157
    types 156
    values 158
resident set size (RSS) 185, 186
reverse algorithm 85
row vector 113
running service code
    profiling 285

S

saturation Prometheus query
    used, for measuring saturation 372
saturation
    about 369
    measuring 372
scalar multiplication
    about 119
    practical example 120, 121
scavenging 241
search algorithms
    about 46
    binary search 47, 48
    linear search 46
selects 71, 72
semaphores 73, 74, 75
sequence containers 89
sequence containers implementations
    array 90
    deque 91
    forward list 94
    list 92
    vector 90
service-level agreements (SLA) 369
service-level indicators (SLIs) 368, 371
service-level objectives (SLOs) 368, 371
set 99
SignalFX
    reference link 360
simplicity
    maintaining, in Go 138
soft clustering 330
Software Development Kit (SDK) 208
sort algorithm 84
sort algorithms

about 43
  heap sort 44, 45
  insertion sort 44
  merge sort 45
  quick sort 46
Sparse library
  reference link 112
sparse matrices
  about 127
  coordinate list matrix 130
  DOK matrix 129
  list of lists (LIL) matrix 129
Sprig
  default functions 179, 180, 181
  exploring 176
  reference link 181
  string functions 176, 177
  string slice functions 178, 179
stack 98, 191
static single assignment (SSA)
  reference link 250
STL, algorithms
  about 84
  binary search 88
  max element 86, 87
  min element 86, 87
  reverse 85
  sort 84

T

TCMalloc
  reference link 197
TensorFlow
  URL 212
text templating 172, 173
thread local storage (tls) 63
time complexity 33
trace 249
trace collection 307, 308, 309, 310, 312

tracing format 306
tracing instrumentation
  implementing 305
tracing window
  movement 312, 313, 314, 315, 316, 317
traffic
  about 368
  measuring 372
Translation Lookaside Buffer (TLB) 184
trees
  exploring 48
  types 156

U

unbuffered channels 69, 70
upstream pprof
  used, for extending capabilities 295, 296

V

values 158
vectors
  about 90, 113
  computations 113, 114, 115
vendor directory 143
vendoring dependencies 247
vendoring
  improvements 247
Viper
  resulting sets 171, 172
  used, for configuration programming 168, 170
virtual memory size (VSZ) 185, 186
virtual memory space (VMS) 185
virtual memory
  benefits 184
VM
  creating, with GPU 218, 220, 221, 222

W

WaitGroups 75, 76

Made in the USA
Columbia, SC
16 August 2020